SwiftUI Essentials

iOS Edition

SwiftUI Essentials – iOS Edition

ISBN-13: 978-1-951442-05-7

Rev: 1.0

Table of Contents

1. Start Here

The goal of this book is to teach the skills necessary to build iOS 13 applications using SwiftUI, Xcode 11 and the Swift 5 programming language.

Beginning with the basics, this book provides an outline of the steps necessary to set up an iOS development environment together with an introduction to the use of Swift Playgrounds to learn and experiment with Swift.

The book also includes in depth chapters introducing the Swift 5 programming language including data types, control flow, functions, object-oriented programming, property wrappers and error handling.

An introduction to the key concepts of SwiftUI and project architecture is followed by a guided tour of Xcode in SwiftUI development mode. The book also covers the creation of custom SwiftUI views and explains how these views are combined to create user interface layouts including the use of stacks, frames and forms.

Other topics covered include data handling using state properties and both observable and environment objects, as are key user interface design concepts such as modifiers, lists, tabbed views, context menus and user interface navigation.

The book also includes chapters covering graphics drawing, user interface animation, view transitions and gesture handling.

Chapters are also provided explaining how to integrate SwiftUI views into existing UIKit-based projects and explains the integration of UIKit code into SwiftUI.

Finally, the book explains how to package up a completed app and upload it to the App Store for publication.

Along the way, the topics covered in the book are put into practice through detailed tutorials, the source code for which is also available for download.

The aim of this book, therefore, is to teach you the skills necessary to build your own apps for iOS 13 using SwiftUI. Assuming you are ready to download the iOS 13 SDK and Xcode 11 and have an Intel-based Mac you are ready to get started.

1.1 For Swift Programmers

This book has been designed to address the needs of both existing Swift programmers and those who are new to both Swift and iOS app development. If you are familiar with the Swift 5.1 programming language, you can probably skip the Swift specific chapters. If you are not yet familiar with the new language features of Swift 5.1, however, we recommend that you at least read the sections covering *implicit returns from single expressions*, *opaque return types* and *property wrappers*. These features are central to the implementation and understanding of SwiftUI.

1.2 For Non-Swift Programmers

If you are new to programming in Swift (or programming in general) then the entire book is appropriate for you. Just start at the beginning and keep going.

1.3 Source Code Download

The source code and Xcode project files for the examples contained in this book are available for download at:

https://www.ebookfrenzy.com/retail/swiftui/

1.4 Download the eBook

Thank you for purchasing the print edition of this book. Your purchase includes a color copy of the book in PDF format.

If you would like to download the PDF version of this book, please email proof of purchase (for example a receipt, delivery notice or photo of the physical book) to *feedback@ebookfrenzy.com* and we will provide you with a download link.

1.5 Feedback

We want you to be satisfied with your purchase of this book. If you find any errors in the book, or have any comments, questions or concerns please contact us at *feedback@ebookfrenzy.com*.

1.6 Errata

While we make every effort to ensure the accuracy of the content of this book, it is inevitable that a book covering a subject area of this size and complexity may include some errors and oversights. Any known issues with the book will be outlined, together with solutions at the following URL:

https://www.ebookfrenzy.com/errata/swiftui.html

In the event that you find an error not listed in the errata, please let us know by emailing our technical support team at *feedback@ebookfrenzy.com*.

2. Joining the Apple Developer Program

The first step in the process of learning to develop iOS 13 based applications involves gaining an understanding of the advantages of enrolling in the Apple Developer Program and deciding the point at which it makes sense to pay to join. With these goals in mind, this chapter will outline the costs and benefits of joining the developer program and, finally, walk through the steps involved in enrolling.

2.1 Downloading Xcode 11 and the iOS 13 SDK

The latest versions of both the iOS SDK and Xcode can be downloaded free of charge from the Mac App Store. Since the tools are free, this raises the question of whether to enroll in the Apple Developer Program, or to wait until it becomes necessary later in your app development learning curve.

2.2 Apple Developer Program

Membership in the Apple Developer Program currently costs $99 per year to enroll as an individual developer. Organization level membership is also available.

Prior to the introduction of iOS 9 and Xcode 7, one of the key advantages of the developer program was that it permitted the creation of certificates and provisioning profiles to test your applications on physical iOS devices. Fortunately, this is no longer the case and all that is now required to test apps on physical iOS devices is an Apple ID.

Clearly much can be achieved without the need to pay to join the Apple Developer program. There are, however, areas of app development which cannot be fully tested without program membership. Of particular significance is the fact that iCloud access, Apple Pay, Game Center and In-App Purchasing can only be enabled and tested with Apple Developer Program membership.

Of further significance is the fact that Apple Developer Program members have access to technical support from Apple's iOS support engineers (though the annual fee initially covers the submission of only two support incident reports more can be purchased) and membership of the Apple Developer forums which can be an invaluable resource for obtaining assistance and guidance from other iOS developers and for finding solutions to problems that others have encountered and subsequently resolved.

Program membership also provides early access to the pre-release Beta versions of both Xcode and iOS.

By far the most important aspect of the Apple Developer Program is that membership is a mandatory requirement in order to publish an application for sale or download in the App Store.

Clearly, program membership is going to be required at some point before your application reaches the App Store. The only question remaining is when exactly to sign up.

2.3 When to Enroll in the Apple Developer Program?

Clearly, there are many benefits to Apple Developer Program membership and, eventually, membership will be necessary to begin selling applications. As to whether to pay the enrollment fee now or later will depend on individual circumstances. If you are still in the early stages of learning to develop iOS applications or have yet to come up with a compelling idea for an application to develop then much of what you need is provided without program membership. As your skill level increases and your ideas for applications to develop take shape you can, after all, always enroll in the developer program later.

If, on the other hand, you are confident that you will reach the stage of having an application ready to publish or know that you will need access to more advanced features such as iCloud, In-App Purchasing and Apple Pay then it is worth joining the developer program sooner rather than later.

2.4 Enrolling in the Apple Developer Program

If your goal is to develop iOS applications for your employer, then it is first worth checking whether the company already has membership. That being the case, contact the program administrator in your company and ask them to send you an invitation from within the Apple Developer Program Member Center to join the team. Once they have done so, Apple will send you an email entitled *You Have Been Invited to Join an Apple Developer Program* containing a link to activate your membership. If you or your company is not already a program member, you can enroll online at:

https://developer.apple.com/programs/enroll/

Apple provides enrollment options for businesses and individuals. To enroll as an individual, you will need to provide credit card information in order to verify your identity. To enroll as a company, you must have legal signature authority (or access to someone who does) and be able to provide documentation such as a Dun & Bradstreet D-U-N-S number and documentation confirming legal entity status.

Acceptance into the developer program as an individual member typically takes less than 24 hours with notification arriving in the form of an activation email from Apple. Enrollment as a company can take considerably longer (sometimes weeks or even months) due to the burden of the additional verification requirements.

While awaiting activation you may log into the Member Center with restricted access using your Apple ID and password at the following URL:

https://developer.apple.com/membercenter

Once logged in, clicking on the *Your Account* tab at the top of the page will display the prevailing status of your application to join the developer program as *Enrollment Pending*. Once the activation email has arrived, log into the Member Center again and note that access is now available to a wide range of options and resources as illustrated in Figure 2-1:

Figure 2-1

2.5 Summary

An important early step in the iOS 13 application development process involves identifying the best time to enroll in the Apple Developer Program. This chapter has outlined the benefits of joining the program, provided some guidance to keep in mind when considering developer program membership and walked briefly through the enrollment process. The next step is to download and install the iOS 13 SDK and Xcode 11 development environment.

Chapter 3

3. Installing Xcode 11 and the iOS 13 SDK

iOS apps are developed using the iOS SDK in conjunction with Apple's Xcode development environment. Xcode is an integrated development environment (IDE) within which you will code, compile, test and debug your iOS applications.

In this chapter we will cover the steps involved in installing both Xcode 11 and the iOS 13 SDK on macOS.

3.1 Identifying Your macOS Version

When developing with SwiftUI, the Xcode 11 environment requires that the version of macOS running on the system be version 10.15 or later. If you are unsure of the version of macOS on your Mac, you can find this information by clicking on the Apple menu in the top left-hand corner of the screen and selecting the *About This Mac* option from the menu. In the resulting dialog check the *Version* line.

If the "About This Mac" dialog does not indicate that macOS 10.15 or later is running, click on the *Software Update...* button to download and install the appropriate operating system upgrades.

Figure 3-1

7

3.2 **Installing Xcode 11 and the iOS 13 SDK**

The best way to obtain the latest versions of Xcode and the iOS SDK is to download them from the Apple Mac App Store. Launch the App Store on your macOS system, enter Xcode into the search box and click on the *Get* button to initiate the installation.

3.3 **Starting Xcode**

Having successfully installed the SDK and Xcode, the next step is to launch it so that we are ready to start development work. To start up Xcode, open the Finder and search for *Xcode*. Since you will be making frequent use of this tool take this opportunity to drag and drop it into your dock for easier access in the future. Click on the Xcode icon in the dock to launch the tool. The first time Xcode runs you may be prompted to install additional components. Follow these steps, entering your username and password when prompted to do so.

Once Xcode has loaded, and assuming this is the first time you have used Xcode on this system, you will be presented with the *Welcome* screen from which you are ready to proceed:

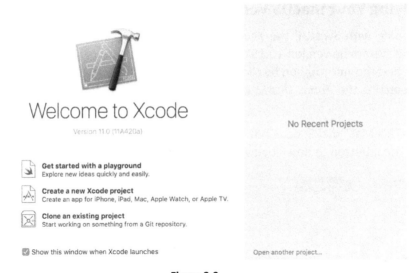

Figure 3-2

3.4 **Adding Your Apple ID to the Xcode Preferences**

Regardless of whether or not you choose to enroll in the Apple Developer Program it is worth adding your Apple ID to Xcode now that it is installed and running. Select the *Xcode -> Preferences...* menu option followed by the *Accounts* tab. On the Accounts screen, click on the + button highlighted in Figure 3-3, select *Apple ID* from the resulting panel and click on the *Continue* button. When prompted, enter your Apple ID and associated password and click on the *Sign In* button to add the account to the preferences.

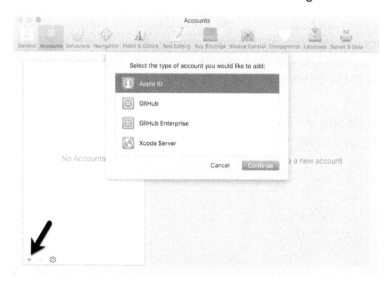

Figure 3-3

3.5 Developer and Distribution Signing Identities

Once the Apple ID has been entered the next step is to generate signing identities. To view the current signing identities, select the newly added Apple ID in the Accounts panel and click on the *Manage Certificates...* button at which point a list of available signing identities will be listed. To create a signing identity, simply click on the + button highlighted in Figure 3-4 and make the appropriate selection from the menu:

Figure 3-4

If the Apple ID has been used to enroll in the Apple Developer program, the option to create an *Apple Distribution* certificate will appear in the menu which will, when clicked, generate the signing identity required to submit the app to the Apple App Store. If you have not yet signed up for the Apple Developer program, select the *Apple Development* option to allow apps to be tested during development.

Having installed the iOS SDK and successfully launched Xcode 11 we can now look at Xcode in more detail, starting with Playgrounds.

4. An Introduction to Xcode 11 Playgrounds

Before introducing the Swift programming language in the chapters that follow, it is first worth learning about a feature of Xcode known as *Playgrounds*. This is a feature of Xcode designed to make learning Swift and experimenting with the iOS SDK much easier. The concepts covered in this chapter can be put to use when experimenting with many of the introductory Swift code examples contained in the chapters that follow.

4.1 What is a Playground?

A playground is an interactive environment where Swift code can be entered and executed with the results appearing in real-time. This makes an ideal environment in which to learn the syntax of Swift and the visual aspects of iOS app development without the need to work continuously through the edit/compile/run/debug cycle that would ordinarily accompany a standard Xcode iOS project. With support for rich text comments, playgrounds are also a good way to document code for future reference or as a training tool.

4.2 Creating a New Playground

To create a new Playground, start Xcode and select the *Get started with a playground* option from the welcome screen or select the *File -> New -> Playground...* menu option. Choose the iOS option on the resulting panel and select the Blank template.

The Blank template is useful for trying out Swift coding. The Single View template, on the other hand, provides a view controller environment for trying out code that requires a user interface layout. The game and map templates provide preconfigured playgrounds that allow you to experiment with the iOS MapKit and SpriteKit frameworks respectively.

On the next screen, name the playground *LearnSwift* and choose a suitable file system location into which the playground should be saved before clicking on the *Create* button.

Once the playground has been created, the following screen will appear ready for Swift code to be entered:

Figure 4-1

The panel on the left-hand side of the window (marked A in Figure 4-1) is the *playground editor* where the lines of Swift code are entered. The right-hand panel (marked B) is referred to as the *results panel* and is where the results of each Swift expression entered into the playground editor panel are displayed.

The cluster of three buttons at the right-hand side of the toolbar (marked C) are used to hide and display other panels within the playground window. The left most button displays the Navigator panel which provides access to the folders and files that make up the playground (marked A in Figure 4-2 below). The middle button, on the other hand, displays the Debug view (B) which displays code output and information about coding or runtime errors. The right most button displays the Utilities panel (C) where a variety of properties relating to the playground may be configured.

Figure 4-2

By far the quickest way to gain familiarity with the playground environment is to work through some simple examples.

4.3 A Basic Swift Playground Example

Perhaps the simplest of examples in any programming language (that at least does something tangible) is to write some code to output a single line of text. Swift is no exception to this rule so, within the playground window, begin adding another line of Swift code so that it reads as follows:

```
import UIKit

var str = "Hello , playground"

print("Welcome to Swift")
```

All that the additional line of code does is make a call to the built-in Swift *print* function which takes as a parameter a string of characters to be displayed on the console. Those familiar with other programming languages will note the absence of a semi-colon at the end of the line of code. In Swift, semi-colons are optional and generally only used as a separator when multiple statements occupy the same line of code.

Note that although some extra code has been entered, nothing yet appears in the results panel. This is because the code has yet to be executed. One option to run the code is to click on the Execute Playground button located in the bottom left-hand corner of the main panel as indicated by the arrow in Figure 4-3:

Figure 4-3

When clicked, this button will execute all the code in the current playground page from the first line of code to the last. Another option is to execute the code in stages using the run button located in the margin of the code editor as shown in Figure 4-4:

Figure 4-4

This button executes the line numbers with the shaded blue background including the line on which the button is currently positioned. In the above figure, for example, the button will execute lines 1 through 3 and then stop.

The position of the run button can be moved by hovering the mouse pointer over the line numbers in the editor. In Figure 4-5, for example, the run button is now positioned on line 5 and will execute lines 4 and 5 when clicked. Note that lines 1 to 3 are no longer highlighted in blue indicating that these have already been executed and are not eligible to be run this time:

```
      ⊞  <  >   ⬚ LearnSwift
      1  import UIKit
      2
      3  var str = "Hello , playground"
      4
     ⊙  print("Welcome to Swift")
```

Figure 4-5

This technique provides an easy way to execute the code in stages making it easier to understand how the code functions and to identify problems in code execution.

To reset the playground so that execution can be performed from the start of the code, simply click on the stop button as indicated in Figure 4-6:

Figure 4-6

Using this incremental execution technique, execute lines 1 through 3 and note that output now appears in the results panel indicating that the variable has been initialized:

```
      ⊞  <  >   ⬚ LearnSwift
      1  import UIKit
      2
      3  var str = "Hello , playground"                          "Hello , playground"  ▣
      4
     ⊙  print("Welcome to Swift")
      6
```

Figure 4-7

Next, execute the remaining lines up to and including line 5 at which point the "Welcome to Swift" output should appear both in the results panel and Debug panel:

Figure 4-8

4.4 Viewing Results

Playgrounds are particularly useful when working and experimenting with Swift algorithms. This can be useful when combined with the Quick Look feature. Remaining within the playground editor, enter the following lines of code beneath the existing print statement:

```
var x = 10

for index in 1...20 {
    let y = index * x
    x -= 1
    print(y)
}
```

This expression repeats a loop 20 times, performing arithmetic expressions on each iteration of the loop. Once the code has been entered into the editor, click on the run button positioned at line 13 to execute these new lines of code. The playground will execute the loop and display in the results panel the number of times the loop was performed. More interesting information, however, may be obtained by hovering the mouse pointer over the results line so that two additional buttons appear as shown in Figure 4-9:

```
 5   print("Welcome to Swift")                    "Welcome to Swift\n"
 6
 7   var x = 10                                    10
 8
 9   for index in 1...20 {
10       let y = index * x                         (20 times)
11       x -= 1                                     (20 times)
12       print(y)                                   (20 times)
13   }
```

Figure 4-9

The left most of the two buttons is the *Quick Look* button which, when selected, will show a popup panel displaying the results as shown in Figure 4-10:

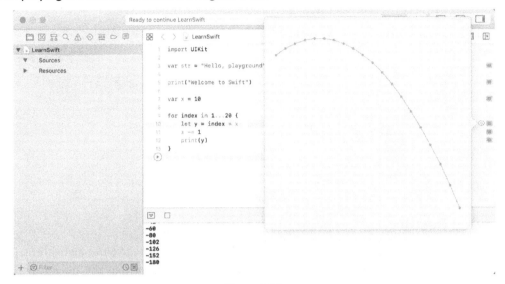

Figure 4-10

The right-most button is the *Show Result* button which, when selected, displays the results in-line with the code:

Figure 4-11

4.5 Adding Rich Text Comments

Rich text comments allow the code within a playground to be documented in a way that is easy to format and read. A single line of text can be marked as being rich text by preceding it with a //: marker. For example:

```
//: This is a single line of documentation text
```

Blocks of text can be added by wrapping the text in /*: and */ comment markers:

```
/*:
This is a block of documentation text that is intended
```

```
to span multiple lines
*/
```

The rich text uses the Markup language and allows text to be formatted using a lightweight and easy to use syntax. A heading, for example, can be declared by prefixing the line with a '#' character while text is displayed in italics when wrapped in '*' characters. Bold text, on the other hand, involves wrapping the text in '**' character sequences. It is also possible to configure bullet points by prefixing each line with a single '*'. Among the many other features of Markup are the ability to embed images and hyperlinks into the content of a rich text comment.

To see rich text comments in action, enter the following markup content into the playground editor immediately after the *print("Welcome to Swift")* line of code:

```
/*:
# Welcome to Playgrounds
This is your *first* playground which is intended to demonstrate:
* The use of **Quick Look**
* Placing results **in-line** with the code
*/
```

As the comment content is added it is said to be displayed in *raw markup* format. To display in *rendered markup* format, either select the *Editor -> Show Rendered Markup* menu option, or enable the *Render Documentation* option located under *Playground Settings* in the Inspector panel (marked C in Figure 4-2). If the Inspector panel is not currently visible, click on the right most of the three view buttons (marked C in Figure 4-1) to display it. Once rendered, the above rich text should appear as illustrated in Figure 4-12:

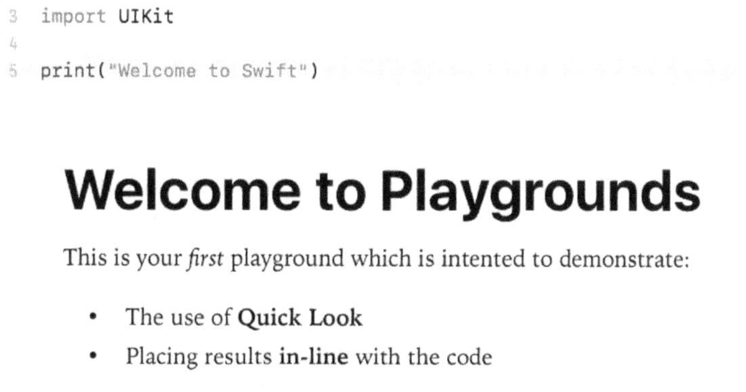

```
3   import UIKit
4
5   print("Welcome to Swift")
```

Welcome to Playgrounds

This is your *first* playground which is intented to demonstrate:

* The use of **Quick Look**
* Placing results **in-line** with the code

Figure 4-12

Detailed information about the Markup syntax can be found online at the following URL:

https://developer.apple.com/library/content/documentation/Xcode/Reference/xcode_markup_for matting_ref/index.html

4.6 **Working with Playground Pages**

A playground can consist of multiple pages, with each page containing its own code, resources and rich text comments. So far, the playground used in this chapter contains a single page. Add an additional page to the playground now by selecting the LearnSwift entry at the top of the Navigator panel, right-clicking and selecting the *New Playground Page* menu option. If the Navigator panel is not currently visible, click on the left most of the three view buttons (marked C in Figure 4-1) to display it. Note that two pages are now listed in the Navigator named "Untitled Page" and "Untitled Page 2". Select and then click a second time on the "Untitled Page 2" entry so that the name becomes editable and change the name to *UIKit Examples* as outlined in Figure 4-13:

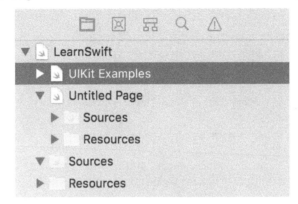

Figure 4-13

Note that the newly added page has Markup links which, when clicked, navigate to the previous or next page in the playground.

4.7 **Working with UIKit in Playgrounds**

Prior to the introduction of SwiftUI, iOS apps were developed using UIKit and a range of UIKit-based frameworks. Unsurprisingly, UIKit can be used within Xcode playgrounds.

While it is also possible to use SwiftUI within a playground, this requires some additional steps that involve integrating SwiftUI into UIKit (a topic which is not covered until much later in this book). In practice, however, Xcode provides a Live Preview canvas which provides many of the features of playgrounds when developing with SwiftUI. As will be discussed later, it may still be necessary to use UIKit when working with SwiftUI, so for completeness, the use of UIKit in a playground will be covered in this section.

When working with UIKit within a playground page it is necessary to import the iOS UIKit Framework. The UIKit Framework contains most of the classes necessary to implement user interfaces for iOS applications when not using SwiftUI. An extremely powerful feature of playgrounds is that it is also possible to work with UIKit along with many of the other frameworks that comprise the iOS SDK.

The following code, for example, imports the UIKit framework, creates a UILabel instance and sets color, text and font properties on it:

```
import UIKit

let myLabel = UILabel(frame: CGRect(x: 0, y: 0, width: 200, height: 50))

myLabel.backgroundColor = UIColor.red
myLabel.text = "Hello Swift"
myLabel.textAlignment = .center
myLabel.font = UIFont(name: "Georgia", size: 24)
myLabel
```

Enter this code into the playground editor on the UIKit Examples page (the existing code can be removed) and run the code. This code provides a good example of how the Quick Look feature can be useful. Each line of the example Swift code configures a different aspect of the appearance of the UILabel instance. Clicking on the Quick Look button for the first line of code will display an empty view (since the label exists but has yet to be given any visual attributes). Clicking on the Quick Look button in the line of code which sets the background color, on the other hand, will show the red label:

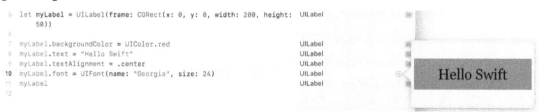

Figure 4-14

Similarly, the quick look view for the line where the text property is set will show the red label with the "Hello Swift" text left aligned:

Figure 4-15

The font setting quick look view on the other hand displays the UILabel with centered text and the larger Georgia font:

Figure 4-16

4.8 **Adding Resources to a Playground**

Another useful feature of playgrounds is the ability to bundle and access resources such as image files in a playground. Within the Navigator panel, click on the right facing arrow (known as a *disclosure arrow*) to the left of the UIKit Examples page entry to unfold the page contents (Figure 4-17) and note the presence of a folder named *Resources*:

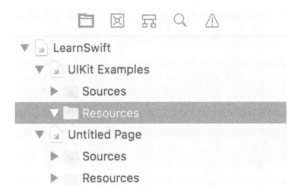

Figure 4-17

If you have not already done so, download and unpack the code samples archive from the following URL:

https://www.ebookfrenzy.com/retail/swiftui/

Open a Finder window, navigate to the *playground_images* folder within the code samples folder and drag and drop the image file named *waterfall.png* onto the *Resources* folder beneath the UIKit Examples page in the Playground Navigator panel:

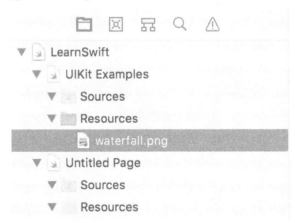

Figure 4-18

With the image added to the resources, add code to the page to create an image object and display the waterfall image on it:

```
let image = UIImage(named: "waterfall")
```

With the code added, run the new statement and use either the Quick Look or inline option to view the results of the code:

```
13   let image = UIImage(named: "waterfall")                                   w 1,280 h 853
```

```
14
```

Figure 4-19

4.9 **Working with Enhanced Live Views**

So far in this chapter, all of the UIKit examples have involved presenting static user interface elements using the Quick Look and in-line features. It is, however, also possible to test dynamic user interface behavior within a playground using the Xcode Enhanced Live Views feature. To demonstrate live views in action, create a new page within the playground named *Live View Example*. Within the newly added page, remove the existing lines of Swift code before adding import statements for the UIKit framework and an additional playground module named PlaygroundSupport:

```
import UIKit
import PlaygroundSupport
```

The PlaygroundSupport module provides a number of useful features for playgrounds including the ability to present a live view within the playground timeline.

Beneath the import statements, add the following code:

```
import UIKit
import PlaygroundSupport


let container = UIView(frame: CGRect(x: 0,y: 0,width: 200,height: 200))
container.backgroundColor = UIColor.white
let square = UIView(frame: CGRect(x: 50,y: 50,width: 100,height: 100))
square.backgroundColor = UIColor.red

container.addSubview(square)

UIView.animate(withDuration: 5.0, animations: {
    square.backgroundColor = UIColor.blue
    let rotation = CGAffineTransform(rotationAngle: 3.14)
    square.transform = rotation
})
```

The code creates a UIView object to act as a container view and assigns it a white background color. A smaller view is then drawn positioned in the center of the container view and colored red. The second view is then added as a child of the container view. An animation is then used to change the color of the smaller view to blue and to rotate it through 360 degrees.

Once the code has been executed, clicking on any of the Quick Look buttons will show a snapshot of the views at each stage in the code sequence. None of the quick look views, however, show the dynamic animation. To see how the animation code works it will be necessary to use the live view playground feature.

The PlaygroundSupport module includes a class named PlaygroundPage that allows playground code to interact with the pages that make up a playground. This is achieved through a range of methods and properties of the class, one of which is the *current* property. This property, in turn, provides access to the current playground page. In order to execute the code within the playground, the *liveView* property of the current page needs to be set to our new container. To display the Live View panel, enable the Xcode *Editor -> Live View* menu option as shown in Figure 4-20:

Figure 4-20

Once the live view panel is visible, add the code to assign the container to the live view of the current page as follows:

```
import UIKit
import PlaygroundSupport

let container = UIView(frame: CGRect(x: 0,y: 0,width: 200,height: 200))

PlaygroundPage.current.liveView = container

container.backgroundColor = UIColor.white
let square = UIView(frame: CGRect(x: 50,y: 50,width: 100,height: 100))
square.backgroundColor = UIColor.red

container.addSubview(square)

UIView.animate(withDuration: 5.0, animations: {
```

```
    square.backgroundColor = UIColor.blue
    let rotation = CGAffineTransform(rotationAngle: 3.14)
    square.transform = rotation
})
```

Once the call has been added, re-execute the code at which point the views should appear in the timeline (Figure 4-21). During the 5 second animation duration, the red square should rotate through 360 degrees while gradually changing color to blue:

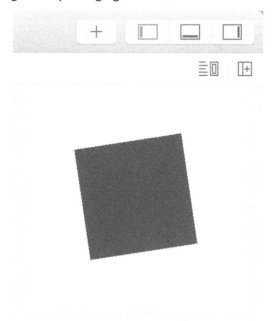

Figure 4-21

To repeat the execution of the code in the playground page, click on the stop button highlighted in Figure 4-6 to reset the playground and change the stop button into the run button (Figure 4-3). Click the run button to repeat the execution.

4.10 Summary

This chapter has introduced the concept of playgrounds. Playgrounds provide an environment in which Swift code can be entered and the results of that code viewed dynamically. This provides an excellent environment both for learning the Swift programming language and for experimenting with many of the classes and APIs included in the iOS SDK without the need to create Xcode projects and repeatedly edit, compile and run code.

5. Swift Data Types, Constants and Variables

If you are new to the Swift programming language then the next few chapters are recommended reading. Although SwiftUI makes the development of apps easier, it will still be necessary to learn Swift programming both to understand SwiftUI and develop fully functional apps.

If, on the other hand, you are familiar with the Swift programming language you can skip the Swift specific chapters that follow (though if you are not familiar with the new features of Swift 5.1 you should at least read the sections and chapters relating to *implicit returns from single expressions*, *opaque return types* and *property wrappers* before moving on to the SwiftUI chapters).

Prior to the introduction of iOS 8, the stipulated programming language for the development of iOS applications was Objective-C. When Apple announced iOS 8, however, the company also introduced an alternative to Objective-C in the form of the Swift programming language.

Due entirely to the popularity of iOS, Objective-C had become one of the more widely used programming languages. With origins firmly rooted in the 40-year-old C Programming Language, however, and despite recent efforts to modernize some aspects of the language syntax, Objective-C was beginning to show its age.

Swift, on the other hand, is a relatively new programming language designed specifically to make programming easier, faster and less prone to programmer error. Starting with a clean slate and no burden of legacy, Swift is a new and innovative language with which to develop applications for iOS, macOS, watchOS and tvOS with the advantage that much of the syntax will be familiar to those with experience of other programming languages.

The introduction of Swift aside, it is still perfectly acceptable to continue to develop applications using Objective-C. Indeed, it is also possible to mix both Swift and Objective-C within the same application code base. That being said, Apple clearly sees the future of development in terms of Swift rather than Objective-C. In recognition of this fact, all of the examples in this book are implemented using Swift. Before moving on to those examples, however, the next several chapters will provide an overview and introduction to Swift programming. The intention of these chapters is to provide enough information so that you can begin to confidently program using Swift. For an exhaustive and in-depth guide to all the features, intricacies and capabilities of Swift, some time spent reading Apple's excellent book entitled "The Swift Programming Language" (available free of charge from within the Apple Books app) is strongly recommended.

5.1 **Using a Swift Playground**

Both this and the following few chapters are intended to introduce the basics of the Swift programming language. As outlined in the previous chapter, entitled *An Introduction to Swift Playgrounds* the best way to learn Swift is to experiment within a Swift playground environment. Before starting this chapter, therefore, create a new playground and use it to try out the code in both this and the other Swift introduction chapters that follow.

5.2 **Swift Data Types**

When we look at the different types of software that run on computer systems and mobile devices, from financial applications to graphics intensive games, it is easy to forget that computers are really just binary machines. Binary systems work in terms of 0 and 1, true or false, set and unset. All the data sitting in RAM, stored on disk drives and flowing through circuit boards and buses are nothing more than sequences of 1s and 0s. Each 1 or 0 is referred to as a *bit* and bits are grouped together in blocks of 8, each group being referred to as a *byte*. When people talk about 32-bit and 64-bit computer systems they are talking about the number of bits that can be handled simultaneously by the CPU bus. A 64-bit CPU, for example, is able to handle data in 64-bit blocks, resulting in faster performance than a 32-bit based system.

Humans, of course, don't think in binary. We work with decimal numbers, letters and words. In order for a human to easily (easily being a relative term in this context) program a computer, some middle ground between human and computer thinking is needed. This is where programming languages such as Swift come into play. Programming languages allow humans to express instructions to a computer in terms and structures we understand, and then compile that down to a format that can be executed by a CPU.

One of the fundamentals of any program involves data, and programming languages such as Swift define a set of *data types* that allow us to work with data in a format we understand when programming. For example, if we want to store a number in a Swift program, we could do so with syntax similar to the following:

```
var mynumber = 10
```

In the above example, we have created a variable named *mynumber* and then assigned to it the value of 10. When we compile the source code down to the machine code used by the CPU, the number 10 is seen by the computer in binary as:

```
1010
```

Now that we have a basic understanding of the concept of data types and why they are necessary we can take a closer look at some of the more commonly used data types supported by Swift.

5.2.1 Integer Data Types

Swift integer data types are used to store whole numbers (in other words a number with no decimal places). Integers can be *signed* (capable of storing positive, negative and zero values) or *unsigned* (positive and zero values only).

Swift provides support for 8, 16, 32 and 64-bit integers (represented by the Int8, Int16, Int32 and Int64 types respectively). The same variants are also available for unsigned integers (UInt8, UInt16, UInt32 and UInt64).

In general, Apple recommends using the *Int* data type rather than one of the above specifically sized data types. The Int data type will use the appropriate integer size for the platform on which the code is running.

All integer data types contain bounds properties which can be accessed to identify the minimum and maximum supported values of that particular type. The following code, for example, outputs the minimum and maximum bounds for the 32-bit signed integer data type:

```
print("Int32 Min = \(Int32.min) Int32 Max = \(Int32.max)")
```

When executed, the above code will generate the following output:

```
Int32 Min = -2147483648 Int32 Max = 2147483647
```

5.2.2 Floating Point Data Types

The Swift floating point data types are able to store values containing decimal places. For example, 4353.1223 would be stored in a floating-point data type. Swift provides two floating point data types in the form of *Float* and *Double*. Which type to use depends on the size of value to be stored and the level of precision required. The Double type can be used to store up to 64-bit floating point numbers with a level of precision of 15 decimal places or greater. The Float data type, on the other hand, is limited to 32-bit floating point numbers and offers a level of precision as low as 6 decimal places depending on the native platform on which the code is running.

5.2.3 Bool Data Type

Swift, like other languages, includes a data type for the purpose of handling true or false (1 or 0) conditions. Two Boolean constant values (*true* and *false*) are provided by Swift specifically for working with Boolean data types.

5.2.4 Character Data Type

The Swift Character data type is used to store a single character of rendered text such as a letter, numerical digit, punctuation mark or symbol. Internally characters in Swift are stored in the form of *grapheme clusters*. A grapheme cluster is made of two or more Unicode scalars that are combined to represent a single visible character.

The following lines assign a variety of different characters to Character type variables:

```
var myChar1 = "f"
var myChar2 = ":"
var myChar3 = "X"
```

Characters may also be referenced using Unicode code points. The following example assigns the 'X' character to a variable using Unicode:

```
var myChar4 = "\u{0058}"
```

5.2.5 String Data Type

The String data type is a sequence of characters that typically make up a word or sentence. In addition to providing a storage mechanism, the String data type also includes a range of string manipulation features allowing strings to be searched, matched, concatenated and modified. Strings in Swift are represented internally as collections of characters (where a character is, as previously discussed, comprised of one or more Unicode scalar values).

Strings can also be constructed using combinations of strings, variables, constants, expressions, and function calls using a concept referred to as *string interpolation*. For example, the following code creates a new string from a variety of different sources using string interpolation before outputting it to the console:

```
var userName = "John"
var inboxCount = 25
let maxCount = 100

var message = "\(userName) has \(inboxCount) messages. Message capacity
remaining is \(maxCount - inboxCount)"

print(message)
```

When executed, the code will output the following message:

```
John has 25 messages. Message capacity remaining is 75 messages.
```

A multiline string literal may be declared by encapsulating the string within triple quotes as follows:

```
var multiline = """

    The console glowed with flashing warnings.
    Clearly time was running out.

    "I thought you said you knew how to fly this!" yelled Mary.

    "It was much easier on the simulator" replied her brother,
     trying to keep the panic out of his voice.

"""

print(multiline)
```

The above code will generate the following output when run:

```
    The console glowed with flashing warnings.
    Clearly time was running out.
```

```
"I thought you said you knew how to fly this!" yelled Mary.

"It was much easier on the simulator" replied her brother,
trying to keep the panic out of his voice.
```

The amount by which each line is indented within a multiline literal is calculated as the number of characters by which the line is indented minus the number of characters by which the closing triple quote line is indented. If, for example, the fourth line in the above example had a 10-character indentation and the closing triple quote was indented by 5 characters, the actual indentation of the fourth line within the string would be 5 characters. This allows multiline literals to be formatted tidily within Swift code while still allowing control over indentation of individual lines.

5.2.6 Special Characters/Escape Sequences

In addition to the standard set of characters outlined above, there is also a range of *special characters* (also referred to as *escape sequences*) available for specifying items such as a new line, tab or a specific Unicode value within a string. These special characters are identified by prefixing the character with a backslash (a concept referred to as *escaping*). For example, the following assigns a new line to the variable named newline:

```
var newline = "\n"
```

In essence, any character that is preceded by a backslash is considered to be a special character and is treated accordingly. This raises the question as to what to do if you actually want a backslash character. This is achieved by *escaping* the backslash itself:

```
var backslash = "\\"
```

Commonly used special characters supported by Swift are as follows:

- **\n** - New line
- **\r** - Carriage return
- **\t** - Horizontal tab
- **** - Backslash
- **\"** - Double quote (used when placing a double quote into a string declaration)
- **\'** - Single quote (used when placing a single quote into a string declaration)
- **\u{*nn*}** – Single byte Unicode scalar where *nn* is replaced by two hexadecimal digits representing the Unicode character.
- **\u{*nnnn*}** – Double byte Unicode scalar where *nnnn* is replaced by four hexadecimal digits representing the Unicode character.
- **\U{*nnnnnnnn*}** – Four-byte Unicode scalar where *nnnnnnnn* is replaced by eight hexadecimal digits representing the Unicode character.

5.3 **Swift Variables**

Variables are essentially locations in computer memory reserved for storing the data used by an application. Each variable is given a name by the programmer and assigned a value. The name assigned to the variable may then be used in the Swift code to access the value assigned to that variable. This access can involve either reading the value of the variable or changing the value. It is, of course, the ability to change the value of variables which gives them the name *variable*.

5.4 **Swift Constants**

A constant is like a variable in that it provides a named location in memory to store a data value. Constants differ in one significant way in that once a value has been assigned to a constant it cannot subsequently be changed.

Constants are particularly useful if there is a value which is used repeatedly throughout the application code. Rather than use the value each time, it makes the code easier to read if the value is first assigned to a constant which is then referenced in the code. For example, it might not be clear to someone reading your Swift code why you used the value 5 in an expression. If, instead of the value 5, you use a constant named interestRate the purpose of the value becomes much clearer. Constants also have the advantage that if the programmer needs to change a widely used value, it only needs to be changed once in the constant declaration and not each time it is referenced.

As with variables, constants have a type, a name and a value. Unlike variables, however, once a value has been assigned to a constant, that value cannot subsequently be changed.

5.5 **Declaring Constants and Variables**

Variables are declared using the *var* keyword and may be initialized with a value at creation time. If the variable is declared without an initial value, it must be declared as being *optional* (a topic which will be covered later in this chapter). The following, for example, is a typical variable declaration:

```
var userCount = 10
```

Constants are declared using the *let* keyword.

```
let maxUserCount = 20
```

For greater code efficiency and execution performance, Apple recommends the use of constants rather than variables whenever possible.

5.6 **Type Annotations and Type Inference**

Swift is categorized as a *type safe* programming language. This essentially means that once the data type of a variable has been identified, that variable cannot subsequently be used to store data of any other type without inducing a compilation error. This contrasts to *loosely typed* programming languages where a variable, once declared, can subsequently be used to store other data types.

There are two ways in which the type of a constant or variable will be identified. One approach is to use a *type annotation* at the point the variable or constant is declared in the code. This is achieved by placing a colon after the constant or variable name followed by the type declaration. The following line of code, for example, declares a variable named userCount as being of type Int:

```
var userCount: Int = 10
```

In the absence of a type annotation in a declaration, the Swift compiler uses a technique referred to as *type inference* to identify the type of the constant or variable. When relying on type inference, the compiler looks to see what type of value is being assigned to the constant or variable at the point that it is initialized and uses that as the type. Consider, for example, the following variable and constant declarations:

```
var signalStrength = 2.231
let companyName = "My Company"
```

During compilation of the above lines of code, Swift will infer that the signalStrength variable is of type Double (type inference in Swift defaults to Double for all floating-point numbers) and that the companyName constant is of type String.

When a constant is declared without a type annotation it must be assigned a value at the point of declaration:

```
let bookTitle = "SwiftUI Essentials"
```

If a type annotation is used when the constant is declared, however, the value can be assigned later in the code. For example:

```
let bookTitle: String
.
.
if iosBookType {
        bookTitle = "SwiftUI Essentials"
} else {
        bookTitle = "Android Studio Development Essentials"
}
```

It is important to note that a value may only be assigned to a constant once. A second attempt to assign a value to a constant will result in a syntax error.

5.7 The Swift Tuple

Before proceeding, now is a good time to introduce the Swift tuple. The tuple is perhaps one of the simplest, yet most powerful features of the Swift programming language. A tuple is, quite simply, a way to temporarily group together multiple values into a single entity. The items stored in a tuple can be of any type and there are no restrictions requiring that those values all be of the same type. A tuple could, for example, be constructed to contain an Int value, a Float value and a String as follows:

```
let myTuple = (10, 432.433, "This is a String")
```

The elements of a tuple can be accessed using a number of different techniques. A specific tuple value can be accessed simply by referencing the index position (with the first value being at index position 0). The code below, for example, extracts the string resource (at index position 2 in the tuple) and assigns it to a new string variable:

```
let myTuple = (10, 432.433, "This is a String")
let myString = myTuple.2
print(myString)
```

Alternatively, all the values in a tuple may be extracted and assigned to variables or constants in a single statement:

```
let (myInt, myFloat, myString) = myTuple
```

This same technique can be used to extract selected values from a tuple while ignoring others by replacing the values to be ignored with an underscore character. The following code fragment extracts the integer and string values from the tuple and assigns them to variables, but ignores the floating-point value:

```
var (myInt, _, myString) = myTuple
```

When creating a tuple, it is also possible to assign a name to each value:

```
let myTuple = (count: 10, length: 432.433, message: "This is a String")
```

The names assigned to the values stored in a tuple may then be used to reference those values in code. For example, to output the *message* string value from the myTuple instance, the following line of code could be used:

```
print(myTuple.message)
```

Perhaps the most powerful use of tuples is, as will be seen in later chapters, the ability to return multiple values from a function.

5.8 The Swift Optional Type

The Swift optional data type is a new concept that does not exist in most other programming languages. The purpose of the optional type is to provide a safe and consistent approach to handling situations where a variable or constant may not have any value assigned to it.

Variables are declared as being optional by placing a ? character after the type declaration. The following code declares an optional Int variable named index:

```
var index: Int?
```

The variable *index* can now either have an integer value assigned to it or have nothing assigned to it. Behind the scenes, and as far as the compiler and runtime are concerned, an optional with no value assigned to it actually has a value of nil.

An optional can easily be tested (typically using an if statement) to identify whether it has a value assigned to it as follows:

```
var index: Int?

if index != nil {
    // index variable has a value assigned to it
} else {
    // index variable has no value assigned to it
}
```

If an optional has a value assigned to it, that value is said to be "wrapped" within the optional. The value wrapped in an optional may be accessed using a concept referred to as *forced unwrapping*. This simply means that the underlying value is extracted from the optional data type, a procedure that is performed by placing an exclamation mark (!) after the optional name.

To explore this concept of unwrapping optional types in more detail, consider the following code:

```
var index: Int?

index = 3

var treeArray = ["Oak", "Pine", "Yew", "Birch"]

if index != nil {
    print(treeArray[index!])
} else {
    print("index does not contain a value")
}
```

The code simply uses an optional variable to hold the index into an array of strings representing the names of tree types (Swift arrays will be covered in more detail in the chapter entitled *Working with Array and Dictionary Collections in Swift*). If the index optional variable has a value assigned to it, the tree name at that location in the array is printed to the console. Since the index is an optional type, the value has been unwrapped by placing an exclamation mark after the variable name:

```
print(treeArray[index!])
```

Had the index not been unwrapped (in other words the exclamation mark omitted from the above line), the compiler would have issued an error similar to the following:

```
Value of optional type 'Int?' must be unwrapped to a value of type 'Int'
```

As an alternative to forced unwrapping, the value assigned to an optional may be allocated to a temporary variable or constant using *optional binding*, the syntax for which is as follows:

```
if let constantname = optionalName {


}

if var variablename = optionalName {
```

```
}
```

The above constructs perform two tasks. In the first instance, the statement ascertains whether the designated optional contains a value. Second, in the event that the optional has a value, that value is assigned to the declared constant or variable and the code within the body of the statement is executed. The previous forced unwrapping example could, therefore, be modified as follows to use optional binding instead:

```
var index: Int?

index = 3

var treeArray = ["Oak", "Pine", "Yew", "Birch"]

if let myvalue = index {
    print(treeArray[myvalue])
} else {
    print("index does not contain a value")
}
```

In this case the value assigned to the index variable is unwrapped and assigned to a temporary constant named *myvalue* which is then used as the index reference into the array. Note that the myvalue constant is described as temporary since it is only available within the scope of the if statement. Once the if statement completes execution, the constant will no longer exist. For this reason, there is no conflict in using the same temporary name as that assigned to the optional. The following is, for example, valid code:

```
.
.
if let index = index {
    print(treeArray[index])
} else {
.
.
```

Optional binding may also be used to unwrap multiple optionals and include a Boolean test condition, the syntax for which is as follows:

```
if let constname1 = optName1, let constname2 = optName2,
    let optName3 = ..., <boolean statement> {

}
```

The following code, for example, uses optional binding to unwrap two optionals within a single statement:

```
var pet1: String?
var pet2: String?

pet1 = "cat"
pet2 = "dog"

if let firstPet = pet1, let secondPet = pet2 {
    print(firstPet)
    print(secondPet)
} else {
    print("insufficient pets")
}
```

The code fragment below, on the other hand, also makes use of the Boolean test clause condition:

```
if let firstPet = pet1, let secondPet = pet2, petCount > 1 {
    print(firstPet)
    print(secondPet)
} else {
    print("insufficient pets")
}
```

In the above example, the optional binding will not be attempted unless the value assigned to *petCount* is greater than 1.

It is also possible to declare an optional as being *implicitly unwrapped*. When an optional is declared in this way, the underlying value can be accessed without having to perform forced unwrapping or optional binding. An optional is declared as being implicitly unwrapped by replacing the question mark (?) with an exclamation mark (!) in the declaration. For example:

```
var index: Int! // Optional is now implicitly unwrapped

index = 3

var treeArray = ["Oak", "Pine", "Yew", "Birch"]

if index != nil {
    print(treeArray[index])

} else {
    print("index does not contain a value")
}
```

With the index optional variable now declared as being implicitly unwrapped, it is no longer necessary to unwrap the value when it is used as an index into the array in the above print call.

One final observation with regard to optionals in Swift is that only optional types are able to have no value or a value of nil assigned to them. In Swift it is not, therefore, possible to assign a nil value to a non-optional variable or constant. The following declarations, for instance, will all result in errors from the compiler since none of the variables are declared as optional:

```
var myInt = nil // Invalid code
var myString: String = nil // Invalid Code
let myConstant = nil // Invalid code
```

5.9 Type Casting and Type Checking

When writing Swift code, situations will occur where the compiler is unable to identify the specific type of a value. This is often the case when a value of ambiguous or unexpected type is returned from a method or function call. In this situation it may be necessary to let the compiler know the type of value that your code is expecting or requires using the *as* keyword (a concept referred to as *type casting*).

The following code, for example, lets the compiler know that the value returned from the *object(forKey:)* method needs to be treated as a String type:

```
let myValue = record.object(forKey: "comment") as! String
```

In fact, there are two types of casting which are referred to as *upcasting* and *downcasting*. Upcasting occurs when an object of a particular class is cast to one of its superclasses. Upcasting is performed using the *as* keyword and is also referred to as *guaranteed conversion* since the compiler can tell from the code that the cast will be successful. The UIButton class, for example, is a subclass of the UIControl class as shown in the fragment of the UIKit class hierarchy shown in Figure 5-1:

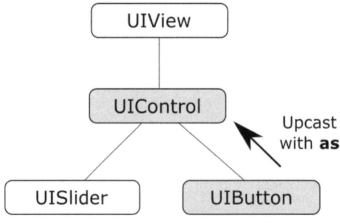

Figure 5-1

Since UIButton is a subclass of UIControl, the object can be safely upcast as follows:

```
let myButton: UIButton = UIButton()

let myControl = myButton as UIControl
```

Downcasting, on the other hand, occurs when a conversion is made from one class to another where there is no guarantee that the cast can be made safely or that an invalid casting attempt will be caught by the compiler. When an invalid cast is made in downcasting and not identified by the compiler it will most likely lead to an error at runtime.

Downcasting usually involves converting from a class to one of its subclasses. Downcasting is performed using the *as!* keyword syntax and is also referred to as *forced conversion*. Consider, for example, the UIKit UIScrollView class which has as subclasses both the UITableView and UITextView classes as shown in Figure 5-2:

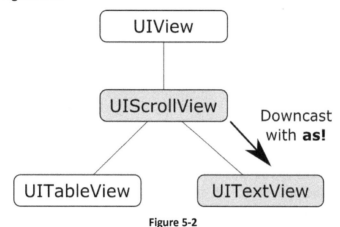

Figure 5-2

In order to convert a UIScrollView object to a UITextView class a downcast operation needs to be performed. The following code attempts to downcast a UIScrollView object to UITextView using the *guaranteed conversion* or *upcast* approach:

```
let myScrollView: UIScrollView = UIScrollView()

let myTextView = myScrollView as UITextView
```

The above code will result in the following error:

```
'UIScrollView' is not convertible to 'UITextView'
```

The compiler is indicating that a UIScrollView instance cannot be safely converted to a UITextView class instance. This does not necessarily mean that it is incorrect to do so, the compiler is simply stating that it cannot guarantee the safety of the conversion for you. The downcast conversion could instead be forced using the *as!* annotation:

```
let myTextView = myScrollView as! UITextView
```

Now the code will compile without an error. As an example of the dangers of downcasting, however, the above code will crash on execution stating that UIScrollView cannot be cast to UITextView. Forced downcasting should, therefore, be used with caution.

A safer approach to downcasting is to perform an optional binding using *as?*. If the conversion is performed successfully, an optional value of the specified type is returned, otherwise the optional value will be nil:

```
if let myTextView = myScrollView as? UITextView {
    print("Type cast to UITextView succeeded")
} else {
    print("Type cast to UITextView failed")
}
```

It is also possible to *type check* a value using the *is* keyword. The following code, for example, checks that a specific object is an instance of a class named MyClass:

```
if myobject is MyClass {
        // myobject is an instance of MyClass
}
```

5.10 **Summary**

This chapter has begun the introduction to Swift by exploring data types together with an overview of how to declare constants and variables. The chapter has also introduced concepts such as type safety, type inference and optionals, each of which is an integral part of Swift programming and designed specifically to make code writing less prone to error.

6. Swift Operators and Expressions

So far we have looked at using variables and constants in Swift and also described the different data types. Being able to create variables, however, is only part of the story. The next step is to learn how to use these variables and constants in Swift code. The primary method for working with data is in the form of *expressions*.

6.1 Expression Syntax in Swift

The most basic Swift expression consists of an *operator*, two *operands* and an *assignment*. The following is an example of an expression:

```
var myresult = 1 + 2
```

In the above example, the (+) operator is used to add two operands (1 and 2) together. The *assignment operator* (=) subsequently assigns the result of the addition to a variable named *myresult*. The operands could just have easily been variables (or a mixture of constants and variables) instead of the actual numerical values used in the example.

In the remainder of this chapter we will look at the basic types of operators available in Swift.

6.2 The Basic Assignment Operator

We have already looked at the most basic of assignment operators, the = operator. This assignment operator simply assigns the result of an expression to a variable. In essence, the = assignment operator takes two operands. The left-hand operand is the variable or constant to which a value is to be assigned and the right-hand operand is the value to be assigned. The right-hand operand is, more often than not, an expression which performs some type of arithmetic or logical evaluation, the result of which will be assigned to the variable or constant. The following examples are all valid uses of the assignment operator:

```
var x: Int? // Declare an optional Int variable
var y = 10 // Declare and initialize a second Int variable

x = 10 // Assign a value to x
x = x! + y // Assign the result of x + y to x
x = y // Assign the value of y to x
```

6.3 Swift Arithmetic Operators

Swift provides a range of operators for the purpose of creating mathematical expressions. These operators primarily fall into the category of *binary* operators in that they take two operands. The exception is the *unary negative operator* (-) which serves to indicate that a value is negative rather than positive. This contrasts with the *subtraction operator* (-) which takes two operands (i.e. one value to be subtracted from another). For example:

```
var x = -10 // Unary - operator used to assign -10 to variable x
x = x - 5 // Subtraction operator. Subtracts 5 from x
```

The following table lists the primary Swift arithmetic operators:

Operator	Description
-(unary)	Negates the value of a variable or expression
*	Multiplication
/	Division
+	Addition
-	Subtraction
%	Remainder/Modulo

Table 6-1

Note that multiple operators may be used in a single expression.

For example:

```
x = y * 10 + z - 5 / 4
```

6.4 Compound Assignment Operators

In an earlier section we looked at the basic assignment operator (=). Swift provides a number of operators designed to combine an assignment with a mathematical or logical operation. These are primarily of use when performing an evaluation where the result is to be stored in one of the operands. For example, one might write an expression as follows:

```
x = x + y
```

The above expression adds the value contained in variable x to the value contained in variable y and stores the result in variable x. This can be simplified using the addition compound assignment operator:

```
x += y
```

The above expression performs exactly the same task as $x = x + y$ but saves the programmer some typing.

Numerous compound assignment operators are available in Swift. The most frequently used of which are outlined in the following table:

Operator	Description
x += y	Add x to y and place result in x
x -= y	Subtract y from x and place result in x
x *= y	Multiply x by y and place result in x
x /= y	Divide x by y and place result in x
x %= y	Perform Modulo on x and y and place result in x

Table 6-2

6.5 Comparison Operators

Swift also includes a set of logical operators useful for performing comparisons. These operators all return a Boolean result depending on the result of the comparison. These operators are *binary operators* in that they work with two operands.

Comparison operators are most frequently used in constructing program flow control logic. For example, an *if* statement may be constructed based on whether one value matches another:

```
if x == y {
    // Perform task
}
```

The result of a comparison may also be stored in a *Bool* variable. For example, the following code will result in a *true* value being stored in the variable result:

```
var result: Bool?
var x = 10
var y = 20

result = x < y
```

Clearly 10 is less than 20, resulting in a *true* evaluation of the *x < y* expression. The following table lists the full set of Swift comparison operators:

Operator	Description
x == y	Returns true if x is equal to y

x > y	Returns true if x is greater than y
x >= y	Returns true if x is greater than or equal to y
x < y	Returns true if x is less than y
x <= y	Returns true if x is less than or equal to y
x != y	Returns true if x is not equal to y

Table 6-3

6.6 Boolean Logical Operators

Swift also provides a set of so-called logical operators designed to return Boolean *true* or *false* values. These operators both return Boolean results and take Boolean values as operands. The key operators are NOT (!), AND (&&) and OR (||).

The NOT (!) operator simply inverts the current value of a Boolean variable, or the result of an expression. For example, if a variable named *flag* is currently true, prefixing the variable with a '!' character will invert the value to false:

```
var flag = true // variable is true
var secondFlag = !flag // secondFlag set to false
```

The OR (||) operator returns true if one of its two operands evaluates to true, otherwise it returns false. For example, the following code evaluates to true because at least one of the expressions either side of the OR operator is true:

```
if (10 < 20) || (20 < 10) {
        print("Expression is true")
}
```

The AND (&&) operator returns true only if both operands evaluate to be true. The following example will return false because only one of the two operand expressions evaluates to true:

```
if (10 < 20) && (20 < 10) {
        print("Expression is true")
}
```

6.7 Range Operators

Swift includes several useful operators that allow ranges of values to be declared. As will be seen in later chapters, these operators are invaluable when working with looping in program logic.

The syntax for the *closed range operator* is as follows:

x...y

This operator represents the range of numbers starting at x and ending at y where both x and y are included within the range. The range operator 5...8, for example, specifies the numbers 5, 6, 7 and 8.

The *half-open range operator*, on the other hand uses the following syntax:

x..<y

In this instance, the operator encompasses all the numbers from x up to, but not including, y. A half-closed range operator 5..<8, therefore, specifies the numbers 5, 6 and 7.

Finally, the *one-sided range* operator specifies a range that can extend as far as possible in a specified range direction until the natural beginning or end of the range is reached (or until some other condition is met). A one-sided range is declared by omitting the number from one side of the range declaration, for example:

x...

or

...y

The previous chapter, for example, explained that a String in Swift is actually a collection of individual characters. A range to specify the characters in a string starting with the character at position 2 through to the last character in the string (regardless of string length) would be declared as follows:

2...

Similarly, to specify a range that begins with the first character and ends with the character at position 6, the range would be specified as follows:

...6

6.8 The Ternary Operator

Swift supports the *ternary operator* to provide a shortcut way of making decisions within code. The syntax of the ternary operator (also known as the conditional operator) is as follows:

```
condition ? true expression : false expression
```

The way the ternary operator works is that *condition* is replaced with an expression that will return either *true* or *false*. If the result is true then the expression that replaces the *true expression* is evaluated. Conversely, if the result was *false* then the *false expression* is evaluated. Let's see this in action:

```
let x = 10
let y = 20

print("Largest number is \(x > y ? x : y)")
```

The above code example will evaluate whether x is greater than y. Clearly this will evaluate to false resulting in y being returned to the print call for display to the user:

```
Largest number is 20
```

6.9 Bitwise Operators

As previously discussed, computer processors work in binary. These are essentially streams of ones and zeros, each one referred to as a bit. Bits are formed into groups of 8 to form bytes. As such, it is not surprising that we, as programmers, will occasionally end up working at this level in our code. To facilitate this requirement, Swift provides a range of *bit operators*.

Those familiar with bitwise operators in other languages such as C, C++, C#, Objective-C and Java will find nothing new in this area of the Swift language syntax. For those unfamiliar with binary numbers, now may be a good time to seek out reference materials on the subject in order to understand how ones and zeros are formed into bytes to form numbers. Other authors have done a much better job of describing the subject than we can do within the scope of this book.

For the purposes of this exercise we will be working with the binary representation of two numbers. First, the decimal number 171 is represented in binary as:

```
10101011
```

Second, the number 3 is represented by the following binary sequence:

```
00000011
```

Now that we have two binary numbers with which to work, we can begin to look at the Swift bitwise operators:

6.9.1 Bitwise NOT

The Bitwise NOT is represented by the tilde (~) character and has the effect of inverting all of the bits in a number. In other words, all the zeros become ones and all the ones become zeros. Taking our example 3 number, a Bitwise NOT operation has the following result:

```
00000011 NOT
========
11111100
```

The following Swift code, therefore, results in a value of -4:

```
let y = 3
let z = ~y

print("Result is \(z)")
```

6.9.2 Bitwise AND

The Bitwise AND is represented by a single ampersand (&). It makes a bit by bit comparison of two numbers. Any corresponding position in the binary sequence of each number where both bits are 1 results in a 1 appearing in the same position of the resulting number. If either bit position contains a 0 then a zero appears in the result. Taking our two example numbers, this would appear as follows:

```
10101011 AND
00000011
========
00000011
```

As we can see, the only locations where both numbers have 1s are the last two positions. If we perform this in Swift code, therefore, we should find that the result is 3 (00000011):

```
let x = 171
let y = 3
let z = x & y

print("Result is \(z)")
```

6.9.3 Bitwise OR

The bitwise OR also performs a bit by bit comparison of two binary sequences. Unlike the AND operation, the OR places a 1 in the result if there is a 1 in the first or second operand. The operator is represented by a single vertical bar character (|). Using our example numbers, the result will be as follows:

```
10101011 OR
00000011
========
10101011
```

If we perform this operation in a Swift example the result will be 171:

```
let x = 171
let y = 3
let z = x | y

print("Result is \(z)")
```

6.9.4 Bitwise XOR

The bitwise XOR (commonly referred to as *exclusive OR* and represented by the caret '^' character) performs a similar task to the OR operation except that a 1 is placed in the result if one or other corresponding bit positions in the two numbers is 1. If both positions are a 1 or a 0 then the corresponding bit in the result is set to a 0. For example:

```
10101011 XOR
```

```
00000011
=========
10101000
```

The result in this case is 10101000 which converts to 168 in decimal. To verify this we can, once again, try some Swift code:

```
let x = 171
let y = 3
let z = x ^ y

print("Result is \(z)")
```

6.9.5 Bitwise Left Shift

The bitwise left shift moves each bit in a binary number a specified number of positions to the left. Shifting an integer one position to the left has the effect of doubling the value.

As the bits are shifted to the left, zeros are placed in the vacated right most (low order) positions. Note also that once the left most (high order) bits are shifted beyond the size of the variable containing the value, those high order bits are discarded:

```
10101011 Left Shift one bit
=========
101010110
```

In Swift the bitwise left shift operator is represented by the '<<' sequence, followed by the number of bit positions to be shifted. For example, to shift left by 1 bit:

```
let x = 171
let z = x << 1

print("Result is \(z)")
```

When compiled and executed, the above code will display a message stating that the result is 342 which, when converted to binary, equates to 101010110.

6.9.6 Bitwise Right Shift

A bitwise right shift is, as you might expect, the same as a left except that the shift takes place in the opposite direction. Shifting an integer one position to the right has the effect of halving the value.

Note that since we are shifting to the right there is no opportunity to retain the lower most bits regardless of the data type used to contain the result. As a result, the low order bits are discarded. Whether or not the vacated high order bit positions are replaced with zeros or ones depends on whether the *sign bit* used to indicate positive and negative numbers is set or not.

```
10101011 Right Shift one bit
```

```
========
01010101
```

The bitwise right shift is represented by the '>>' character sequence followed by the shift count:

```
let x = 171
let z = x >> 1

print("Result is \(z)")
```

When executed, the above code will report the result of the shift as being 85, which equates to binary 01010101.

6.10 Compound Bitwise Operators

As with the arithmetic operators, each bitwise operator has a corresponding compound operator that allows the operation and assignment to be performed using a single operator:

Operator	Description
x &= y	Perform a bitwise AND of x and y and assign result to x
x |= y	Perform a bitwise OR of x and y and assign result to x
x ^= y	Perform a bitwise XOR of x and y and assign result to x
x <<= n	Shift x left by n places and assign result to x
x >>= n	Shift x right by n places and assign result to x

Table 6-4

6.11 Summary

Operators and expressions provide the underlying mechanism by which variables and constants are manipulated and evaluated within Swift code. This can take the simplest of forms whereby two numbers are added using the addition operator in an expression and the result stored in a variable using the assignment operator. Operators fall into a range of categories, details of which have been covered in this chapter.

7. Swift Control Flow

Regardless of the programming language used, application development is largely an exercise in applying logic, and much of the art of programming involves writing code that makes decisions based on one or more criteria. Such decisions define which code gets executed, how many times it is executed and, conversely, which code gets by-passed when the program is executing. This is often referred to as *control flow* since it controls the *flow* of program execution. Flow control typically falls into the categories of *looping control* (how often code is executed) and *conditional flow control* (whether code is executed). This chapter is intended to provide an introductory overview of both types of flow control in Swift.

7.1 Looping Control Flow

This chapter will begin by looking at control flow in the form of loops. Loops are essentially sequences of Swift statements which are to be executed repeatedly until a specified condition is met. The first looping statement we will explore is the *for-in* loop.

7.2 The Swift *for-in* Statement

The *for-in* loop is used to iterate over a sequence of items contained in a collection or number range and provides a simple to use looping option.

The syntax of the for-in loop is as follows:

```
for constant name in collection or range {
        // code to be executed
}
```

In this syntax, *constant name* is the name to be used for a constant that will contain the current item from the collection or range through which the loop is iterating. The code in the body of the loop will typically use this constant name as a reference to the current item in the loop cycle. The *collection* or *range* references the item through which the loop is iterating. This could, for example, be an array of string values, a range operator or even a string of characters (the topic of collections will be covered in greater detail within the chapter entitled *Working with Array and Dictionary Collections in Swift*).

Consider, for example, the following for-in loop construct:

```
for index in 1...5 {
        print("Value of index is \(index)")
}
```

The loop begins by stating that the current item is to be assigned to a constant named *index*. The statement then declares a closed range operator to indicate that the for loop is to iterate through a range of numbers, starting at 1 and ending at 5. The body of the loop simply prints out a message to the console panel indicating the current value assigned to the *index* constant, resulting in the following output:

```
Value of index is 1
Value of index is 2
Value of index is 3
Value of index is 4
Value of index is 5
```

As will be demonstrated in the *Working with Array and Dictionary Collections in Swift* chapter of this book, the *for-in* loop is of particular benefit when working with collections such as arrays and dictionaries.

The declaration of a constant name in which to store a reference to the current item is not mandatory. In the event that a reference to the current item is not required in the body of the *for* loop, the constant name in the *for* loop declaration can be replaced by an underscore character. For example:

```
var count = 0

for _ in 1...5 {
    // No reference to the current value is required.
    count += 1
}
```

7.2.1 The while Loop

The Swift *for* loop described previously works well when it is known in advance how many times a particular task needs to be repeated in a program. There will, however, be instances where code needs to be repeated until a certain condition is met, with no way of knowing in advance how many repetitions are going to be needed to meet that criteria. To address this need, Swift provides the *while* loop.

Essentially, the *while* loop repeats a set of tasks while a specified condition is met. The *while* loop syntax is defined as follows:

```
while condition {
    // Swift statements go here
}
```

In the above syntax, *condition* is an expression that will return either *true* or *false* and the *// Swift statements go here* comment represents the code to be executed while the *condition* expression is *true*. For example:

```
var myCount = 0
```

```
while  myCount < 100 {
      myCount += 1
}
```

In the above example, the *while* expression will evaluate whether the *myCount* variable is less than 100. If it is already greater than 100, the code in the braces is skipped and the loop exits without performing any tasks.

If, on the other hand, *myCount* is not greater than 100 the code in the braces is executed and the loop returns to the *while* statement and repeats the evaluation of *myCount*. This process repeats until the value of *myCount* is greater than 100, at which point the loop exits.

7.3 The *repeat ... while* loop

The *repeat ... while* loop replaces the Swift 1.x *do .. while* loop. It is often helpful to think of the *repeat ... while* loop as an inverted *while* loop. The *while* loop evaluates an expression before executing the code contained in the body of the loop. If the expression evaluates to *false* on the first check then the code is not executed. The *repeat ... while* loop, on the other hand, is provided for situations where you know that the code contained in the body of the loop will *always* need to be executed at least once. For example, you may want to keep stepping through the items in an array until a specific item is found. You know that you have to at least check the first item in the array to have any hope of finding the entry you need. The syntax for the *repeat ... while* loop is as follows:

```
repeat {
        // Swift statements here
} while conditional expression
```

In the *repeat ... while* example below the loop will continue until the value of a variable named *i* equals 0:

```
var i = 10

repeat {
        i -= 1
} while (i > 0)
```

7.4 Breaking from Loops

Having created a loop, it is possible that under certain conditions you might want to break out of the loop before the completion criteria have been met (particularly if you have created an infinite loop). One such example might involve continually checking for activity on a network socket. Once activity has been detected it will most likely be necessary to break out of the monitoring loop and perform some other task.

For the purpose of breaking out of a loop, Swift provides the *break* statement which breaks out of the current loop and resumes execution at the code directly after the loop. For example:

```
var j = 10

for _ in 0 ..< 100
{
    j += j

    if j > 100 {
        break
    }

    print("j = \(j)")
}
```

In the above example the loop will continue to execute until the value of j exceeds 100 at which point the loop will exit and execution will continue with the next line of code after the loop.

7.5 The *continue* Statement

The *continue* statement causes all remaining code statements in a loop to be skipped, and execution to be returned to the top of the loop. In the following example, the print function is only called when the value of variable *i* is an even number:

```
var i = 1

while i < 20
{
        i += 1

        if (i % 2) != 0 {
            continue
        }

        print("i = \(i)")
}
```

The *continue* statement in the above example will cause the print call to be skipped unless the value of *i* can be divided by 2 with no remainder. If the *continue* statement is triggered, execution will skip to the top of the while loop and the statements in the body of the loop will be repeated (until the value of *i* exceeds 19).

7.6 Conditional Flow Control

In the previous chapter we looked at how to use logical expressions in Swift to determine whether something is *true* or *false*. Since programming is largely an exercise in applying logic, much of the art of programming involves writing code that makes decisions based on one or more criteria. Such decisions define which code gets executed and, conversely, which code gets by-passed when the program is executing. This is often referred to as *flow control* since it controls the *flow* of program execution.

7.7 **Using the if Statement**

The *if* statement is perhaps the most basic of flow control options available to the Swift programmer. Programmers who are familiar with C, Objective-C, C++ or Java will immediately be comfortable using Swift *if* statements.

The basic syntax of the Swift *if* statement is as follows:

```
if boolean expression {
    // Swift code to be performed when expression evaluates to true
}
```

Unlike some other programming languages, it is important to note that the braces ({}) are mandatory in Swift, even if only one line of code is executed after the *if* expression.

Essentially if the *Boolean expression* evaluates to *true* then the code in the body of the statement is executed. The body of the statement is enclosed in braces ({}). If, on the other hand, the expression evaluates to *false* the code in the body of the statement is skipped.

For example, if a decision needs to be made depending on whether one value is greater than another, we would write code similar to the following:

```
let x = 10

if x > 9 {
    print("x is greater than 9!")
}
```

Clearly, x is indeed greater than 9 causing the message to appear in the console panel.

7.8 **Using if ... else ... Statements**

The next variation of the *if* statement allows us to also specify some code to perform if the expression in the *if* statement evaluates to *false*. The syntax for this construct is as follows:

```
if boolean expression {
    // Code to be executed if expression is true
} else {
    // Code to be executed if expression is false
}
```

Using the above syntax, we can now extend our previous example to display a different message if the comparison expression evaluates to be *false*:

```
let x = 10

if x > 9 {
```

```
        print("x is greater than 9!")
} else {
        print("x is less than 9!")

}
```

In this case, the second print statement would execute if the value of x was less than 9.

7.9 **Using if ... else if ... Statements**

So far we have looked at *if* statements which make decisions based on the result of a single logical expression. Sometimes it becomes necessary to make decisions based on a number of different criteria. For this purpose, we can use the *if ... else if ...* construct, an example of which is as follows:

```
let x = 9;

if x == 10 {
        print("x is 10")
} else if x == 9 {
        print("x is 9")
} else if x == 8 {
        print("x is 8")
}
```

This approach works well for a moderate number of comparisons but can become cumbersome for a larger volume of expression evaluations. For such situations, the Swift *switch* statement provides a more flexible and efficient solution. For more details on using the *switch* statement refer to the next chapter entitled *The Swift Switch Statement*.

7.10 **The guard Statement**

The guard statement is a Swift language feature introduced as part of Swift 2. A guard statement contains a Boolean expression which must evaluate to true in order for the code located *after* the guard statement to be executed. The guard statement must include an *else* clause to be executed in the event that the expression evaluates to false. The code in the else clause must contain a statement to exit the current code flow (i.e. a *return, break, continue* or *throw* statement). Alternatively, the else block may call any other function or method that does not itself return.

The syntax for the guard statement is as follows:

```
guard <boolean expressions> else {
    // code to be executed if expression is false
    <exit statement here>
}

// code here is executed if expression is true
```

The guard statement essentially provides an "early exit" strategy from the current function or loop in the event that a specified requirement is not met.

The following code example implements a guard statement within a function:

```
func multiplyByTen(value: Int?) {

    guard let number = value, number < 10 else {
        print("Number is too high")
        return
    }

    let result = number * 10
    print(result)
}
```

The function takes as a parameter an integer value in the form of an optional. The guard statement uses optional binding to unwrap the value and verify that it is less than 10. In the event that the variable could not be unwrapped, or that its value is greater than 9, the else clause is triggered, the error message printed, and the return statement executed to exit the function.

If the optional contains a value less than 10, the code after the guard statement executes to multiply the value by 10 and print the result. A particularly important point to note about the above example is that the unwrapped *number* variable is available to the code outside of the guard statement. This would not have been the case had the variable been unwrapped using an *if* statement.

7.11 Summary

The term *flow control* is used to describe the logic that dictates the execution path that is taken through the source code of an application as it runs. This chapter has looked at the two types of flow control provided by Swift (looping and conditional) and explored the various Swift constructs that are available to implement both forms of flow control logic.

Chapter 8

8. The Swift Switch Statement

In *Swift Control Flow* we looked at how to control program execution flow using the *if* and *else* statements. While these statement constructs work well for testing a limited number of conditions, they quickly become unwieldy when dealing with larger numbers of possible conditions. To simplify such situations, Swift has inherited the *switch* statement from the C programming language. Those familiar with the switch statement from other programming languages should be aware, however, that the Swift switch statement has some key differences from other implementations. In this chapter we will explore the Swift implementation of the *switch* statement in detail.

8.1 Why Use a switch Statement?

For a small number of logical evaluations of a value the *if ... else if ...* construct is perfectly adequate. Unfortunately, any more than two or three possible scenarios can quickly make such a construct both time consuming to write and difficult to read. For such situations, the *switch* statement provides an excellent alternative.

8.2 Using the switch Statement Syntax

The syntax for a basic Swift *switch* statement implementation can be outlined as follows:

```
switch expression
{
    case match1:
        statements

    case match2:
        statements

    case match3, match4:
        statements

    default:
        statements
}
```

In the above syntax outline, *expression* represents either a value, or an expression which returns a value. This is the value against which the *switch* operates.

For each possible match a *case* statement is provided, followed by a *match* value. Each potential match must be of the same type as the governing expression. Following on from the *case* line are the Swift statements that are to be executed in the event of the value matching the case condition.

Finally, the *default* section of the construct defines what should happen if none of the case statements present a match to the *expression*.

8.3 A Swift switch Statement Example

With the above information in mind we may now construct a simple *switch* statement:

```
let value = 4

switch (value)
{
     case 0:
        print("zero")

     case 1:
        print("one")

     case 2:
        print("two")

     case 3:
        print("three")

     case 4:
        print("four")

     case 5:
        print("five")

     default:
        print("Integer out of range")
}
```

8.4 Combining case Statements

In the above example, each case had its own set of statements to execute. Sometimes a number of different matches may require the same code to be executed. In this case, it is possible to group case matches together with a common set of statements to be executed when a match for any of the cases is found. For example, we can modify the switch construct in our example so that the same code is executed regardless of whether the value is 0, 1 or 2:

```
let value = 1
```

```
switch (value)
{
     case 0, 1, 2:
       print("zero, one or two")

     case 3:
       print("three")

     case 4:
       print("four")

     case 5:
       print("five")

     default:
       print("Integer out of range")
}
```

8.5 Range Matching in a switch Statement

The case statements within a switch construct may also be used to implement range matching. The following switch statement, for example, checks a temperature value for matches within three number ranges:

```
let temperature = 83

switch (temperature)
{
     case 0...49:
       print("Cold")

     case 50...79:
       print("Warm")

     case 80...110:
       print("Hot")

     default:
       print("Temperature out of range")
}
```

8.6 **Using the where statement**

The *where* statement may be used within a switch case match to add additional criteria required for a positive match. The following switch statement, for example, checks not only for the range in which a value falls, but also whether the number is odd or even:

```
let temperature = 54

switch (temperature)
{
     case 0...49 where temperature % 2 == 0:
        print("Cold and even")

     case 50...79 where temperature % 2 == 0:
        print("Warm and even")

     case 80...110 where temperature % 2 == 0:
        print("Hot and even")

     default:
        print("Temperature out of range or odd")
}
```

8.7 **Fallthrough**

Those familiar with switch statements in other languages such as C and Objective-C will notice that it is no longer necessary to include a *break* statement after each case declaration. Unlike other languages, Swift automatically breaks out of the statement when a matching case condition is met. The fallthrough effect of other switch implementations (whereby the execution path continues through the remaining case statements) can be emulated using the *fallthrough* statement:

```
let temperature = 10

switch (temperature)
{
     case 0...49 where temperature % 2 == 0:
        print("Cold and even")
     fallthrough

     case 50...79 where temperature % 2 == 0:
        print("Warm and even")
        fallthrough

     case 80...110 where temperature % 2 == 0:
        print("Hot and even")
        fallthrough
```

```
    default:
        print("Temperature out of range or odd")
}
```

Although *break* is less commonly used in Swift switch statements, it is useful when no action needs to be taken for the default case. For example:

```
.
.
.
    default:
        break
}
```

8.8 **Summary**

While the *if.. else..* construct serves as a good decision-making option for small numbers of possible outcomes, this approach can become unwieldy in more complex situations. As an alternative method for implementing flow control logic in Swift when many possible outcomes exist as the result of an evaluation, the *switch* statement invariably makes a more suitable option. As outlined in this chapter, however, developers familiar with switch implementations from other programming languages should be aware of some subtle differences in the way that the Swift switch statement works.

9. An Overview of Swift 5 Functions, Methods and Closures

Swift functions, methods and closures are a vital part of writing well-structured and efficient code and provide a way to organize programs while avoiding code repetition. In this chapter we will look at how functions, methods and closures are declared and used within Swift.

9.1 What is a Function?

A function is a named block of code that can be called upon to perform a specific task. It can be provided data on which to perform the task and is capable of returning results to the code that called it. For example, if a particular arithmetic calculation needs to be performed in a Swift program, the code to perform the arithmetic can be placed in a function. The function can be programmed to accept the values on which the arithmetic is to be performed (referred to as *parameters*) and to return the result of the calculation. At any point in the program code where the calculation is required the function is simply called, parameter values passed through as *arguments* and the result returned.

The terms *parameter* and *argument* are often used interchangeably when discussing functions. There is, however, a subtle difference. The values that a function is able to accept when it is called are referred to as *parameters*. At the point that the function is actually called and passed those values, however, they are referred to as *arguments*.

9.2 What is a Method?

A method is essentially a function that is associated with a particular class, structure or enumeration. If, for example, you declare a function within a Swift class (a topic covered in detail in the chapter entitled *The Basics of Object-Oriented Programming in Swift*), it is considered to be a method. Although the remainder of this chapter refers to functions, the same rules and behavior apply equally to methods unless otherwise stated.

9.3 How to Declare a Swift Function

A Swift function is declared using the following syntax:

```
func <function name> (<para name>: <para type>,
                      <para name>: <para type>, ... ) -> <return type> {
        // Function code
}
```

This combination of function name, parameters and return type are referred to as the *function signature*. Explanations of the various fields of the function declaration are as follows:

- **func** – The prefix keyword used to notify the Swift compiler that this is a function.
- **<function name>** - The name assigned to the function. This is the name by which the function will be referenced when it is called from within the application code.
- **<para name>** - The name by which the parameter is to be referenced in the function code.
- **<para type>** - The type of the corresponding parameter.
- **<return type>** - The data type of the result returned by the function. If the function does not return a result then no return type is specified.
- **Function code** - The code of the function that does the work.

As an example, the following function takes no parameters, returns no result and simply displays a message:

```
func sayHello() {
    print("Hello")
}
```

The following sample function, on the other hand, takes an integer and a string as parameters and returns a string result:

```
func buildMessageFor(name: String, count: Int) -> String {
    return("\(name), you are customer number \(count)")
}
```

9.4 Implicit Returns from Single Expressions

In the previous example, the *return* statement was used to return the string value from within the *buildMessageFor()* function. It is worth noting that if a function contains a single expression (as was the case in this example), the return statement may be omitted. The *buildMessageFor()* method could, therefore, be rewritten as follows:

```
func buildMessageFor(name: String, count: Int) -> String {
    "\(name), you are customer number \(count)"
}
```

The return statement can only be omitted if the function contains a single expression. The following code, for example, will fail to compile since the function contains two expressions requiring the use of the return statement:

```
func buildMessageFor(name: String, count: Int) -> String {
    let uppername = name.uppercased()
    "\(uppername), you are customer number \(count)" // Invalid
expression
}
```

9.5 **Calling a Swift Function**

Once declared, functions are called using the following syntax:

```
<function name> (<arg1>, <arg2>, ... )
```

Each argument passed through to a function must match the parameters the function is configured to accept. For example, to call a function named *sayHello* that takes no parameters and returns no value, we would write the following code:

```
sayHello()
```

9.6 **Handling Return Values**

To call a function named *buildMessage* that takes two parameters and returns a result, on the other hand, we might write the following code:

```
let message = buildMessageFor(name: "John", count: 100)
```

In the above example, we have created a new variable called *message* and then used the assignment operator (=) to store the result returned by the function.

When developing in Swift, situations may arise where the result returned by a method or function call is not used. When this is the case, the return value may be discarded by assigning it to '_'. For example:

```
_ = buildMessageFor(name: "John", count: 100)
```

9.7 **Local and External Parameter Names**

When the preceding example functions were declared, they were configured with parameters that were assigned names which, in turn, could be referenced within the body of the function code. When declared in this way, these names are referred to as *local parameter names*.

In addition to local names, function parameters may also have *external parameter names*. These are the names by which the parameter is referenced when the function is called. By default, function parameters are assigned the same local and external parameter names. Consider, for example, the previous call to the *buildMessageFor* method:

```
let message = buildMessageFor(name: "John", count: 100)
```

As declared, the function uses "name" and "count" as both the local and external parameter names.

The default external parameter names assigned to parameters may be removed by preceding the local parameter names with an underscore (_) character as follows:

```
func buildMessageFor(_ name: String, _ count: Int) -> String {
      return("\(name), you are customer number \(count)")
}
```

With this change implemented, the function may now be called as follows:

```
let message = buildMessageFor("John", 100)
```

Alternatively, external parameter names can be added simply by declaring the external parameter name before the local parameter name within the function declaration. In the following code, for example, the external names of the first and second parameters have been set to "username" and "usercount" respectively:

```
func buildMessageFor(username name: String, usercount count: Int)
                                            -> String {
        return("\(name), you are customer number \(count)")
}
```

When declared in this way, the external parameter name must be referenced when calling the function:

```
let message = buildMessageFor(username: "John", usercount: 100)
```

Regardless of the fact that the external names are used to pass the arguments through when calling the function, the local names are still used to reference the parameters within the body of the function. It is important to also note that when calling a function using external parameter names for the arguments, those arguments must still be placed in the same order as that used when the function was declared.

9.8 Declaring Default Function Parameters

Swift provides the ability to designate a default parameter value to be used in the event that the value is not provided as an argument when the function is called. This simply involves assigning the default value to the parameter when the function is declared. When using default parameters, it is important that the parameters for which a default is being declared be placed at the end of the parameter list so that the compiler does not become confused about which parameters have been omitted during a function call. Swift also provides a default external name based on the local parameter name for defaulted parameters (unless one is already provided) which must then be used when calling the function.

To see default parameters in action the *buildMessageFor* function will be modified so that the string "Customer" is used as a default in the event that a customer name is not passed through as an argument:

```
func buildMessageFor(_ name: String = "Customer", count: Int ) -> String
{
        return ("\(name), you are customer number \(count)")
}
```

The function can now be called without passing through a name argument:

```
let message = buildMessageFor(count: 100)
print(message)
```

When executed, the above function call will generate output to the console panel which reads:

```
Customer, you are customer 100
```

9.9 Returning Multiple Results from a Function

A function can return multiple result values by wrapping those results in a tuple. The following function takes as a parameter a measurement value in inches. The function converts this value into yards, centimeters and meters, returning all three results within a single tuple instance:

```
func sizeConverter(_ length: Float) -> (yards: Float, centimeters: Float,
                                        meters: Float) {

    let yards = length * 0.0277778
    let centimeters = length * 2.54
    let meters = length * 0.0254

    return (yards, centimeters, meters)
}
```

The return type for the function indicates that the function returns a tuple containing three values named yards, centimeters and meters respectively, all of which are of type Float:

```
-> (yards: Float, centimeters: Float, meters: Float)
```

Having performed the conversion, the function simply constructs the tuple instance and returns it.

Usage of this function might read as follows:

```
let lengthTuple = sizeConverter(20)

print(lengthTuple.yards)
print(lengthTuple.centimeters)
print(lengthTuple.meters)
```

9.10 Variable Numbers of Function Parameters

It is not always possible to know in advance the number of parameters a function will need to accept when it is called within application code. Swift handles this possibility through the use of *variadic parameters*. Variadic parameters are declared using three periods (…) to indicate that the function accepts zero or more parameters of a specified data type. Within the body of the function, the parameters are made available in the form of an array object. The following function, for example, takes as parameters a variable number of String values and then outputs them to the console panel:

```
func displayStrings(_ strings: String...)
{
    for string in strings {
        print(string)
    }
}
```

```
displayStrings("one", "two", "three", "four")
```

9.11 Parameters as Variables

All parameters accepted by a function are treated as constants by default. This prevents changes being made to those parameter values within the function code. If changes to parameters need to be made within the function body, therefore, shadow copies of those parameters must be created. The following function, for example, is passed length and width parameters in inches, creates shadow variables of the two values and converts those parameters to centimeters before calculating and returning the area value:

```
func calcuateArea(length: Float, width: Float) -> Float {

    var length = length
    var width = width

    length = length * 2.54
    width = width * 2.54
    return length * width
}

print(calcuateArea(length: 10, width: 20))
```

9.12 Working with In-Out Parameters

When a variable is passed through as a parameter to a function, we now know that the parameter is treated as a constant within the body of that function. We also know that if we want to make changes to the parameter value we have to create a shadow copy as outlined in the above section. Since this is a copy, any changes made to the variable are not, by default, reflected in the original variable. Consider, for example, the following code:

```
var myValue = 10

func doubleValue ( _ value: Int) -> Int {
    var value = value
    value += value
    return(value)
}

print("Before function call myValue = \(myValue)")

print("doubleValue call returns \(doubleValue(myValue))")

print("After function call myValue = \(myValue)")
```

The code begins by declaring a variable named *myValue* initialized with a value of 10. A new function is then declared which accepts a single integer parameter. Within the body of the function, a shadow copy of the value is created, doubled and returned.

The remaining lines of code display the value of the *myValue* variable before and after the function call is made. When executed, the following output will appear in the console:

```
Before function call myValue = 10
doubleValue call returns 20
After function call myValue = 10
```

Clearly, the function has made no change to the original myValue variable. This is to be expected since the mathematical operation was performed on a copy of the variable, not the *myValue* variable itself.

In order to make any changes made to a parameter persist after the function has returned, the parameter must be declared as an *in-out parameter* within the function declaration. To see this in action, modify the *doubleValue* function to include the *inout* keyword, and remove the creation of the shadow copy as follows:

```
func doubleValue (_ value: inout Int) -> Int {
    var value = value
    value += value
    return(value)
}
```

Finally, when calling the function, the inout parameter must now be prefixed with an & modifier:

```
print("doubleValue call returned \(doubleValue(&myValue))")
```

Having made these changes, a test run of the code should now generate output clearly indicating that the function modified the value assigned to the original *myValue* variable:

```
Before function call myValue = 10
doubleValue call returns 20
After function call myValue = 20
```

9.13 Functions as Parameters

An interesting feature of functions within Swift is that they can be treated as data types. It is perfectly valid, for example, to assign a function to a constant or variable as illustrated in the declaration below:

```
func inchesToFeet (_ inches: Float) -> Float {

    return inches * 0.0833333
}

let toFeet = inchesToFeet
```

The above code declares a new function named *inchesToFeet* and subsequently assigns that function to a constant named *toFeet*. Having made this assignment, a call to the function may be made using the constant name instead of the original function name:

```
let result = toFeet(10)
```

On the surface this does not seem to be a particularly compelling feature. Since we could already call the function without assigning it to a constant or variable data type it does not seem that much has been gained.

The possibilities that this feature offers become more apparent when we consider that a function assigned to a constant or variable now has the capabilities of many other data types. In particular, a function can now be passed through as an argument to another function, or even returned as a result from a function.

Before we look at what is, essentially, the ability to plug one function into another, it is first necessary to explore the concept of function data types. The data type of a function is dictated by a combination of the parameters it accepts and the type of result it returns. In the above example, since the function accepts a floating-point parameter and returns a floating-point result, the function's data type conforms to the following:

```
(Float) -> Float
```

A function which accepts an Int and a Double as parameters and returns a String result, on the other hand, would have the following data type:

```
(Int, Double) -> String
```

In order to accept a function as a parameter, the receiving function simply declares the data type of the function it is able to accept.

For the purposes of an example, we will begin by declaring two unit conversion functions and assigning them to constants:

```
func inchesToFeet ( _ inches: Float) -> Float {

    return inches * 0.0833333
}

func inchesToYards ( _ inches: Float) -> Float {

    return inches * 0.0277778
}

let toFeet = inchesToFeet
let toYards = inchesToYards
```

The example now needs an additional function, the purpose of which is to perform a unit conversion and print the result in the console panel. This function needs to be as general purpose as possible, capable of performing a variety of different measurement unit conversions. In order to demonstrate functions as parameters, this new function will take as a parameter a function type that matches both the inchesToFeet and inchesToYards function data type together with a value to be converted. Since the data type of these functions is equivalent to (Float) -> Float, our general-purpose function can be written as follows:

```
func outputConversion(_ converterFunc: (Float) -> Float, value: Float) {

    let result = converterFunc(value)

    print("Result of conversion is \(result)")
}
```

When the outputConversion function is called, it will need to be passed a function matching the declared data type. That function will be called to perform the conversion and the result displayed in the console panel. This means that the same function can be called to convert inches to both feet and yards, simply by "plugging in" the appropriate converter function as a parameter. For example:

```
outputConversion(toYards, value: 10) // Convert to Yards
outputConversion(toFeet, value: 10) // Convert to Inches
```

Functions can also be returned as a data type simply by declaring the type of the function as the return type. The following function is configured to return either our toFeet or toYards function type (in other words a function which accepts and returns a Float value) based on the value of a Boolean parameter:

```
func decideFunction(_ feet: Bool) -> (Float) -> Float
{
    if feet {
        return toFeet
    } else {
        return toYards
    }
}
```

9.14 Closure Expressions

Having covered the basics of functions in Swift it is now time to look at the concept of *closures* and *closure expressions*. Although these terms are often used interchangeably there are some key differences.

Closure expressions are self-contained blocks of code. The following code, for example, declares a closure expression and assigns it to a constant named sayHello and then calls the function via the constant reference:

```
let sayHello = { print("Hello") }
sayHello()
```

Closure expressions may also be configured to accept parameters and return results. The syntax for this is as follows:

```
{(<para name>: <para type>, <para name> <para type>, ... ) ->
                                        <return type> in
        // Closure expression code here
}
```

The following closure expression, for example, accepts two integer parameters and returns an integer result:

```
let multiply = {(_ val1: Int, _ val2: Int) -> Int in
        return val1 * val2
}
let result = multiply(10, 20)
```

Note that the syntax is similar to that used for declaring Swift functions with the exception that the closure expression does not have a name, the parameters and return type are included in the braces and the *in* keyword is used to indicate the start of the closure expression code. Functions are, in fact, just named closure expressions.

Closure expressions are often used when declaring completion handlers for asynchronous method calls. In other words, when developing iOS applications, it will often be necessary to make calls to the operating system where the requested task is performed in the background allowing the application to continue with other tasks. Typically, in such a scenario, the system will notify the application of the completion of the task and return any results by calling the completion handler that was declared when the method was called. Frequently the code for the completion handler will be implemented in the form of a closure expression. Consider the following code from an example used later in the book:

```
eventstore.requestAccess(to: .reminder, completion: {(granted: Bool,
                    error: Error?) -> Void in
    if !granted {
            print(error!.localizedDescription)
    }
})
```

When the tasks performed by the *requestAccess(to:)* method call are complete it will execute the closure expression declared as the *completion:* parameter. The completion handler is required by the method to accept a Boolean value and an Error object as parameters and return no results, hence the following declaration:

```
{(granted: Bool, error: Error?) -> Void in
```

In actual fact, the Swift compiler already knows about the parameter and return value requirements for the completion handler for this method call and is able to infer this information without it being declared in the closure expression. This allows a simpler version of the closure expression declaration to be written:

```
eventstore.requestAccess(to: .reminder, completion: {(granted, error) in
    if !granted {
            print(error!.localizedDescription)
    }
})
```

9.15 Closures in Swift

A *closure* in computer science terminology generally refers to the combination of a self-contained block of code (for example a function or closure expression) and one or more variables that exist in the context surrounding that code block. Consider, for example the following Swift function:

```
func functionA() -> () -> Int {

    var counter = 0

    func functionB() -> Int {
        return counter + 10
    }
    return functionB
}

let myClosure = functionA()
let result = myClosure()
```

In the above code, *functionA* returns a function named *functionB*. In actual fact functionA is returning a closure since functionB relies on the *counter* variable which is declared outside the functionB's local scope. In other words, functionB is said to have *captured* or *closed over* (hence the term closure) the counter variable and, as such, is considered a closure in the traditional computer science definition of the word.

To a large extent, and particularly as it relates to Swift, the terms *closure* and *closure expression* have started to be used interchangeably. The key point to remember, however, is that both are supported in Swift.

9.16 Summary

Functions, closures and closure expressions are self-contained blocks of code that can be called upon to perform a specific task and provide a mechanism for structuring code and promoting reuse. This chapter has introduced the concepts of functions and closures in terms of declaration and implementation.

10. The Basics of Object-Oriented Programming in Swift

Swift provides extensive support for developing object-oriented applications. The subject area of object-oriented programming is, however, large. It is not an exaggeration to state that entire books have been dedicated to the subject. As such, a detailed overview of object-oriented software development is beyond the scope of this book. Instead, we will introduce the basic concepts involved in object-oriented programming and then move on to explaining the concept as it relates to Swift application development. Once again, while we strive to provide the basic information you need in this chapter, we recommend reading a copy of Apple's *The Swift Programming Language* book for more extensive coverage of this subject area.

10.1 What is an Instance?

Objects (also referred to as class *instances*) are self-contained modules of functionality that can be easily used and re-used as the building blocks for a software application.

Instances consist of data variables (called *properties*) and functions (called *methods*) that can be accessed and called on the instance to perform tasks and are collectively referred to as *class members*.

10.2 What is a Class?

Much as a blueprint or architect's drawing defines what an item or a building will look like once it has been constructed, a class defines what an instance will look like when it is created. It defines, for example, what the methods will do and what the properties will be.

10.3 Declaring a Swift Class

Before an instance can be created, we first need to define the class 'blueprint' for the instance. In this chapter we will create a bank account class to demonstrate the basic concepts of Swift object-oriented programming.

In declaring a new Swift class we specify an optional *parent class* from which the new class is derived and also define the properties and methods that the class will contain. The basic syntax for a new class is as follows:

```
class NewClassName: ParentClass {
    // Properties
    // Instance Methods
    // Type methods
```

```
}
```

The *Properties* section of the declaration defines the variables and constants that are to be contained within the class. These are declared in the same way that any other variable or constant would be declared in Swift.

The *Instance methods* and *Type methods* sections define the methods that are available to be called on the class and instances of the class. These are essentially functions specific to the class that perform a particular operation when called upon and will be described in greater detail later in this chapter.

To create an example outline for our BankAccount class, we would use the following:

```
class BankAccount {

}
```

Now that we have the outline syntax for our class, the next step is to add some instance properties to it.

When naming classes, note that the convention is for first character of each word to be declared in uppercase (a concept referred to as UpperCamelCase). This contrasts with property and function names where lower case is used for the first character (referred to as lowerCamelCase).

10.4 **Adding Instance Properties to a Class**

A key goal of object-oriented programming is a concept referred to as *data encapsulation*. The idea behind data encapsulation is that data should be stored within classes and accessed only through methods defined in that class. Data encapsulated in a class are referred to as *properties* or *instance variables*.

Instances of our BankAccount class will be required to store some data, specifically a bank account number and the balance currently held within the account. Properties are declared in the same way any other variables and constants are declared in Swift. We can, therefore, add these variables as follows:

```
class BankAccount {
    var accountBalance: Float = 0
    var accountNumber: Int = 0
}
```

Having defined our properties, we can now move on to defining the methods of the class that will allow us to work with our properties while staying true to the data encapsulation model.

10.5 **Defining Methods**

The methods of a class are essentially code routines that can be called upon to perform specific tasks within the context of that class.

Methods come in two different forms, *type methods* and *instance methods*. Type methods operate at the level of the class, such as creating a new instance of a class. Instance methods, on the other hand, operate only on the instances of a class (for example performing an arithmetic operation on two property variables and returning the result).

Instance methods are declared within the opening and closing braces of the class to which they belong and are declared using the standard Swift function declaration syntax.

Type methods are declared in the same way as instance methods with the exception that the declaration is preceded by the *class* keyword.

For example, the declaration of a method to display the account balance in our example might read as follows:

```
class BankAccount {

    var accountBalance: Float = 0
    var accountNumber: Int = 0

    func displayBalance()
    {
        print("Number \(accountNumber)")
        print("Current balance is \(accountBalance)")
    }
}
```

The method is an *instance method* so it is not preceded by the *class* keyword.

When designing the BankAccount class it might be useful to be able to call a type method on the class itself to identify the maximum allowable balance that can be stored by the class. This would enable an application to identify whether the BankAccount class is suitable for storing details of a new customer without having to go through the process of first creating a class instance. This method will be named *getMaxBalance* and is implemented as follows:

```
class BankAccount {

    var accountBalance: Float = 0
    var accountNumber: Int = 0

    func displayBalance()
    {
        print("Number \(accountNumber)")
        print("Current balance is \(accountBalance)")
    }

    class func getMaxBalance() -> Float {
        return 100000.00
```

```
    }
}
```

10.6 Declaring and Initializing a Class Instance

So far all we have done is define the blueprint for our class. In order to do anything with this class, we need to create instances of it. The first step in this process is to declare a variable to store a reference to the instance when it is created. We do this as follows:

```
var account1: BankAccount = BankAccount()
```

When executed, an instance of our BankAccount class will have been created and will be accessible via the *account1* variable.

10.7 Initializing and Deinitializing a Class Instance

A class will often need to perform some initialization tasks at the point of creation. These tasks can be implemented by placing an *init* method within the class. In the case of the BankAccount class, it would be useful to be able to initialize the account number and balance properties with values when a new class instance is created. To achieve this, the *init* method could be written in the class as follows:

```
class BankAccount {

    var accountBalance: Float = 0
    var accountNumber: Int = 0

    init(number: Int, balance: Float)
    {
        accountNumber = number
        accountBalance = balance
    }

    func displayBalance()
    {
        print("Number \(accountNumber)")
        print("Current balance is \(accountBalance)")
    }
}
```

When creating an instance of the class, it will now be necessary to provide initialization values for the account number and balance properties as follows:

```
var account1 = BankAccount(number: 12312312, balance: 400.54)
```

Conversely, any cleanup tasks that need to be performed before a class instance is destroyed by the Swift runtime system can be performed by implementing the deinitializer within the class definition:

```
class BankAccount {

    var accountBalance: Float = 0
    var accountNumber: Int = 0

    init(number: Int, balance: Float)
    {
        accountNumber = number
        accountBalance = balance
    }

    deinit {
        // Perform any necessary clean up here
    }

    func displayBalance()
    {
        print("Number \(accountNumber)")
        print("Current balance is \(accountBalance)")
    }
}
```

10.8 Calling Methods and Accessing Properties

Now is probably a good time to recap what we have done so far in this chapter. We have now created a new Swift class named *BankAccount*. Within this new class we declared some properties to contain the bank account number and current balance together with an initializer and a method to display the current balance information. In the preceding section we covered the steps necessary to create and initialize an instance of our new class. The next step is to learn how to call the instance methods and access the properties we built into our class. This is most easily achieved using *dot notation*.

Dot notation involves accessing an instance variable, or calling an instance method by specifying a class instance followed by a dot followed in turn by the name of the property or method:

```
classInstance.propertyName
classInstance.instanceMethod()
```

For example, to get the current value of our *accountBalance* instance variable:

```
var balance1 = account1.accountBalance
```

Dot notation can also be used to set values of instance properties:

```
account1.accountBalance = 6789.98
```

The same technique is used to call methods on a class instance. For example, to call the *displayBalance* method on an instance of the BankAccount class:

```
account1.displayBalance()
```

Type methods are also called using dot notation, though they must be called on the class type instead of a class instance:

```
ClassName.typeMethod()
```

For example, to call the previously declared *getMaxBalance* type method, the BankAccount class is referenced:

```
var maxAllowed = BankAccount.getMaxBalance()
```

10.9 **Stored and Computed Properties**

Class properties in Swift fall into two categories referred to as *stored properties* and *computed properties*. Stored properties are those values that are contained within a constant or variable. Both the account name and number properties in the BankAccount example are stored properties.

A computed property, on the other hand, is a value that is derived based on some form of calculation or logic at the point at which the property is set or retrieved. Computed properties are implemented by creating *getter* and optional corresponding *setter* methods containing the code to perform the computation. Consider, for example, that the BankAccount class might need an additional property to contain the current balance less any recent banking fees. Rather than use a stored property, it makes more sense to use a computed property which calculates this value on request. The modified BankAccount class might now read as follows:

```
class BankAccount {

    var accountBalance: Float = 0
    var accountNumber: Int = 0;
    let fees: Float = 25.00

    var balanceLessFees: Float {
        get {
            return accountBalance - fees
        }
    }

    init(number: Int, balance: Float)
    {
        accountNumber = number
        accountBalance = balance
    }
```

```
.
.
.
}
```

The above code adds a getter that returns a computed property based on the current balance minus a fee amount. An optional setter could also be declared in much the same way to set the balance value less fees:

```
var balanceLessFees: Float {
    get {
        return accountBalance - fees
    }

    set(newBalance)
    {
        accountBalance = newBalance - fees
    }
}
```

The new setter takes as a parameter a floating-point value from which it deducts the fee value before assigning the result to the current balance property. Although these are computed properties, they are accessed in the same way as stored properties using dot-notation. The following code gets the current balance less the fees value before setting the property to a new value:

```
var balance1 = account1.balanceLessFees
account1.balanceLessFees = 12123.12
```

10.10 Lazy Stored Properties

There are several different ways in which a property can be initialized, the most basic being direct assignment as follows:

```
var myProperty = 10
```

Alternatively, a property may be assigned a value within the initializer:

```
class MyClass {
  let title: String

  init(title: String) {
    self.title = title
  }
}
```

For more complex requirements, a property may be initialized using a closure:

```
class MyClass {
```

```
    var myProperty: String = {
        var result = resourceIntensiveTask()
        result = processData(data: result)
        return result
    }()
.
.
.
}
```

Particularly in the case of a complex closure, there is the potential for the initialization to be resource intensive and time consuming. When declared in this way, the initialization will be performed every time an instance of the class is created, regardless of when (or even if) the property is actually used within the code of the app. Also, situations may arise where the value assigned to the property may not be known until a later stage in the execution process, for example after data has been retrieved from a database or user input has been obtained from the user. A far more efficient solution in such situations would be for the initialization to take place only when the property is first accessed. Fortunately, this can be achieved by declaring the property as *lazy* as follows:

```
class MyClass {

    lazy var myProperty: String = {
        var result = resourceIntensiveTask()
        result = processData(data: result)
        return result
    }()
.
.
.
}
```

When a property is declared as being lazy, it is only initialized when it is first accessed, allowing any resource intensive activities to be deferred until the property is needed and any initialization on which the property is dependent to be completed.

Note that lazy properties must be declared as variables (*var*).

10.11 Using self in Swift

Programmers familiar with other object-oriented programming languages may be in the habit of prefixing references to properties and methods with *self* to indicate that the method or property belongs to the current class instance. The Swift programming language also provides the *self* property type for this purpose and it is, therefore, perfectly valid to write code which reads as follows:

```
class MyClass {
    var myNumber = 1
```

```
func addTen() {
    self.myNumber += 10
  }
}
```

In this context, the *self* prefix indicates to the compiler that the code is referring to a property named *myNumber* which belongs to the MyClass class instance. When programming in Swift, however, it is no longer necessary to use self in most situations since this is now assumed to be the default for references to properties and methods. To quote The Swift Programming Language guide published by Apple, "in practice you don't need to write *self* in your code very often". The function from the above example, therefore, can also be written as follows with the *self* reference omitted:

```
func addTen() {
    myNumber += 10
}
```

In most cases, use of self is optional in Swift. That being said, one situation where it is still necessary to use *self* is when referencing a property or method from within a closure expression. The use of self, for example, is mandatory in the following closure expression:

```
document?.openWithCompletionHandler({(success: Bool) -> Void in
    if success {
        self.ubiquityURL = resultURL
    }
})
```

It is also necessary to use self to resolve ambiguity such as when a function parameter has the same name as a class property. In the following code, for example, the first print statement will output the value passed through to the function via the myNumber parameter while the second print statement outputs the number assigned to the myNumber class property (in this case 10):

```
class MyClass {

    var myNumber = 10 // class property

    func addTen(myNumber: Int) {
        print(myNumber) // Output the function parameter value
        print(self.myNumber) // Output the class property value
    }
}
```

Whether or not to use self in most other situations is largely a matter of programmer preference. Those who prefer to use self when referencing properties and methods can continue to do so in Swift. Code that is written without use of the *self* property type (where doing so is not mandatory) is, however, just as valid when programming in Swift.

10.12 **Understanding Swift Protocols**

By default, there are no specific rules to which a Swift class must conform as long as the class is syntactically correct. In some situations, however, a class will need to meet certain criteria in order to work with other classes. This is particularly common when writing classes that need to work with the various frameworks that comprise the iOS SDK. A set of rules that define the minimum requirements which a class must meet is referred to as a *Protocol*. A protocol is declared using the *protocol* keyword and simply defines the methods and properties that a class must contain in order to be in conformance. When a class *adopts* a protocol, but does not meet all of the protocol requirements, errors will be reported stating that the class fails to conform to the protocol.

Consider the following protocol declaration. Any classes that adopt this protocol must include both a readable String value called *name* and a method named *buildMessage()* which accepts no parameters and returns a String value.

```
protocol MessageBuilder {

    var name: String { get }
    func buildMessage() -> String
}
```

Below, a class has been declared which adopts the MessageBuilder protocol:

```
class MyClass: MessageBuilder {

}
```

Unfortunately, as currently implemented, MyClass will generate a compilation error because it contains neither the *name* variable nor the *buildMessage()* method as required by the protocol it has adopted. To conform to the protocol, the class would need to meet both requirements, for example:

```
class MyClass: MessageBuilder {

    var name: String

    init(name: String) {
      self.name = name
    }

    func buildMessage() -> String {
        "Hello " + name
    }
}
```

10.13 **Opaque Return Types**

Now that protocols have been explained it is a good time to introduce the concept of opaque return types. As we have seen in previous chapters, if a function returns a result, the type of that result must be included in the function declaration. The following function, for example, is configured to return an Int result:

```
func doubleFunc1 (value: Int) -> Int {
    return value * 2
}
```

Instead of specifying a specific return type (also referred to as a *concrete type*), opaque return types allow a function to return any type as long as it conforms to a specified protocol. Opaque return types are declared by preceding the protocol name with the *some* keyword. The following changes to the *doubleFunc1()* function, for example, declare that a result will be returned of any type that conforms to the Equitable protocol:

```
func doubleFunc1(value: Int) -> some Equatable {
    value * 2
}
```

To conform to the Equatable protocol, which is a standard protocol provided with Swift, a type must allow the underlying values to be compared for equality. Opaque return types can, however, be used for any protocol, including those you create yourself.

Given that both the Int and String concrete types are in conformance with the Equatable protocol, it is possible to also create a function that returns a String result:

```
func doubleFunc2(value: String) -> some Equatable {
    value + value
}
```

Although these two methods return entirely different concrete types, the only thing known about these types is that they conform to the Equatable protocol. We therefore know the capabilities of the type, but not the actual type.

In fact, we only know the concrete type returned in these examples because we have access to the source code of the functions. If these functions resided in a library or API framework for which the source is not available to us, we would not know the exact type being returned. This is intentional and designed to hide the underlying return type used within public APIs. By masking the concrete return type, programmers will not come to rely on a function returning a specific concrete type or risk accessing internal objects which were not intended to be accessed. This also has the benefit that the developer of the API can make changes to the underlying implementation (including returning a different protocol compliant type) without having to worry about breaking dependencies in any code that uses the API.

This raises the question of what happens when an incorrect assumption is made when working with opaque return type. Consider, for example, that the assumption could be made that the results from the *doubleFunc1()* and *doubleFunc2()* functions can be compared for equality:

```
let intOne = doubleFunc1(value: 10)
let stringOne = doubleFunc2(value: "Hello")


if (intOne == stringOne) {
    print("They match")
}
```

Working on the premise that we do not have access to the source code for these two functions there is no way to know whether the above code is valid. Fortunately, although we, as programmers, have no way of knowing the concrete type returned by the functions, the Swift compiler has access to this hidden information. The above code will, therefore, generate the following syntax error long before we get to the point of trying to execute invalid code:

```
Binary operator '==' cannot be applied to operands of type 'some
 Equatable' (result of 'doubleFunc1(value:)') and 'some Equatable'
(result of 'doubleFunc2(value:)')
```

Opaque return types are a fundamental foundation of the implementation of the SwiftUI APIs and are used widely when developing apps in SwiftUI (the *some* keyword will appear frequently in SwiftUI View declarations). SwiftUI advocates the creation of apps by composing together small, reusable building blocks and refactoring large view declarations into collections of small, lightweight subviews. Each of these building blocks will typically conform to the View protocol. By declaring these building blocks as returning opaque types that conform to the View protocol, these building blocks become remarkably flexible and interchangeable, resulting in code that is cleaner and easier to reuse and maintain.

10.14 Summary

Object-oriented programming languages such as Swift encourage the creation of classes to promote code reuse and the encapsulation of data within class instances. This chapter has covered the basic concepts of classes and instances within Swift together with an overview of stored and computed properties and both instance and type methods. The chapter also introduced the concept of protocols which serve as templates to which classes must conform and explained how they form the basis of opaque return types.

11. An Introduction to Swift Subclassing and Extensions

In *The Basics of Object-Oriented Programming in Swift* we covered the basic concepts of object-oriented programming and worked through an example of creating and working with a new class using Swift. In that example, our new class was not derived from any base class and, as such, did not inherit any traits from a parent or super class. In this chapter we will introduce the concepts of subclassing, inheritance and extensions in Swift.

11.1 Inheritance, Classes and Subclasses

The concept of inheritance brings something of a real-world view to programming. It allows a class to be defined that has a certain set of characteristics (such as methods and properties) and then other classes to be created which are derived from that class. The derived class inherits all of the features of the parent class and typically then adds some features of its own.

By deriving classes we create what is often referred to as a *class hierarchy*. The class at the top of the hierarchy is known as the *base class* or *root class* and the derived classes as *subclasses* or *child classes*. Any number of subclasses may be derived from a class. The class from which a subclass is derived is called the *parent class* or *super class*.

Classes need not only be derived from a root class. For example, a subclass can also inherit from another subclass with the potential to create large and complex class hierarchies.

In Swift a subclass can only be derived from a single direct parent class. This is a concept referred to as *single inheritance*.

11.2 A Swift Inheritance Example

As with most programming concepts, the subject of inheritance in Swift is perhaps best illustrated with an example. In *The Basics of Object-Oriented Programming in Swift* we created a class named *BankAccount* designed to hold a bank account number and corresponding current balance. The BankAccount class contained both properties and instance methods. A simplified declaration for this class is reproduced below:

```swift
class BankAccount {

    var accountBalance: Float
    var accountNumber: Int

    init(number: Int, balance: Float)
```

```
    {
        accountNumber = number
        accountBalance = balance
    }

    func displayBalance()
    {
        print("Number \(accountNumber)")
        print("Current balance is \(accountBalance)")
    }
}
```

Though this is a somewhat rudimentary class, it does everything necessary if all you need it to do is store an account number and account balance. Suppose, however, that in addition to the BankAccount class you also needed a class to be used for savings accounts. A savings account will still need to hold an account number and a current balance and methods will still be needed to access that data. One option would be to create an entirely new class, one that duplicates all of the functionality of the BankAccount class together with the new features required by a savings account. A more efficient approach, however, would be to create a new class that is a *subclass* of the BankAccount class. The new class will then inherit all the features of the BankAccount class but can then be extended to add the additional functionality required by a savings account.

To create a subclass of BankAccount that we will call SavingsAccount, we simply declare the new class, this time specifying BankAccount as the parent class:

```
class SavingsAccount: BankAccount {


}
```

Note that although we have yet to add any instance variables or methods, the class has actually inherited all the methods and properties of the parent BankAccount class. We could, therefore, create an instance of the SavingsAccount class and set variables and call methods in exactly the same way we did with the BankAccount class in previous examples. That said, we haven't really achieved anything unless we take steps to extend the class.

11.3 Extending the Functionality of a Subclass

So far we have been able to create a subclass that contains all the functionality of the parent class. For this exercise to make sense, however, we now need to extend the subclass so that it has the features we need to make it useful for storing savings account information. To do this, we simply add the properties and methods that provide the new functionality, just as we would for any other class we might wish to create:

```
class SavingsAccount: BankAccount {

    var interestRate: Float = 0.0
```

```
func calculateInterest() -> Float
{
    return interestRate * accountBalance
}
}
```

11.4 Overriding Inherited Methods

When using inheritance, it is not unusual to find a method in the parent class that almost does what you need, but requires modification to provide the precise functionality you require. That being said, it is also possible you'll inherit a method with a name that describes exactly what you want to do, but it actually does not come close to doing what you need. One option in this scenario would be to ignore the inherited method and write a new method with an entirely new name. A better option is to *override* the inherited method and write a new version of it in the subclass.

Before proceeding with an example, there are two rules that must be obeyed when overriding a method. First, the overriding method in the subclass must take exactly the same number and type of parameters as the overridden method in the parent class. Second, the new method must have the same return type as the parent method.

In our BankAccount class we have a method named *displayBalance* that displays the bank account number and current balance held by an instance of the class. In our SavingsAccount subclass we might also want to output the current interest rate assigned to the account. To achieve this, we simply declare a new version of the *displayBalance* method in our SavingsAccount subclass, prefixed with the *override* keyword:

```
class SavingsAccount: BankAccount {

    var interestRate: Float

    func calculateInterest() -> Float
    {
        return interestRate * accountBalance
    }

    override func displayBalance()
    {
        print("Number \(accountNumber)")
        print("Current balance is \(accountBalance)")
        print("Prevailing interest rate is \(interestRate)")
    }
}
```

It is also possible to make a call to the overridden method in the super class from within a subclass. The *displayBalance* method of the super class could, for example, be called to display the account number and balance, before the interest rate is displayed, thereby eliminating further code duplication:

```
override func displayBalance()
{
        super.displayBalance()
        print("Prevailing interest rate is \(interestRate)")
}
```

11.5 Initializing the Subclass

As the SavingsAccount class currently stands, it inherits the init initializer method from the parent BankAccount class which was implemented as follows:

```
init(number: Int, balance: Float)
{
        accountNumber = number
        accountBalance = balance
}
```

Clearly this method takes the necessary steps to initialize both the account number and balance properties of the class. The SavingsAccount class, however, contains an additional property in the form of the interest rate variable. The SavingsAccount class, therefore, needs its own initializer to ensure that the interestRate property is initialized when instances of the class are created. This method can perform this task and then make a call to the *init* method of the parent class to complete the initialization of the remaining variables:

```
class SavingsAccount: BankAccount {

    var interestRate: Float

    init(number: Int, balance: Float, rate: Float)
    {
        interestRate = rate
        super.init(number: number, balance: balance)
    }
    .
    .
    .
}
```

Note that to avoid potential initialization problems, the *init* method of the superclass must always be called *after* the initialization tasks for the subclass have been completed.

11.6 **Using the SavingsAccount Class**

Now that we have completed work on our SavingsAccount class, the class can be used in some example code in much the same way as the parent BankAccount class:

```
let savings1 = SavingsAccount(number: 12311, balance: 600.00,
                                            rate: 0.07)

print(savings1.calculateInterest())
savings1.displayBalance()
```

11.7 **Swift Class Extensions**

Another way to add new functionality to a Swift class is to use an extension. Extensions can be used to add features such as methods, initializers, computed properties and subscripts to an existing class without the need to create and reference a subclass. This is particularly powerful when using extensions to add functionality to the built-in classes of the Swift language and iOS SDK frameworks.

A class is extended using the following syntax:

```
extension ClassName {
    // new features here
}
```

For the purposes of an example, assume that we need to add some additional properties to the standard Double class that will return the value raised to the power 2 and 3. This functionality can be added using the following extension declaration:

```
extension Double {

    var squared: Double {
        return self * self
    }

    var cubed: Double {
        return self * self * self
    }
}
```

Having extended the Double class with two new computed properties we can now make use of the properties as we would any other properties of the Double class:

```
let myValue: Double = 3.0
print(myValue.squared)
```

When executed, the print statement will output the value of 9.0. Note that when declaring the myValue constant we were able to declare it as being of type Double and access the extension properties without the need to use a subclass. In fact, because these properties were added as an extension, rather than using a subclass, we can now access these properties directly on Double values:

```
print(3.0.squared)
print(6.0.cubed)
```

Extensions provide a quick and convenient way to extend the functionality of a class without the need to use subclasses. Subclasses, however, still have some advantages over extensions. It is not possible, for example, to override the existing functionality of a class using an extension and extensions cannot contain stored properties.

11.8 Summary

Inheritance extends the concept of object re-use in object-oriented programming by allowing new classes to be derived from existing classes, with those new classes subsequently extended to add new functionality. When an existing class provides some, but not all, of the functionality required by the programmer, inheritance allows that class to be used as the basis for a new subclass. The new subclass will inherit all the capabilities of the parent class, but may then be extended to add the missing functionality.

Swift extensions provide a useful alternative option to adding functionality to existing classes without the need to create a subclass.

12. An Introduction to Swift Structures

Having covered Swift classes in the preceding chapters, this chapter will introduce the use of structures in Swift. Although at first glance structures and classes look similar, there are some important differences that need to be understood when deciding which to use. This chapter will outline how to declare and use structures, explore the differences between structures and classes and introduce the concepts of value and reference types.

12.1 An Overview of Swift Structures

As with classes, structures form the basis of object-oriented programming and provide a way to encapsulate data and functionality into re-usable instances. Structure declarations resemble classes with the exception that the *struct* keyword is used in place of the *class* keyword. The following code, for example, declares a simple structure consisting of a String variable, initializer and method:

```swift
struct SampleStruct {

    var name: String

    init(name: String) {
        self.name = name
    }

    func buildHelloMsg() {
        "Hello " + name
    }
}
```

Consider the above structure declaration in comparison to the equivalent class declaration:

```swift
class SampleClass {

    var name: String

    init(name: String) {
        self.name = name
    }

    func buildHelloMsg() {
        "Hello " + name
```

```
    }
}
```

Other than the use of the *struct* keyword instead of *class*, the two declarations are identical. Instances of each type are also created using the same syntax:

```
let myStruct = SampleStruct(name: "Mark")
let myClass = SampleClass(name: "Mark")
```

In common with classes, structures may be extended and are also able to adopt protocols and contain initializers.

Given the commonality between classes and structures, it is important to gain an understanding of how the two differ. Before exploring the most significant difference it is first necessary to understand the concepts of *value types* and *reference types*.

12.2 Value Types vs. Reference Types

While on the surface structures and classes look alike, major differences in behavior occur when structure and class instances are copied or passed as arguments to methods or functions. This occurs because structure instances are value type while class instances are reference type.

When a structure instance is copied or passed to a method, an actual copy of the instance is created, together with any data contained within the instance. This means that the copy has its own version of the data which is unconnected with the original structure instance. In effect, this means that there can be multiple copies of a structure instance within a running app, each with its own local copy of the associated data. A change to one instance has no impact on any other instances.

In contrast, when a class instance is copied or passed as an argument, the only thing duplicated or passed is a reference to the location in memory where that class instance resides. Any changes made to the instance using those references will be performed on the same instance. In other words, there is only one class instance but multiple references pointing to it. A change to the instance data using any one of those references changes the data for all other references.

To demonstrate reference and value types in action, consider the following code:

```
struct SampleStruct {

    var name: String

    init(name: String) {
        self.name = name
    }

    func buildHelloMsg() {
        "Hello " + name
    }
}
```

```
let myStruct1 = SampleStruct(name: "Mark")
print(myStruct1.name)
```

When the code executes, the name "Mark" will be displayed. Now change the code so that a copy of the myStruct1 instance is made, the name property changed and the names from each instance displayed:

```
let myStruct1 = SampleStruct(name: "Mark")
var myStruct2 = myStruct1
myStruct2.name = "David"

print(myStruct1.name)
print(myStruct2.name)
```

When executed, the output will read as follows:

```
Mark
David
```

Clearly, the change of name only applied to myStruct2 since this is an actual copy of myStruct1 containing its own copy of the data as shown in Figure 12-1:

Figure 12-1

Contrast this with the following class example:

```
class SampleClass {

    var name: String

    init(name: String) {
        self.name = name
    }

    func buildHelloMsg() {
        "Hello " + name
    }
}

let myClass1 = SampleClass(name: "Mark")
var myClass2 = myClass1
```

```
myClass2.name = "David"

print(myClass1.name)
print(myClass2.name)
```

When this code executes, the following output will be generated:

```
David
David
```

In this case, the name property change is reflected for both myClass1 and myClass2 because both are references pointing to the same class instance as illustrated in Figure 12-2 below:

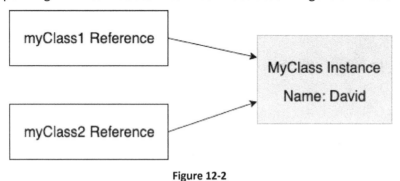

Figure 12-2

In addition to these value and reference type differences, structures do not support inheritance and sub-classing in the way that classes do. In other words, it is not possible for one structure to inherit from another structure. Unlike classes, structures also cannot contain a de-initializer (deinit) method. Finally, while it is possible to identify the type of a class instance at runtime, the same is not true of a struct.

12.3 When to use Structures or Classes

In general, structures are recommended whenever possible because they are both more efficient than classes and safer to use in multi-threaded code. Classes should be used when inheritance is needed, only one instance of the encapsulated data is required, or extra steps need to be taken to free up resources when an instance is de-initialized.

12.4 Summary

Swift structures and classes both provide a mechanism for creating instances that define properties, store values and define methods. Although the two mechanisms appear to be similar, there are significant behavioral differences when structure and class instances are either copied or passed to a method. Classes are categorized as being reference type instances while structures are value type. When a structure instance is copied or passed, an entirely new copy of the instance is created containing its own data. Class instances, on the other hand, are passed and copied by reference, with each reference pointing to the same class instance. Other features unique to classes include support for inheritance and deinitialization and the ability to identify the class type at runtime. Structures should typically be used in place of classes unless specific class features are required.

13. An Introduction to Swift Property Wrappers

Now that the topics of Swift classes and structures have been covered, this chapter will introduce a related topic in the form of property wrappers. Introduced in Swift 5.1, property wrappers provide a way to reduce the amount of duplicated code involved in writing getters, setters and computed properties in class and structure implementations.

13.1 Understanding Property Wrappers

When values are assigned or accessed via a property within a class or structure instance it is sometimes necessary to perform some form of transformation or validation on that value before it is stored or read. As outlined in the chapter entitled *The Basics of Object-Oriented Programming in Swift*, this type of behavior can be implemented through the creation of computed properties. Frequently, patterns emerge where a computed property is common to multiple classes or structures. Prior to the introduction of Swift 5.1, the only way to share the logic of a computed property was to duplicate the code and embed it into each class or structure implementation. Not only is this inefficient, but a change in the behavior of the computation must be manually propagated across all the entities that use it.

To address this shortcoming, Swift 5.1 introduced a feature known as *property wrappers*. Property wrappers essentially allow the capabilities of computed properties to be separated from individual classes and structures and reused throughout the app code base.

13.2 A Simple Property Wrapper Example

Perhaps the best way to understand property wrappers is to study a very simple example. Imagine a structure with a String property intended to contain a city name. Such a structure might read as follows:

```
struct Address {
    var city: String
}
```

If the class was required to store the city name in uppercase, regardless of how it was entered by the user, a computed property such as the following might be added to the structure:

```
struct Address {

    private var cityname: String = ""
```

```
    var city: String {
        get { cityname }
        set { cityname = newValue.uppercased() }
    }
}
```

When a city name is assigned to the property, the setter within the computed property converts it to uppercase before storing it in the private *cityname* variable. This structure can be tested using the following code:

```
var address = Address()
```

```
address.city = "London"
print(address.city)
```

When executed, the output from the above code would read as follows:

```
LONDON
```

Clearly the computed property performs the task of converting the city name string to uppercase, but if the same behavior is needed in other structures or classes the code would need to be duplicated in those declarations. In this example this is only a small amount of code, but that won't necessarily be the case for more complex computations.

Instead of using a computed property, this logic can instead be implemented as a property wrapper. The following declaration, for example, implements a property wrapper named FixCase designed to convert a string to uppercase:

```
@propertyWrapper
struct FixCase {
    private(set) var value: String = ""

    var wrappedValue: String {
        get { value }
        set { value = newValue.uppercased() }
    }

    init(wrappedValue initialValue: String) {
        self.wrappedValue = initialValue
    }
}
```

Property wrappers are declared using the @propertyWrapper directive and are implemented in a class or structure (with structures being the preferred choice). All property wrappers must contain a wrappedValue property containing the getter and setter code that changes or validates the value. An optional initializer may also be included which is passed the value being assigned. In this case, the initial value is simply assigned to the wrappedValue property where it is converted to uppercase and stored in the private variable.

Now that this property wrapper has been defined, it can be reused by applying it to other property variables wherever the same behavior is needed. To use this property wrapper, simply prefix property declarations with the @FixCase directive in any class or structure declarations where the behavior is needed, for example:

```
struct Contact {
    @FixCase var name: String
    @FixCase var city: String
    @FixCase var country: String
}
```

```
var contact = Contact(name: "John Smith", city: "London", country:
"United Kingdom")
print("\(contact.name), \(contact.city), \(contact.country)")
```

When executed, the following output will appear:

```
JOHN SMITH, LONDON, UNITED KINGDOM
```

13.3 Supporting Multiple Variables and Types

In the above example, the property wrapper accepted a single value in the form of the value to be assigned to the property being wrapped. More complex property wrappers may also be implemented that accept other values that can be used when performing the computation. These additional values are placed within parentheses after the property wrapper name. A property wrapper designed to restrict a value within a specified range might read as follows:

```
struct Demo {
    @MinMaxVal(min: 10, max: 150) var value: Int = 100
}
```

The code to implement the above MinMaxVal property wrapper could be written as follows:

```
@propertyWrapper
struct MinMaxVal {
  var value: Int
  let max: Int
  let min: Int

    init(wrappedValue: Int, min: Int, max: Int) {
    value = wrappedValue
    self.min = min
    self.max = max
  }
```

```
  var wrappedValue: Int {
    get { return value }
    set {
      if newValue > max {
        value = max
      } else if newValue < min {
        value = min
      } else {
        value = newValue
      }
    }
  }
}
```

Note that the *init()* method has been implemented to accept the min and max values in addition to the wrapped value. The wrappedValue setter checks the value and modifies it to the min or max number if it falls above or below the specified range.

The above property wrapper can be tested using the following code:

```
struct Demo {
    @MinMaxVal(min: 100, max: 200) var value: Int = 100
}

var demo = Demo()
demo.value = 150
print(demo.value)

demo.value = 250
print(demo.value)
```

When executed, the first print statement will output 150 because it falls within the acceptable range, while the second print statement will show that the wrapper restricted the value to the maximum permitted value (in this case 200).

As currently implemented, the property wrapper will only work with integer (Int) values. The wrapper would be more useful if it could be used with any variable type which can be compared with another value of the same type. Fortunately, protocol wrappers can be implemented to work with any types that conform to a specific protocol. Since the purpose of this wrapper is to perform comparisons, it makes sense to modify it to support any data types that conform to the Comparable protocol which is included with the Foundation framework. Types that conform to the Comparable protocol are able to be used in equality, greater-than and less-than comparisons. A wide range of types such as String, Int, Date, Date Interval and Character conform to this protocol.

To implement the wrapper so that it can be used with any types that conform to the Comparable protocol, the declaration needs to be modified as follows:

```
@propertyWrapper
struct MinMaxVal<V: Comparable> {
  var value: V
  let max: V
  let min: V

    init(wrappedValue: V, min: V, max: V) {
    value = wrappedValue
    self.min = min
    self.max = max
  }

  var wrappedValue: V {
    get { return value }
    set {
       if newValue > max {
         value = max
       } else if newValue < min {
         value = min
       } else {
         value = newValue
       }
    }
  }
}
```

The modified wrapper will still work with Int values as before but can now also be used with any of
the other types that conform to the Comparable protocol. In the following example, a string value
is evaluated to ensure that it fits alphabetically within the min and max string values:

```
struct Demo {
    @MinMaxVal(min: "Apple", max: "Orange") var value: String = ""
}

var demo = Demo()
demo.value = "Banana"
print(demo.value)
// Banana <--- Value fits within alphabetical range and is stored.

demo.value = "Pear"
print(demo.value)
// Orange <--- Value is outside of the alphabetical range so is changed
to the max value.
```

Similarly, this same wrapper will also work with Date instances, as in the following example where the value is limited to a date between the current date and one month in the future:

```
struct DateDemo {
    @MinMaxVal(min: Date(), max: Calendar.current.date(byAdding: .month,
            value: 1, to: Date())! ) var value: Date = Date()
}
```

The following code and output demonstrate the wrapper in action using Date values:

```
var dateDemo = DateDemo()

print(dateDemo.value)
// 2019-08-23 20:05:13 +0000. <--- Property set to today by default.

dateDemo.value = Calendar.current.date(byAdding: .day, value: 10, to:
Date())! // <--- Property is set to 10 days into the future.
print(dateDemo.value)
// 2019-09-02 20:05:13 +0000 <--- Property is within acceptable range and
is stored.
dateDemo.value = Calendar.current.date(byAdding: .month, value: 2, to:
Date())! // <--- Property is set to 2 months into the future.

print(dateDemo.value)
// 2019-09-23 20:08:54 +0000 <--- Property is outside range and set to
max date (i.e. 1 month into the future).
```

13.4 Summary

Introduced with Swift 5.1, property wrappers allow the behavior that would normally be placed in the getters and setters of a property implementation to be extracted and reused through the codebase of an app project avoiding the duplication of code within the class and structure declarations. Property wrappers are declared in the form of structures using the @propertyWrapper directive.

Property wrappers are a powerful Swift feature and allow you to add your own custom behavior to the Swift language. In addition to creating your own property wrappers, you will also encounter them when working with the iOS SDK. In fact, pre-defined property wrappers are used extensively when working with SwiftUI as will be covered in later chapters.

14. Working with Array and Dictionary Collections in Swift

Arrays and dictionaries in Swift are objects that contain collections of other objects. In this chapter, we will cover some of the basics of working with arrays and dictionaries in Swift.

14.1 Mutable and Immutable Collections

Collections in Swift come in mutable and immutable forms. The contents of immutable collection instances cannot be changed after the object has been initialized. To make a collection immutable, assign it to a *constant* when it is created. Collections are mutable, on the other hand, if assigned to a *variable*.

14.2 Swift Array Initialization

An array is a data type designed specifically to hold multiple values in a single ordered collection. An array, for example, could be created to store a list of String values. Strictly speaking, a single Swift based array is only able to store values that are of the same type. An array declared as containing String values, therefore, could not also contain an Int value. As will be demonstrated later in this chapter, however, it is also possible to create mixed type arrays. The type of an array can be specified specifically using type annotation or left to the compiler to identify using type inference.

An array may be initialized with a collection of values (referred to as an *array literal*) at creation time using the following syntax:

var variableName: [type] = [value 1, value2, value3, ...]

The following code creates a new array assigned to a variable (thereby making it mutable) that is initialized with three string values:

```
var treeArray = ["Pine", "Oak", "Yew"]
```

Alternatively, the same array could have been created immutably by assigning it to a constant:

```
let treeArray = ["Pine", "Oak", "Yew"]
```

In the above instance, the Swift compiler will use type inference to decide that the array contains values of String type and prevent values of other types being inserted into the array elsewhere within the application code.

Alternatively, the same array could have been declared using type annotation:

```
var treeArray: [String] = ["Pine", "Oak", "Yew"]
```

Arrays do not have to have values assigned at creation time. The following syntax can be used to create an empty array:

```
var variableName = [type]()
```

Consider, for example, the following code which creates an empty array designated to store floating point values and assigns it to a variable named priceArray:

```
var priceArray = [Float]()
```

Another useful initialization technique allows an array to be initialized to a certain size with each array element pre-set with a specified default value:

```
var nameArray = [String](repeating: "My String", count: 10)
```

When compiled and executed, the above code will create a new 10 element array with each element initialized with a string that reads "My String".

Finally, a new array may be created by adding together two existing arrays (assuming both arrays contain values of the same type). For example:

```
let firstArray = ["Red", "Green", "Blue"]
let secondArray = ["Indigo", "Violet"]

let thirdArray = firstArray + secondArray
```

14.3 Working with Arrays in Swift

Once an array exists, a wide range of methods and properties are provided for working with and manipulating the array content from within Swift code, a subset of which is as follows:

14.3.1 Array Item Count

A count of the items in an array can be obtained by accessing the array's count property:

```
var treeArray = ["Pine", "Oak", "Yew"]
var itemCount = treeArray.count

print(itemCount)
```

Whether or not an array is empty can be identified using the array's Boolean *isEmpty* property as follows:

```
var treeArray = ["Pine", "Oak", "Yew"]

if treeArray.isEmpty {
    // Array is empty
}
```

14.3.2 Accessing Array Items

A specific item in an array may be accessed or modified by referencing the item's position in the array index (where the first item in the array has index position 0) using a technique referred to as *index subscripting*. In the following code fragment, the string value contained at index position 2 in the array (in this case the string value "Yew") is output by the print call:

```
var treeArray = ["Pine", "Oak", "Yew"]

print(treeArray[2])
```

This approach can also be used to replace the value at an index location:

```
treeArray[1] = "Redwood"
```

The above code replaces the current value at index position 1 with a new String value that reads "Redwood".

14.4 Random Items and Shuffling

A call to the *shuffled()* method of an array object will return a new version of the array with the item ordering randomly shuffled, for example:

```
let shuffledTrees = treeArray.shuffled()
```

To access an array item at random, simply make a call to the *randomElement()* method:

```
let randomTree = treeArray.randomElement()
```

14.5 Appending Items to an Array

Items may be added to an array using either the *append* method or + and += operators. The following, for example, are all valid techniques for appending items to an array:

```
treeArray.append("Redwood")
treeArray += ["Redwood"]
treeArray += ["Redwood", "Maple", "Birch"]
```

14.5.1 Inserting and Deleting Array Items

New items may be inserted into an array by specifying the index location of the new item in a call to the array's *insert(at:)* method. An insertion preserves all existing elements in the array, essentially moving them to the right to accommodate the newly inserted item:

```
treeArray.insert("Maple", at: 0)
```

Similarly, an item at a specific array index position may be removed using the *remove(at:)* method call:

```
treeArray.remove(at: 2)
```

To remove the last item in an array, simply make a call to the array's *removeLast* method as follows:

```
treeArray.removeLast()
```

14.6 Array Iteration

The easiest way to iterate through the items in an array is to make use of the for-in looping syntax. The following code, for example, iterates through all of the items in a String array and outputs each item to the console panel:

```
let treeArray = ["Pine", "Oak", "Yew", "Maple", "Birch", "Myrtle"]

for tree in treeArray {
    print(tree)
}
```

Upon execution, the following output would appear in the console:

```
Pine
Oak
Yew
Maple
Birch
Myrtle
```

14.7 Creating Mixed Type Arrays

A mixed type array is an array that can contain elements of different class types. Clearly an array that is either declared or inferred as being of type String cannot subsequently be used to contain non-String class object instances. Interesting possibilities arise, however, when taking into consideration that Swift includes the *Any* type. Any is a special type in Swift that can be used to reference an object of a non-specific class type. It follows, therefore, that an array declared as containing Any object types can be used to store elements of mixed types. The following code, for example, declares and initializes an array containing a mixture of String, Int and Double elements:

```
let mixedArray: [Any] = ["A String", 432, 34.989]
```

The use of the Any type should be used with care since the use of Any masks from Swift the true type of the elements in such an array thereby leaving code prone to potential programmer error. It will often be necessary, for example, to manually cast the elements in an Any array to the correct type before working with them in code. Performing the incorrect cast for a specific element in the array will most likely cause the code to compile without error but crash at runtime. Consider, for the sake of an example, the following mixed type array:

```
let mixedArray: [Any] = [1, 2, 45, "Hello"]
```

Assume that, having initialized the array, we now need to iterate through the integer elements in the array and multiply them by 10. The code to achieve this might read as follows:

```
for object in mixedArray {
    print(object * 10)
```

```
}
```

When entered into Xcode, however, the above code will trigger a syntax error indicating that it is not possible to multiply operands of type Any and Int. In order to remove this error it will be necessary to downcast the array element to be of type Int:

```
for object in mixedArray {
    print(object as! Int * 10)
}
```

The above code will compile without error and work as expected until the final String element in the array is reached at which point the code will crash with the following error:

```
Could not cast value of type 'Swift.String' to 'Swift.Int'
```

The code will, therefore, need to be modified to be aware of the specific type of each element in the array. Clearly, there are both benefits and risks to using Any arrays in Swift.

14.8 **Swift Dictionary Collections**

String dictionaries allow data to be stored and managed in the form of key-value pairs. Dictionaries fulfill a similar purpose to arrays, except each item stored in the dictionary has associated with it a unique key (to be precise, the key is unique to the particular dictionary object) which can be used to reference and access the corresponding value. Currently only String, Int, Double and Bool data types are suitable for use as keys within a Swift dictionary.

14.9 **Swift Dictionary Initialization**

A dictionary is a data type designed specifically to hold multiple values in a single unordered collection. Each item in a dictionary consists of a key and an associated value. The data types of the key and value elements type may be specified specifically using type annotation, or left to the compiler to identify using type inference.

A new dictionary may be initialized with a collection of values (referred to as a *dictionary literal*) at creation time using the following syntax:

var *variableName*: [*key type*: *value type*] = [*key 1: value 1, key 2: value2 ….*]

The following code creates a new array assigned to a variable (thereby making it mutable) that is initialized with four key-value pairs in the form of ISBN numbers acting as keys for corresponding book titles:

```
var bookDict = ["100-432112" : "Wind in the Willows",
                "200-532874" : "Tale of Two Cities",
                "202-546549" : "Sense and Sensibility",
                "104-109834" : "Shutter Island"]
```

In the above instance, the Swift compiler will use type inference to decide that both the key and value elements of the dictionary are of String type and prevent values or keys of other types being inserted into the dictionary.

Alternatively, the same array could have been declared using type annotation:

```
var bookDict: [String: String] =
            ["100-432112" : "Wind in the Willows",
             "200-532874" : "Tale of Two Cities",
             "202-546549" : "Sense and Sensibility",
             "104-109834" : "Shutter Island"]
```

As with arrays, it is also possible to create an empty dictionary, the syntax for which reads as follows:

var *variableName* = [*key type*: *value type*]()

The following code creates an empty dictionary designated to store integer keys and string values:

```
var myDictionary = [Int: String]()
```

14.10 Sequence-based Dictionary Initialization

Dictionaries may also be initialized using sequences to represent the keys and values. This is achieved using the Swift *zip()* function, passing through the keys and corresponding values. In the following example, a dictionary is created using two arrays:

```
let keys = ["100-432112", "200-532874", "202-546549", "104-109834"]
let values = ["Wind in the Willows", "Tale of Two Cities",
              "Sense and Sensibility", "Shutter Island"]

let bookDict = Dictionary(uniqueKeysWithValues: zip(keys, values))
```

This approach allows keys and values to be generated programmatically. In the following example, a number range starting at 1 is being specified for the keys instead of using an array of predefined keys:

```
let values = ["Wind in the Willows", "Tale of Two Cities",
        "Sense and Sensibility", "Shutter Island"]

var bookDict = Dictionary(uniqueKeysWithValues: zip(1..., values))
```

The above code is a much cleaner equivalent to the following dictionary declaration:

```
var bookDict = [1 : "Wind in the Willows",
                2 : "Tale of Two Cities",
                3 : "Sense and Sensibility",
                4 : "Shutter Island"]
```

14.11 Dictionary Item Count

A count of the items in a dictionary can be obtained by accessing the dictionary's count property:

```
print(bookDict.count)
```

14.12 **Accessing and Updating Dictionary Items**

A specific value may be accessed or modified using key subscript syntax to reference the corresponding key. The following code references a key known to be in the bookDict dictionary and outputs the associated value (in this case the book entitled "A Tale of Two Cities"):

```
print(bookDict["200-532874"])
```

When accessing dictionary entries in this way, it is also possible to declare a default value to be used in the event that the specified key does not return a value:

```
print(bookDict["999-546547", default: "Book not found"])
```

Since the dictionary does not contain an entry for the specified key, the above code will output text which reads "Book not found".

Indexing by key may also be used when updating the value associated with a specified key, for example, to change the title of the same book from "A Tale of Two Cities" to "Sense and Sensibility"):

```
bookDict["200-532874"] = "Sense and Sensibility"
```

The same result is also possible by making a call to the *updateValue(forKey:)* method, passing through the key corresponding to the value to be changed:

```
bookDict.updateValue("The Ruins", forKey: "200-532874")
```

14.13 **Adding and Removing Dictionary Entries**

Items may be added to a dictionary using the following key subscripting syntax:

dictionaryVariable[key] = value

For example, to add a new key-value pair entry to the books dictionary:

```
bookDict["300-898871"] = "The Overlook"
```

Removal of a key-value pair from a dictionary may be achieved either by assigning a *nil* value to the entry, or via a call to the *removeValueForKey* method of the dictionary instance. Both code lines below achieve the same result of removing the specified entry from the books dictionary:

```
bookDict["300-898871"] = nil
bookDict.removeValue(forKey: "300-898871")
```

14.14 **Dictionary Iteration**

As with arrays, it is possible to iterate through the dictionary entries by making use of the for-in looping syntax. The following code, for example, iterates through all of the entries in the books dictionary, outputting both the key and value for each entry panel:

```
for (bookid, title) in bookDict {
  print("Book ID: \(bookid) Title: \(title)")
```

```
}
```

Upon execution, the following output would appear in the console:

```
Book ID: 100-432112 Title: Wind in the Willows
Book ID: 200-532874 Title: The Ruins
Book ID: 104-109834 Title: Shutter Island
Book ID: 202-546549 Title: Sense and Sensibility
```

14.15 Summary

Collections in Swift take the form of either dictionaries or arrays. Both provide a way to collect together multiple items within a single object. Arrays provide a way to store an ordered collection of items where those items are accessed by an index value corresponding to the item position in the array. Dictionaries provide a platform for storing key-value pairs, where the key is used to gain access to the stored value. Iteration through the elements of Swift collections can be achieved using the for-in loop construct.

15. Understanding Error Handling in Swift 5

In a perfect world, a running iOS app would never encounter an error. The reality, however, is that it is impossible to guarantee that an error of some form or another will not occur at some point during the execution of the app. It is essential, therefore, to ensure that the code of an app is implemented such that it gracefully handles any errors that may occur. Since the introduction of Swift 2, the task of handling errors has become much easier for the iOS app developer.

This chapter will cover the handling of errors using Swift and introduce topics such as *error types*, *throwing methods and functions*, the *guard* and *defer* statements and *do-catch* statements.

15.1 Understanding Error Handling

No matter how carefully Swift code is designed and implemented, there will invariably be situations that are beyond the control of the app. An app that relies on an active internet connection cannot, for example, control the loss of signal on an iPhone device, or prevent the user from enabling "airplane mode". What the app can do, however, is to implement robust handling of the error (for example displaying a message indicating to the user that the app requires an active internet connection to proceed).

There are two sides to handling errors within Swift. The first involves triggering (or *throwing*) an error when the desired results are not achieved within the method of an iOS app. The second involves catching and handling the error after it is thrown by a method.

When an error is thrown, the error will be of a particular error type which can be used to identify the specific nature of the error and used to decide on the most appropriate course of action to be taken. The error type value can be any value that conforms to the ErrorType protocol.

In addition to implementing methods in an app to throw errors when necessary, it is important to be aware that a number of API methods in the iOS SDK (particularly those relating to file handling) will throw errors which will need to be handled within the code of the app.

15.2 Declaring Error Types

For the sake of an example, consider a method that is required to transfer a file to a remote server. Such a method might fail to transfer the file for a variety of reasons such as there being no network connection, the connection being too slow or the failure to find the file to be transferred. All these possible errors could be represented within an enumeration that conforms to the Error protocol as follows:

```
enum FileTransferError: Error {
    case noConnection
    case lowBandwidth
    case fileNotFound
}
```

Once an error type has been declared, it can be used within a method when throwing errors.

15.3 **Throwing an Error**

A method or function declares that it can throw an error using the *throws* keyword. For example:

```
func transferFile() throws {
}
```

In the event that the function or method returns a result, the *throws* keyword is placed before the return type as follows:

```
func transferFile() throws -> Bool {
}
```

Once a method has been declared as being able to throw errors, code can then be added to throw the errors when they are encountered. This is achieved using the *throw* statement in conjunction with the *guard* statement. The following code declares some constants to serve as status values and then implements the guard and throw behavior for the method:

```
let connectionOK = true
let connectionSpeed = 30.00
let fileFound = false

enum FileTransferError: Error {
    case noConnection
    case lowBandwidth
    case fileNotFound
}

func fileTransfer() throws {

    guard connectionOK else {
        throw FileTransferError.noConnection
    }

    guard connectionSpeed > 30 else {
        throw FileTransferError.lowBandwidth
    }

    guard fileFound else {
```

```
      throw FileTransferError.fileNotFound
    }
}
```

Within the body of the method, each guard statement checks a condition for a true or false result. In the event of a false result, the code contained within the *else* body is executed. In the case of a false result, the throw statement is used to throw one of the error values contained in the FileTransferError enumeration.

15.4 **Calling Throwing Methods and Functions**

Once a method or function is declared as throwing errors, it can no longer be called in the usual manner. Calls to such methods must now be prefixed by the *try* statement as follows:

```
try fileTransfer()
```

In addition to using the try statement, the call must also be made from within a *do-catch* statement to catch and handle any errors that may be thrown. Consider, for example, that the *fileTransfer* method needs to be called from within a method named *sendFile*. The code within this method might be implemented as follows:

```
func sendFile() -> String {

    do {
        try fileTransfer()
    } catch FileTransferError.noConnection {
        return("No Network Connection")
    } catch FileTransferError.lowBandwidth {
        return("File Transfer Speed too Low")
    } catch FileTransferError.fileNotFound {
        return("File not Found")
    } catch {
        return("Unknown error")
    }

    return("Successful transfer")
}
```

The method calls the *fileTransfer* method from within a *do-catch* statement which, in turn, includes catch conditions for each of the three possible error conditions. In each case, the method simply returns a string value containing a description of the error. In the event that no error was thrown, a string value is returned indicating a successful file transfer. Note that a fourth catch condition is included with no pattern matching. This is a "catch all" statement that ensures that any errors not matched by the preceding catch statements are also handled. This is required because do-catch statements must be exhaustive (in other words constructed so as to catch all possible error conditions).

15.5 **Accessing the Error Object**

When a method call fails, it will invariably return an Error object identifying the nature of the failure. A common requirement within the catch statement is to gain access to this object so that appropriate corrective action can be taken within the app code. The following code demonstrates how such an error object is accessed from within a catch statement when attempting to create a new file system directory:

```
do {
    try filemgr.createDirectory(atPath: newDir,
                    withIntermediateDirectories: true,
                    attributes: nil)
    } catch let error {
            print("Error: \(error.localizedDescription)")
}
```

15.6 **Disabling Error Catching**

A throwing method may be forced to run without the need to enclose the call within a do-catch statement by using the *try!* statement as follows:

```
try! fileTransfer
```

In using this approach we are informing the compiler that we know with absolute certainty that the method call will not result in an error being thrown. In the event that an error is thrown when using this technique, the code will fail with a runtime error. As such, this approach should be used sparingly.

15.7 **Using the defer Statement**

The previously implemented *sendFile* method demonstrated a common scenario when handling errors. Each of the catch clauses in the do-catch statement contained a return statement that returned control to the calling method. In such a situation, however, it might be useful to be able to perform some other task before control is returned and regardless of the type of error that was encountered. The *sendFile* method might, for example, need to remove temporary files before returning. This behavior can be achieved using the *defer* statement.

The defer statement allows a sequence of code statements to be declared as needing to be run as soon as the method returns. In the following code, the *sendFile* method has been modified to include a defer statement:

```
func sendFile() -> String {

    defer {
        removeTmpFiles()
        closeConnection()
    }
```

```
do {
    try fileTransfer()
} catch FileTransferError.NoConnection {
    return("No Network Connection")
} catch FileTransferError.LowBandwidth {
    return("File Transfer Speed too Low")
} catch FileTransferError.FileNotFound {
    return("File not Found")
} catch {
    return("Unknown error")
}

    return("Successful transfer")
}
```

With the defer statement now added, the calls to the *removeTmpFiles* and *closeConnection* methods will always be made before the method returns, regardless of which return call gets triggered.

15.8 **Summary**

Error handling is an essential part of creating robust and reliable iOS apps. Since the introduction of Swift 2 it is now much easier to both trigger and handle errors. Error types are created using values that conform to the ErrorType protocol and are most commonly implemented as enumerations. Methods and functions that throw errors are declared as such using the *throw* keyword. The *guard* and *throw* statements are used within the body of these methods or functions to throw errors based on the error type.

A throwable method or function is called using the *try* statement which must be encapsulated within a do-catch statement. A do-catch statement consists of an exhaustive list of catch pattern constructs, each of which contains the code to be executed in the event of a particular error being thrown. Cleanup tasks can be defined to be executed when a method returns through the use of the *defer* statement.

16. An Overview of SwiftUI

Now that Xcode has been installed and the basics of the Swift programing language covered, it is time to start introducing SwiftUI.

First announced at Apple's Worldwide Developer Conference in 2019, SwiftUI is an entirely new approach to developing apps for all Apple operating system platforms. The basic goals of SwiftUI are to make app development easier, faster and less prone to the types of bugs that typically appear when developing software projects. These elements have been combined with SwiftUI specific additions to Xcode that allow SwiftUI projects to be tested in near real-time using a live preview of the app during the development process.

Many of the advantages of SwiftUI originate from the fact that it is both *declarative* and *data driven*, topics which will be explained in this chapter.

The discussion in this chapter is intended as a high-level overview of SwiftUI and does not cover the practical aspects of implementation within a project. Implementation and practical examples will be covered in detail in the remainder of the book.

16.1 UIKit and Interface Builder

To understand the meaning and advantages of SwiftUI's declarative syntax, it helps to understand how user interface layouts were designed before the introduction of SwiftUI. Up until the introduction of SwiftUI, iOS apps were built entirely using UIKit together with a collection of associated frameworks that make up the iOS Software Development Kit (SDK).

To aid in the design of the user interface layouts that make up the screens of an app, Xcode includes a tool called Interface Builder. Interface Builder is a powerful tool that allows storyboards to be created which contain the individual scenes that make up an app (with a scene typically representing a single app screen).

The user interface layout of a scene is designed within Interface Builder by dragging components (such as buttons, labels, text fields and sliders) from a library panel to the desired location on the scene canvas. Selecting a component in a scene provides access to a range of inspector panels where the attributes of the components can be changed.

The layout behavior of the scene (in other words how it reacts to different device screen sizes and changes to device orientation between portrait and landscape) is defined by configuring a range of constraints that dictate how each component is positioned and sized in relation to both the containing window and the other components in the layout.

Finally, any components that need to respond to user events (such as a button tap or slider motion) are connected to methods in the app source code where the event is handled.

At various points during this development process, it is necessary to compile and run the app on a simulator or device to test that everything is working as expected.

16.2 SwiftUI Declarative Syntax

SwiftUI introduces a declarative syntax that provides an entirely different way of implementing user interface layouts and behavior from the UIKit and Interface Builder approach. Instead of manually designing the intricate details of the layout and appearance of components that make up a scene, SwiftUI allows the scenes to be described using a simple and intuitive syntax. In other words, SwiftUI allows layouts to be created by declaring how the user interface should appear without having to worry about the complexity of how the layout is actually built.

This essentially involves declaring the components to be included in the layout, stating the kind of layout manager in which they to be contained (vertical stack, horizontal stack, form, list etc.) and using modifiers to set attributes such as the text on a button, the foreground color of a label, or the method to be called in the event of a tap gesture. Having made these declarations, all the intricate and complicated details of how to position, constrain and render the layout are handled automatically by SwiftUI.

SwiftUI declarations are structured hierarchically, which also makes it easy to create complex views by composing together small, re-usable custom subviews.

While the view layout is being declared and tested, Xcode provides a preview canvas which changes in real-time to reflect the appearance of the layout. Xcode also includes a *live preview* mode which allows the app to be launched within the preview canvas and fully tested without the need to build and run on a simulator or device.

Coverage of the SwiftUI declaration syntax begins with the chapter entitled *Creating Custom Views with SwiftUI*.

16.3 SwiftUI is Data Driven

When we say that SwiftUI is data driven, this is not to say that it is no longer necessary to handle events generated by the user (in other words the interaction between the user and the app user interface). It is still necessary, for example, to know when the user taps a button and to react in some app specific way. Being data driven relates more to the relationship between the underlying app data and the user interface and logic of the app.

Prior to the introduction of SwiftUI, an iOS app would contain code responsible for checking the current values of data within the app. If data is likely to change over time, code has to be written to ensure that the user interface always reflects the latest state of the data (perhaps by writing code to frequently check for changes to the data, or by providing a refresh option for the user to request a data update). Similar problems arise when keeping the user interface state consistent and making sure issues like toggle button settings are stored appropriately. Requirements such as these can become increasingly complex when multiple areas of an app depend on the same data sources.

SwiftUI addresses this complexity by providing several ways to *bind* the data model of an app to the user interface components and logic that provide the app functionality.

When implemented, the data model *publishes* data variables to which other parts of the app can then *subscribe*. Using this approach, changes to the published data are automatically reported to all subscribers. If the binding is made from a user interface component, any data changes will automatically be reflected within the user interface by SwiftUI without the need to write any additional code.

16.4 **SwiftUI vs. UIKit**

With the choice of using UIKit and SwiftUI now available, the obvious question arises as to which is the best option. When making this decision it is important to understand that SwiftUI and UIKit are not mutually exclusive. In fact, several integration solutions are available (a topic area covered starting with the chapter entitled *Integrating UIViews with SwiftUI*).

The first factor to take into consideration during the decision process is that any app that includes SwiftUI-based code will only run on devices running iOS 13 or later. This means, for example, that your app will only be available to users with the following iPhone models:

- iPhone 11
- iPhone 11 Pro
- iPhone 11 Pro Max
- iPhone Xs
- iPhone Xs Max
- iPhone XR
- iPhone X
- iPhone 8
- iPhone 8 Plus
- iPhone 7
- iPhone 7 Plus
- iPhone 6s
- iPhone 6s Plus
- iPhone SE

Apple reported on October 15, 2019 that, based on App Store measurements, 50% of all iPhone devices were running iOS 13, a percentage that will continue to increase with the passage of time.

If supporting devices running older versions of iOS is not of concern and you are starting a new project, it makes sense to use SwiftUI wherever possible. Not only does SwiftUI provide a faster, more efficient app development environment, it also makes it easier to make the same app available on multiple Apple platforms (iOS, iPadOS, macOS, watchOS and tvOS) without making significant code changes.

If you have an existing app developed using UIKit there is no easy migration path to convert that code to SwiftUI, so it probably makes sense to keep using UIKit for that part of the project. UIKit will continue to be a valuable part of the app development toolset and will be extended, supported and enhanced by Apple for the foreseeable future. When adding new features to an existing project, however, consider doing so using SwiftUI and integrating it into the existing UIKit codebase.

When adopting SwiftUI for new projects, it will probably not be possible to avoid using UIKit entirely. Although SwiftUI comes with a wide array of user interface components, it will still be necessary to use UIKit for certain functionality such as map and web view integration.

In addition, for extremely complex user interface layout designs, it may also be necessary to use Interface Builder in situations where layout needs cannot be satisfied using the SwiftUI layout container views.

16.5 Summary

SwiftUI introduces a different approach to app development than that offered by UIKit and Interface Builder. Rather than directly implement the way in which a user interface is to be rendered, SwiftUI allows the user interface to be declared in descriptive terms and then does all the work of deciding the best way to perform the rendering when the app runs.

SwiftUI is also data driven in that data change drives the behavior and appearance of the app. This is achieved through a publisher and subscriber model.

This chapter has provided a very high-level view of SwiftUI. The remainder of this book will explore SwiftUI in greater depth.

17. Using Xcode in SwiftUI Mode

When creating a new project, Xcode now provides a choice of creating either a Storyboard or SwiftUI based user interface for the project. When creating a SwiftUI project, Xcode appears and behaves significantly differently when designing the user interface for an app project compared to the UIKit Storyboard mode.

When working in SwiftUI mode, most of your time as an app developer will be spent in the code editor and preview canvas, both of which will be explored in detail in this chapter.

17.1 Starting Xcode 11

As with all iOS examples in this book, the development of our example will take place within the Xcode 11 development environment. If you have not already installed this tool together with the latest iOS SDK refer first to the *Installing Xcode 11 and the iOS 13 SDK* chapter of this book. Assuming the installation is complete, launch Xcode either by clicking on the icon on the dock (assuming you created one) or use the macOS Finder to locate Xcode in the Applications folder of your system.

When launched for the first time, and until you turn off the *Show this window when Xcode launches* toggle, the screen illustrated in Figure 17-1 will appear by default:

Figure 17-1

If you do not see this window, simply select the *Window -> Welcome to Xcode* menu option to display it. From within this window, click on the option to *Create a new Xcode project*.

17.2 **Creating a SwiftUI Project**

When creating a new project, the project options screen includes an option to select how the user interface is to be implemented. To use SwiftUI, simply change the menu option highlighted in Figure 17-2 to *SwiftUI*:

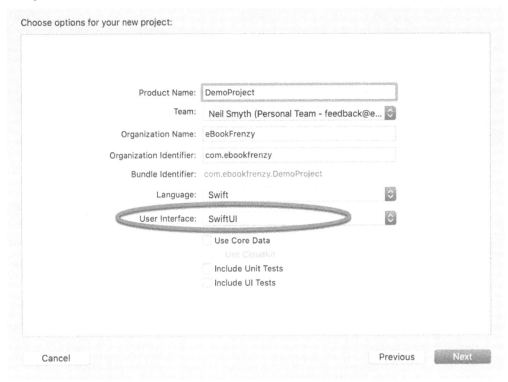

Figure 17-2

Once a new project has been created with SwiftUI selected, the main Xcode panel will appear with the default layout for SwiftUI development displayed.

17.3 **Xcode in SwiftUI Mode**

Before beginning work on a SwiftUI user interface, it is worth taking some time to gain familiarity with how Xcode works in SwiftUI mode. A newly created project includes a single SwiftUI View file named *ContentView.swift* which, when selected from the project navigation panel, will appear within Xcode as shown in Figure 17-3 below:

Figure 17-3

Located to the right of the project navigator (A) is the code editor (B). To the right of this is the preview canvas (C) where any changes made to the SwiftUI layout declaration will appear in real-time.

Selecting a view in the canvas will automatically select and highlight the corresponding entry in the code editor, and vice versa. Attributes for the currently selected item will appear in the attributes inspector panel (D).

During debugging, the debug panel (E) will appear containing debug output from both the iOS frameworks and any diagnostic print statements you have included in your code.

The three panels (A, D and E) can be displayed and hidden using the three buttons located on the right-hand side of the toolbar as shown in Figure 17-4:

Figure 17-4

17.4 The Preview Canvas

The preview canvas provides both a visual representation of the user interface design and a tool for adding and modifying views within the layout design. The canvas may also be used to perform live testing of the running app without the need to launch an iOS simulator. Figure 17-5 illustrates a typical preview canvas for a newly created project:

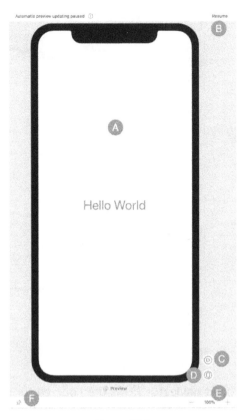

Figure 17-5

If the canvas is not visible it can be displayed using the Xcode *Editor -> Canvas* menu option.

The main canvas area (A) represents the current view as it will appear when running on a physical device. When changes are made to the code in the editor, those changes are reflected within the preview canvas. To avoid continually updating the canvas, and depending on the nature of the changes being made, the preview will occasionally pause live updates. When this happens, the Resume button (B) will appear which, when clicked, will once again begin updating the preview.

By default, the preview displays a static representation of the user interface. To test the user interface in a running version of the app, simply click on the Live Preview button (C). Xcode will then build the app and run it within the preview canvas where you can interact with it as you would in a simulator or on a physical device. When in Live Preview mode, the button changes to a stop button which can be used to exit live mode.

The current version of the app may also be previewed on an attached physical device by clicking on the Preview on Device button (D). As with the preview canvas, the running app on the device will update dynamically as changes are made to the code in the editor.

Right-clicking on either the Live Preview or Preview on Device buttons will provide the option to run in debug mode, attaching the process to the debugger and allowing diagnostic output to appear in the debug area (marked E in Figure 17-3 above).

Figure 17-6

17.5 Preview Pinning

When building an app in Xcode it is likely that it will consist of several SwiftUI View files in addition to the default *ContentView.swift* file. When a SwiftUI View file is selected from the project navigator, both the code editor and preview canvas will change to reflect the currently selected file. Sometimes you may want the user interface layout for one SwiftUI file to appear in the preview canvas while editing the code in a different file. This can be particularly useful if the layout from one file is dependent on or embedded in another view. The pin button (labelled F in Figure 17-5 above) pins the current preview to the canvas so that it remains visible on the canvas after navigating to a different view. The view to which you have navigated will appear beneath the pinned view in the canvas and can be viewed by scrolling.

Finally, the size buttons (E) can be used to zoom in and out of the canvas.

17.6 Modifying the Design

Working with SwiftUI primarily involves adding additional views, customizing those views using modifiers, adding logic and interacting with state and other data instance bindings. All of these tasks can be performed exclusively by modifying the structure in the code editor. The font used to display the "Hello World" Text view, for example, can be changed by adding the appropriate modifier in the editor:

```
Text("Hello World")
    .font(.largeTitle)
```

An alternative to this is to make changes to the SwiftUI views by dragging and dropping items from the Library panel. The Library panel is displayed by clicking on the toolbar button highlighted in Figure 17-7:

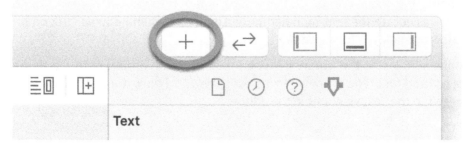

Figure 17-7

When displayed, the Library panel will appear as shown in Figure 17-8:

Figure 17-8

When launched in this way, the Library panel is transient and will disappear either after a selection has been made, or a click is performed outside of the panel. To keep the panel displayed, hold down the Option key when clicking on the Library button.

When first opened, the panel displays a list of views available for inclusion in the user interface design. The list can be browsed, or the search bar used to narrow the list to specific views. The toolbar (highlighted in the above figure) can be used to switch to other categories such as modifiers, commonly used code snippets, images and color resources.

An item within the library can be applied to the user interface design in a number of ways. To apply a font modifier to the "Hello World" Text view, one option is to select the view in either the code or preview canvas, locate the font modifier in the Library panel and double-click on it. Xcode will then automatically apply the font modifier.

Another option is to locate the Library item and then drag and drop it onto the desired location either in the code editor or the preview canvas. In Figure 17-9 below, for example, the font modifier is being dragged to the Text view within the editor:

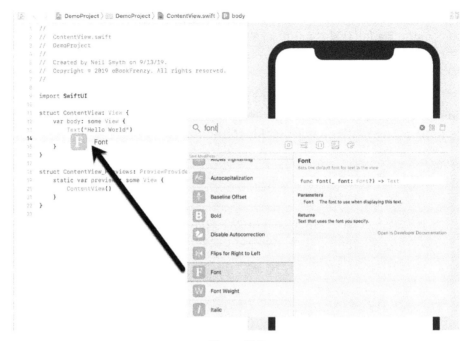

Figure 17-9

The same result can be achieved by dragging an item from the library onto the preview canvas. In the case of Figure 17-10, a Button view is being added to the layout beneath the existing Text view:

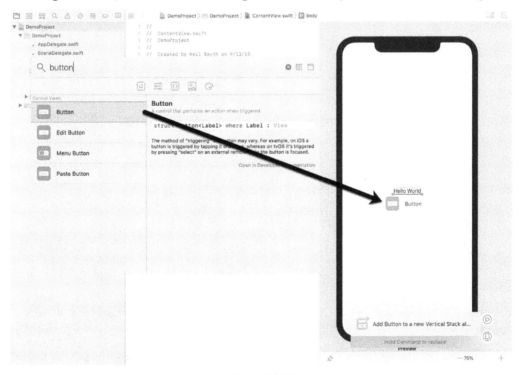

Figure 17-10

In this example, the side along which the view will be placed if released highlights and the preview canvas displays a notification that the Button and existing Text view will automatically be placed in a Vertical Stack container view (stacks will be covered later in the chapter entitled *SwiftUI Stacks and Frames*).

Once a view or modifier has been added to the SwiftUI view file it is highly likely that some customization will be necessary, such as specifying the color for a foreground modifier. One option is, of course, to simply make the changes within the editor, for example:

```
Text("Hello World")
    .font(.largeTitle)
    .foregroundColor(.red)
```

Another option is to select the view in either the editor or preview panel and then make the necessary changes within the Attributes inspector panel:

Figure 17-11

The Attributes inspector will provide the option to make changes to any modifiers already applied to the selected view.

Before moving on to the next topic, it is also worth noting that the Attributes inspector provides yet another way to add modifiers to a view via the Add Modifier menu located at the bottom of the panel. When clicked, this menu will display a long list of modifiers available for the current view type. To apply a modifier, simply select it from the menu. An entry for the new modifier will subsequently appear in the inspector where it can be configured with the required properties.

17.7 **Editor Context Menu**

Holding down the Command key while clicking on the item in the code editor will display the menu shown in Figure 17-12:

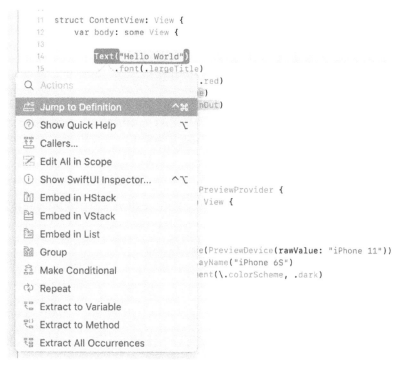

Figure 17-12

This menu provides a list of options which will vary depending on the type of item selected. Options typically include a shortcut to a popup version of the Attributes inspector for the current view, together with options to embed the current view in a stack or list container. This menu is also useful for extracting part of a view into its own self-contained subview. Creating subviews is strongly encouraged to promote reuse, improve performance and unclutter complex design structures.

17.8 **Previewing on Multiple Device Configurations**

Every newly created SwiftUI View file includes an additional declaration at the bottom of the file that resembles the following:

```
struct ContentView_Previews: PreviewProvider {
    static var previews: some View {
        ContentView()
    }
}
```

This structure, which conforms to the PreviewProvider protocol, returns an instance of the primary view within the file. This instructs Xcode to display the preview for that view within the preview canvas (without this declaration, nothing will appear in the canvas).

By default, the preview canvas shows the user interface on a single device based on the current selection in the run target menu to the right of the run and stop button in the Xcode toolbar. To preview on other device models, one option is to simply change the run target and wait for the preview canvas to change.

A better option, however, is to modify the previews structure to specify a different device. In the following example, the canvas previews the user interface on an iPhone SE:

```
struct ContentView_Previews: PreviewProvider {
    static var previews: some View {
        ContentView()
            .previewDevice(PreviewDevice(rawValue: "iPhone SE"))
            .previewDisplayName("iPhone SE")
    }
}
```

In fact, it is possible using this technique to preview multiple device types simultaneously by placing them into a Group view as follows:

```
struct ContentView_Previews: PreviewProvider {
    static var previews: some View {

        Group {
            ContentView()
                .previewDevice(PreviewDevice(rawValue: "iPhone SE"))
                .previewDisplayName("iPhone SE")

            ContentView()
                .previewDevice(PreviewDevice(rawValue: "iPhone 11"))
                .previewDisplayName("iPhone 11")
        }
    }
}
```

When multiple devices are previewed, they appear in a scrollable list within the preview canvas as shown in Figure 17-13:

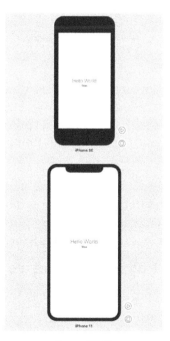

Figure 17-13

The environment modifier may also be used to preview the layout in other configurations, for example, to preview in dark mode:

```
ContentView()
    .previewDevice(PreviewDevice(rawValue: "iPhone SE"))
    .previewDisplayName("iPhone SE")
        .environment(\.colorScheme, .dark)
```

This preview structure is also useful for passing sample data into the enclosing view for testing purposes within the preview canvas, a technique that will be used in later chapters. For example:

```
struct ContentView_Previews: PreviewProvider {
    static var previews: some View {
        ContentView(sampleData: mySampleData)
    }
}
```

17.9 Running the App on a Simulator

Although much can be achieved using the preview canvas, there is no substitute for running the app on physical devices and simulators during testing.

Within the main Xcode project window, the menu located in the top left-hand corner of the window (marked C in Figure 17-14) is used to choose a target simulator. This menu will include both simulators that have been configured and any physical devices connected to the development system:

Figure 17-14

Clicking on the *Run* toolbar button (A) will compile the code and run the app on the selected target. The small panel in the center of the Xcode toolbar (D) will report the progress of the build process together with any problems or errors that cause the build process to fail. Once the app is built, the simulator will start and the app will run. Clicking on the stop button (B) will terminate the running app.

The simulator includes a number of options not available in the live preview for testing different aspects of the app. The Hardware and Debug menus, for example, include options for rotating the simulator through portrait and landscape orientations, testing Face ID authentication and simulating geographical location changes for navigation and map-based apps.

17.10 **Running the App on a Physical iOS Device**

Although the Simulator environment provides a useful way to test an app on a variety of different iOS device models, it is important to also test on a physical iOS device.

If you have entered your Apple ID in the Xcode preferences screen as outlined in the *Joining the Apple Developer Program* chapter and selected a development team for the project, it is possible to run the app on a physical device simply by connecting it to the development Mac system with a USB cable and selecting it as the run target within Xcode.

With a device connected to the development system, and an application ready for testing, refer to the device menu located in the Xcode toolbar. There is a reasonable chance that this will have defaulted to one of the iOS Simulator configurations. Switch to the physical device by selecting this menu and changing it to the device name as shown in Figure 17-5:

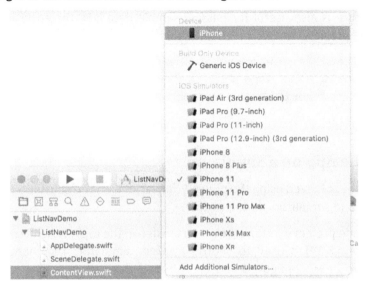

Figure 17-15

With the target device selected, make sure the device is unlocked and click on the run button at which point Xcode will install and launch the app on the device. If you have not yet joined the Apple Developer Program, the following dialog may appear within Xcode indicating that you need to configure your device to trust the developer certificate used to build the app:

Could not launch "DemoProject"

Verify the Developer App certificate for your account is trusted on your device. Open Settings on iPhone and navigate to General -> Device Management, then select your Developer App certificate to trust it. Internal launch error: process launch failed: Security

Details   OK

Figure 17-16

Following the instructions in the dialog, open the Settings app on the device, navigate to *General -> Profiles and Device Management* and select the developer certificate on the resulting screen:

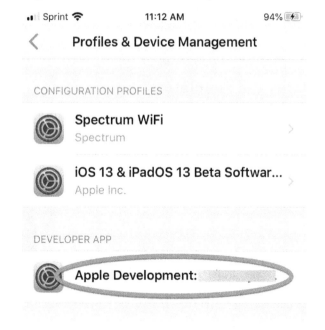

Figure 17-17

In the subsequent certificate screen, tap the *Trust "Apple Development: <email address>"* button followed by the Trust button in the confirmation dialog:

Figure 17-18

Once the certificate is trusted, it should be possible to install and run the app on the device.

As will be discussed later in this chapter, a physical device may also be configured for network testing, whereby apps are installed and tested on the device via a network connection without the need to have the device connected by a USB cable.

17.11 Managing Devices and Simulators

Currently connected iOS devices and the simulators configured for use with Xcode can be viewed and managed using the Xcode Devices window which is accessed via the *Window -> Devices and Simulators* menu option. Figure 17-19 for example, shows a typical Device screen on a system where an iPhone has been detected:

Figure 17-19

A wide range of simulator configurations are set up within Xcode by default and can be viewed by selecting the *Simulators* tab at the top of the dialog. Other simulator configurations can be added by clicking on the + button located in the bottom left-hand corner of the window. Once selected, a dialog will appear allowing the simulator to be configured in terms of device, iOS version and name.

17.12 **Enabling Network Testing**

In addition to testing an app on a physical device connected to the development system via a USB cable, Xcode also supports testing via a network connection. This option is enabled on a per device basis within the Devices and Simulators dialog introduced in the previous section. With the device connected via the USB cable, display this dialog, select the device from the list and enable the *Connect via network* option as highlighted in Figure 17-20:

Figure 17-20

Once the setting has been enabled, the device may continue to be used as the run target for the app even when the USB cable is disconnected. The only requirement being that both the device and development computer be connected to the same Wi-Fi network. Assuming this requirement has been met, clicking on the run button with the device selected in the run menu will install and launch the app over the network connection.

17.13 **Dealing with Build Errors**

If for any reason a build fails, the status window in the Xcode toolbar will report that an error has been detected by displaying "Build" together with the number of errors detected and any warnings. In addition, the left-hand panel of the Xcode window will update with a list of the errors. Selecting an error from this list will take you to the location in the code where corrective action needs to be taken.

17.14 **Monitoring Application Performance**

Another useful feature of Xcode is the ability to monitor the performance of an application while it is running, either on a device or simulator or within the live preview canvas. This information is accessed by displaying the *Debug Navigator*.

When Xcode is launched, the project navigator is displayed in the left-hand panel by default. Along the top of this panel is a bar with a range of other options. The seventh option from the left displays the debug navigator when selected as illustrated in Figure 17-21. When displayed, this panel shows a number of real-time statistics relating to the performance of the currently running application such as memory, CPU usage, disk access, energy efficiency, network activity and iCloud storage access.

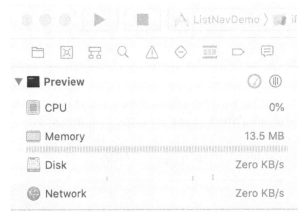

Figure 17-21

When one of these categories is selected, the main panel (Figure 17-22) updates to provide additional information about that particular aspect of the application's performance:

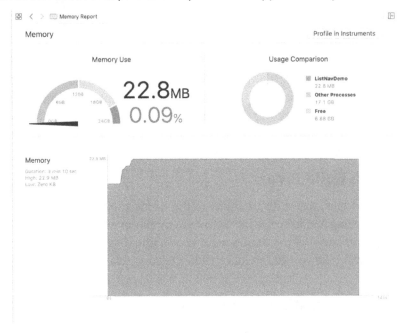

Figure 17-22

Yet more information can be obtained by clicking on the *Profile in Instruments* button in the top right-hand corner of the panel.

17.15 Exploring the User Interface Layout Hierarchy

Xcode also provides an option to break the user interface layout out into a rotatable 3D view that shows how the view hierarchy for a user interface is constructed. This can be particularly useful for identifying situations where one view instance is obscured by another appearing on top of it or a layout is not appearing as intended. This is also useful for learning how SwiftUI works behind the scenes to construct a SwiftUI layout, if only to appreciate how much work SwiftUI is saving us from having to do.

To access the view hierarchy in this mode, begin by previewing the view in debug mode as illustrated in Figure 17-6 above. Once the preview is live, click on the *Debug View Hierarchy* button indicated in Figure 17-23:

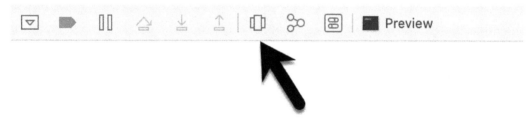

Figure 17-23

Once activated, a 3D "exploded" view of the layout will appear. Clicking and dragging within the view will rotate the hierarchy allowing the layers of views that make up the user interface to be inspected:

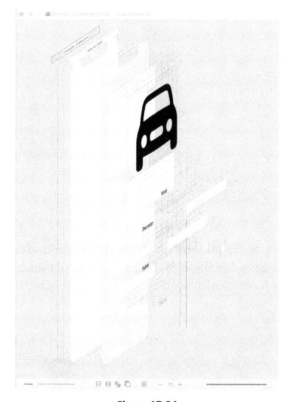

Figure 17-24

Moving the slider in the bottom left-hand corner of the panel will adjust the spacing between the different views in the hierarchy. The two markers in the right-hand slider (Figure 17-25) may also be used to narrow the range of views visible in the rendering. This can be useful, for example, to focus on a subset of views located in the middle of the hierarchy tree:

Figure 17-25

While the hierarchy is being debugged, the left-hand panel will display the entire view hierarchy tree for the layout as shown in Figure 17-26 below:

Figure 17-26

Selecting an object in the hierarchy tree will highlight the corresponding item in the 3D rendering and vice versa. The far right-hand panel will also display the attributes of the selected object. If the panel is not currently visible it can be displayed by clicking on the toolbar button indicated in Figure 17-27:

Figure 17-27

Figure 17-28, for example, shows the inspector panel while a Text view is selected within the view hierarchy.

Figure 17-28

17.16 **Summary**

When creating a new project, Xcode provides the option to use either UIKit Storyboards or SwiftUI as the basis of the user interface of the app. When in SwiftUI mode, most of the work involved in developing an app takes place in the code editor and the preview canvas. New views can be added to the user interface layout and configured either by typing into the code editor or dragging and dropping components from the Library either onto the editor or the preview canvas.

The preview canvas will usually update in real time to reflect code changes as they are typed into the code editor, though will frequently pause updates in response to larger changes. When in the paused state, clicking the Resume button will restart updates. The Attribute inspector allows the properties of a selected view to be changed and new modifiers added. Holding down the Command key while clicking on a view in the editor or canvas displays the context menu containing a range of options such as embedding the view in a container or extracting the selection to a subview.

The preview structure at the end of the SwiftUI View file allows previewing to be performed on multiple device models simultaneously and with different environment settings.

18. The Anatomy of a Basic SwiftUI Project

When a new SwiftUI project is created in Xcode using the Single View App template, Xcode generates a number of different files and folders which form the basis of the project, and on which the finished app will eventually be built.

Although it is not necessary to know in detail about the purpose of each of these files when beginning with SwiftUI development, each of them will become useful as you progress to developing more complex applications.

The goal of this chapter, therefore, is to provide a brief overview of each element of a basic project structure.

18.1 Creating an Example Project

It may be useful to create a sample project to review while working through this chapter. To do so, launch Xcode and, on the welcome screen, select the option to create a new project. On the resulting template selection panel, choose the Single View App option before proceeding to the next screen. On the project options screen, name the project *ProjectDemo* and change the User Interface menu to SwiftUI. Click Next to proceed to the final screen, choose a suitable filesystem location for the project and click on the Create button.

18.2 UIKit and SwiftUI

As discussed previously, before the introduction of SwiftUI, iOS apps were developed using UIKit. In recognition of this reality, Apple has provided a number of ways in which SwiftUI and UIKit code can be integrated within the same project.

It may not be obvious initially, but when creating a new SwiftUI based project, Xcode actually creates a UIKit-based app which uses these integration techniques to host the SwiftUI views that ultimately make up the app. Some of the files described in this chapter are, therefore, UIKit-based and all class names prefixed with "UI" are UIKit classes.

18.3 The AppDelegate.swift File

Every iOS app has one instance of the UIApplication class which is responsible for handling events and managing the different UIWindow objects that will be used by the app to display user interfaces to the user. UIWindow instances are not visible to the user but instead provide containers to hold the visible objects that make up the user interface.

The UIApplication instance has associated with it a delegate which it notifies via method calls of significant events relating to the lifecycle of the app such as the app launching, incoming notifications, low device memory, the pending termination of the app and the creation of new scenes within the app.

By default, the *AppDelegate.swift* file generated by Xcode contains only the methods that are mandatory to comply with the AppDelegate protocol but others can be added for the app to receive notification of other app lifecycle events. These methods can be useful for implementing early app specific initialization tasks such as establishing a network connection or setting up database access. The didFinishLaunchingWithOptions method is particularly useful for adding initialization code since it is the first method to be called after the app has finished launching.

18.4 **The SceneDelegate.swift File**

The entire user interface of an app is represented as a scene in the form of a UIWindowScene object with a UIWindow child. It is important not to confuse this with a UIKit *Storyboard scene* which represents only a single screen within an app user interface. By default, an app will have only one scene, but with the introduction of multi-window support with iOS 13 it is also possible to configure an app to allow the creation of multiple instances of its user interface. On iPhone devices, the user switches between user interface copies using the app switcher while on the iPad, copies of the user interface can also appear side by side.

While multiple scenes all share the same UIApplication object, each of the UIWindowScene instances in a multi-window configuration has its own scene delegate instance.

The SceneDelegate class file implements the UIWindowSceneDelegate protocol and contains methods to handle events such as a new scene object connecting to the current session, the scene transitioning between background and foreground or a scene disconnecting from the app.

All of the SceneDelegate methods are useful for performing initialization and deinitialization tasks during the lifecycle of the app. The most important delegate method in this file, however, is the willConnectTo method which is called each time a new scene object is added to the app.

By default, the willConnectTo delegate method will have been implemented by Xcode to create an instance of the SwiftUI ContentView view declared in the *ContentView.swift* file and make it visible to the user. It is within this method that the gap between the UIKit architecture and SwiftUI is bridged.

In order to embed a SwiftUI view into a UIKit project, the SwiftUI view is embedded into a UIHostingController instance (a topic covered in detail starting with the chapter entitled *Integrating UIViews with SwiftUI*). To achieve this, the willConnectTo delegate method performs the following tasks:

1. Creates an instance of ContentView.
2. Creates a new UIWindow instance.
3. Embeds the ContentView instance into a UIHostingController instance.
4. Assigns the UIHostingController as the root view controller for the newly created UIWindow instance.

5. Replaces the scene's current UIWindow instance with the new one.
6. Makes the window visible to the user.

Figure 18-1 illustrates the hierarchy of a single window app:

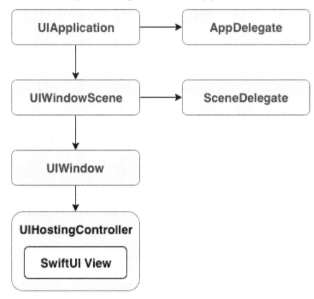

A multi-window app hierarchy, on the other hand, can be represented as shown in Figure 18-2 below. Note that while there is only one AppDelegate, each scene has its own SceneDelegate instance:

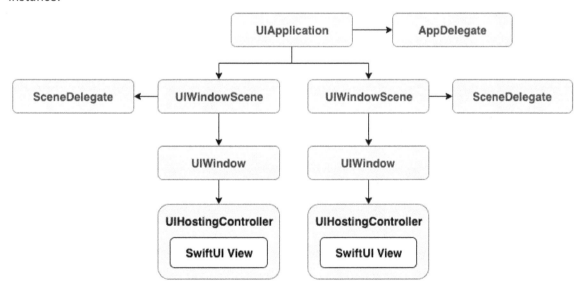

18.5 **ContentView.swift File**

This is a SwiftUI View file that contains the content of the first screen to appear when the app starts. This file and others like it are where most of the work is performed when developing apps in SwiftUI. By default, it contains a single Text view displaying the words "Hello World".

18.6 **Assets.xcassets**

The Assets.xcassets folder contains the asset catalog that is used to store resources used by the app such as images, icons and colors.

18.7 **Info.plist**

The information property list file is an XML file containing key-value pairs used to configure the app. The setting to enable multi-window support, for example, is contained within this file.

18.8 **LaunchScreen.storyboard**

Contains the storyboard file containing the user interface layout for the screen displayed to the user while the app is launching. Since this is a UIKit Storyboard scene, it is designed using the Interface Builder tool rather than SwiftUI.

18.9 **Summary**

When a new SwiftUI project is created in Xcode using the Single View App template, Xcode automatically generates a number of files required for the app to function. All of these files and folders can be modified to add functionality to the app, both in terms of adding resource assets, performing initialization and deinitialization tasks and building the user interface and logic of the app. This chapter has provided a high-level overview of each of these files together with an outline of the internal architecture of a SwiftUI-based iOS app.

19. Creating Custom Views with SwiftUI

A key step in learning to develop apps using SwiftUI is learning how to declare user interface layouts both by making use of the built-in SwiftUI views as well as building your own custom views. This chapter will introduce the basic concepts of SwiftUI views and outline the syntax used to declare user interface layouts and modify view appearance and behavior.

19.1 SwiftUI Views

User interface layouts are composed in SwiftUI by using, creating and combining views. An important first step is to understand what is meant by the term "view". Views in SwiftUI are declared as structures that conform to the View protocol. In order to conform with the View protocol, a structure is required to contain a body property and it is within this body property that the view is declared.

SwiftUI includes a wide range of built-in views that can be used when constructing a user interface including text label, button, text field, menu, toggle and layout manager views. Each of these is a self-contained instance that complies with the View protocol. When building an app with SwiftUI you will use these views to create custom views of your own which, when combined, constitute the appearance and behavior of your user interface.

These custom views will range from subviews that encapsulate a re-useable subset of view components (perhaps a secure text field and a button for logging in to screens within your app) to views that encapsulate the user interface for an entire screen. Regardless of the size and complexity of a custom view or the number of child views encapsulated within, a view is still just an instance that defines some user interface appearance and behavior.

19.2 Creating a Basic View

In Xcode, custom views are contained within SwiftUI View files. When a new SwiftUI project is created, Xcode will create a single SwiftUI View file containing a single custom view consisting of the single Text view component. Additional view files can be added to the project by selecting the *File -> New -> File...* menu option and choosing the SwiftUI View file entry from the template screen.

The default SwiftUI View file is named *ContentView.swift* and reads as follows:

```
import SwiftUI

struct ContentView: View {
    var body: some View {
        Text("Hello World")
    }
```

```
}

struct ContentView_Previews: PreviewProvider {
    static var previews: some View {
        ContentView()
    }
}
```

The view is named ContentView and is declared as conforming to the View protocol. It also includes the mandatory body property which, in turn contains an instance of the built-in Text view component which is initialized with a string which reads "Hello World".

The second structure in the file is needed to create an instance of ContentView so that it appears in the preview canvas, a topic which will be covered in detail in later chapters.

19.3 Adding Additional Views

Additional views can be added to a parent view by placing them in the body. The body property, however, is configured to return a single view. Adding an additional view, as is the case in the following example, will generate a syntax error:

```
struct ContentView: View {
    var body: some View {
        Text("Hello World")
        Text("Goodbye World") // Invalid structure
    }
}
```

To add additional views, those views must be placed in a container view such as a stack or form. The above example could, therefore, be modified to place the two Text views in a vertical stack (VStack) view which, as the name suggests, positions views vertically within the containing view:

```
struct ContentView: View {
    var body: some View {
        VStack {
            Text("Hello World")
            Text("Goodbye World")
        }
    }
}
```

SwiftUI views are hierarchical by nature, starting with parent and child views. This allows views to be nested to multiple levels to create user interfaces of any level of complexity. Consider, for example, the following view hierarchy diagram:

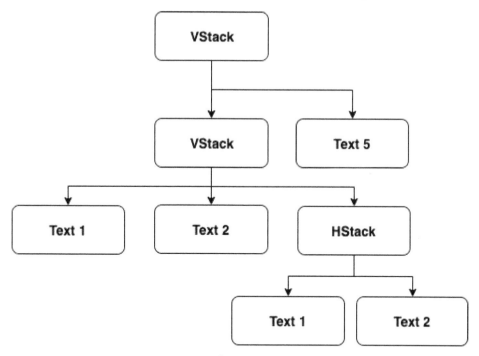

Figure 19-1

The equivalent view declaration for the above view would read as follows:

```
struct ContentView: View {
    var body: some View {
        VStack {
            VStack {
                Text("Text 1")
                Text("Text 2")
                HStack {
                    Text("Text 3")
                    Text("Text 4")
                }
            }
            Text("Text 5")
        }
    }
}
```

A notable exception to the requirement that multiple views be embedded in a container is that multiple Text views count as a single view when concatenated. The following, therefore, is a valid view declaration:

```
struct ContentView: View {
    var body: some View {
```

```
        Text("Hello, ") + Text("how ") + Text("are you?")
    }
}
```

Note that in the above examples the closure for the body property does not have a return statement. This is because the closure essentially contains a single expression (implicit returns from single expressions were covered in the chapter entitled *An Overview of Swift 5 Functions, Methods and Closures*). As soon as extra expressions are added to the closure, however, it will be necessary to add a return statement, for example:

```
struct ContentView: View {
    var body: some View {

        var myString: String = "Welcome to SwiftUI"

        return VStack {
            Text("Hello World")
            Text("Goodbye World")
        }
    }
}
```

19.4 **Working with Subviews**

Apple recommends that views be kept as small and lightweight as possible. This promotes the creation of reusable components, makes view declarations easier to maintain and results in more efficient layout rendering.

If you find that a custom view declaration has become large and complex, identify areas of the view that can be extracted into a subview. As a very simplistic example, the HStack view in the above example could be extracted as a subview named "MyHStackView" as follows:

```
struct ContentView: View {
    var body: some View {
        VStack {
            VStack {
                Text("Text 1")
                Text("Text 2")
                MyHStackView()
            }
            Text("Text 5")
        }
    }
}
```

```
struct MyHStackView: View {
    var body: some View {
        HStack {
            Text("Text 3")
            Text("Text 4")
        }
    }
}
```

19.5 Views as Properties

In addition to creating subviews, views may also be assigned to properties as a way to organize complex view hierarchies. Consider the following example view declaration:

```
struct ContentView: View {

    var body: some View {

        VStack {
            Text("Main Title")
                .font(.largeTitle)
            HStack {
                Text("Car Image")
                Image(systemName: "car.fill")
            }
        }
    }
}
```

Any part of the above declaration can be moved to a property value, and then referenced by name. In the following declaration, the HStack has been assigned to a property named carStack which is then referenced within the VStack layout:

```
struct ContentView: View {

    let carStack = HStack {
        Text("Car Image")
        Image(systemName: "car.fill")
    }

    var body: some View {
        VStack {
            Text("Main Title")
                .font(.largeTitle)
            carStack
        }
```

```
        }
}
```

19.6 Modifying Views

It is unlikely that any of the views provided with SwiftUI will appear and behave exactly as required without some form of customization. These changes are made by applying *modifiers* to the views.

All SwiftUI views have sets of modifiers which can be applied to make appearance and behavior changes. These modifiers take the form of methods that are called on the instance of the view and essentially wrap the original view inside another view which applies the necessary changes. This means that modifiers can be chained together to apply multiple modifications to the same view. The following, for example, changes the font and foreground color of a Text view:

```
Text("Text 1")
      .font(.headline)
      .foregroundColor(.red)
```

Similarly, the following example uses modifiers to configure an Image view to be resizable with the aspect ratio set to fit proportionally within the available space:

```
Image(systemName: "car.fill")
      .resizable()
      .aspectRatio(contentMode: .fit)
```

Modifiers may also be applied to custom subviews. In the following example, the font for both Text views in the previously declared MyHStackView custom view will be changed to use the large title font style:

```
MyHStackView()
      .font(.largeTitle)
```

19.7 Working with Text Styles

In the above example the font used to display text on a view was declared using a built-in text style (in this case the large title style).

iOS provides a way for the user to select a preferred text size which applications are expected to adopt when displaying text. The current text size can be configured on a device via the *Settings -> Display & Brightness -> Text Size* screen which provides a slider to adjust the font size as shown in Figure 19-2:

Figure 19-2

If a font has been declared on a view using a text style, the text size will dynamically adapt to the user's preferred font size. Almost without exception, the built-in iOS apps adopt the preferred size setting selected by the user when displaying text and Apple recommends that third-party apps also conform to the user's chosen text size. The following text style options are currently available:

- headline
- subheadline
- body
- callout
- footnote
- caption

If none of the text styles meet your requirements, it is also possible to apply custom fonts by declaring the font family and size, though this font setting will be fixed in size regardless of the user's preferred text size selection:

```
Text("Sample Text")
    .font(.custom("Copperplate", size: 70))
```

The above custom font selection will render the Text view as follows:

SAMPLE TEXT

Figure 19-3

19.8 Modifier Ordering

When chaining modifiers, it is important to be aware that the order in which they are applied can be significant. Both border and padding modifiers have been applied to the following Text view.

```
Text("Sample Text")
    .border(Color.black)
    .padding()
```

The border modifier draws a black border around the view and the padding modifier adds space around the view. When the above view is rendered it will appear as shown in Figure 19-4:

Figure 19-4

Given that padding has been applied to the text, it might be reasonable to expect there to be a gap between the text and the border. In fact, the border was only applied to the original Text view. Padding was then applied to the modified view returned by the border modifier. The padding is still applied to the view, but outside of the border. For the border to encompass the padding, the order of the modifiers needs to be changed so that the border is drawn on the view returned by the padding modifier:

```
Text("Sample Text")
    .padding()
    .border(Color.black)
```

With the modifier order switched, the view will now be rendered as follows:

Figure 19-5

If you don't see the expected effects when working with chained modifiers, keep in mind this may be because of the order in which they are being applied to the view.

19.9 Custom Modifiers

SwiftUI also allows you to create your own custom modifiers. This can be particularly useful if you have a standard set of modifiers that are frequently applied to views. Suppose that the following modifiers are a common requirement within your view declarations:

```
Text("Text 1")
    .font(.largeTitle)
    .background(Color.white)
    .border(Color.gray, width: 0.2)
    .shadow(color: Color.black, radius: 5, x: 0, y: 5)
```

Instead of applying these four modifiers each time text with this appearance is required, a better solution is to group them into a custom modifier and then reference that modifier each time the modification is needed. Custom modifiers are declared as structs that conform to the ViewModifier protocol and, in this instance, might be implemented as follows:

```
struct StandardTitle: ViewModifier {
    func body(content: Content) -> some View {
        content
            .font(.largeTitle)
            .background(Color.white)
            .border(Color.gray, width: 0.2)
            .shadow(color: Color.black, radius: 5, x: 0, y: 5)
    }
}
```

The custom modifier is then applied when needed by passing it through to the *modifier()* method:

```
Text("Text 1")
    .modifier(StandardTitle())
Text("Text 2")
    .modifier(StandardTitle())
```

With the custom modifier implemented, changes can be made to the StandardTitle implementation and those changes will automatically propagate through to all views that use the modifier. This avoids the need to manually change the modifiers on multiple views.

19.10 Basic Event Handling

Although SwiftUI is described as being data driven, it is still necessary to the handle events that are generated when a user interacts with the views in the user interface. Some views, such as the Button view, are provided solely for the purpose of soliciting user interaction. In fact, the Button view can be used to turn a variety of different views into a "clickable" button. A Button view needs to be declared with the action method to be called when a click is detected together with the view to act as the button content. It is possible, for example, to designate an entire stack of views as a single button. In most cases, however, a Text view will typically be used as the Button content. In the following implementation, a Button view is used to wrap a Text view which, when clicked will call a method named *buttonPressed()*:

```
struct ContentView: View {
    var body: some View {
        Button(action: buttonPressed) {
            Text("Click Me")
        }
    }


    func buttonPressed() {
        // Code to perform action here
    }
}
```

Instead of specifying an action function, the code to be executed when the button is clicked may also be specified as a closure in-line with the declaration:

```
Button(action: {
    // Code to perform action here
}) {
    Text("Click Me")
}
```

Another common requirement is to turn an Image view into a button, for example:

```
Button(action: {
    print("hello")
}) {
    Image(systemName: "square.and.arrow.down")
}
```

19.11 The onAppear and onDisappear Methods

Action methods may be declared on specific views to perform initialization and deinitialization tasks when the view appears and disappears within a layout. This is achieved by using the onAppear and onDisappear instance methods, for example:

```
Text("Hello World")
    .onAppear(perform: {
        // Code here to perform when the view appears
    })
    .onDisappear(perform: {
        // Code here to perform when view disappears
    })
```

19.12 **Building Custom Container Views**

As outlined earlier in this chapter, subviews provide a useful way to divide a view declaration into small, lightweight and reusable blocks. One limitation of subviews, however, is that the content of the container view is static. In other words, it is not possible to dynamically specify the views that are to be included at the point that a subview is included in a layout. The only children included in the subview are those that are specified in the original declaration.

Consider the following subview which consists of three TextViews contained within a VStack and modified with custom spacing and font settings.

```
struct MyVStack: View {
    var body: some View {
        VStack(spacing: 10) {
            Text("Text Item 1")
            Text("Text Item 2")
            Text("Text Item 3")
        }
        .font(.largeTitle)
    }
}
```

To include an instance of MyVStack in a declaration, it would be referenced as follows:

```
MyVStack()
```

Suppose, however, that a VStack with a spacing of 10 and a large font modifier is something that is needed frequently within a project, but in each case, different child views are required to be contained within the stack. While this flexibility isn't possible using subviews, it can be achieved using the SwiftUI ViewBuilder closure attribute when constructing custom container views.

A ViewBuilder takes the form of a Swift closure which can be used to create a custom view comprised of multiple child views, the content of which does not need to be declared until the view is used within a layout declaration. The ViewBuilder closure takes the content views and returns them as a single view which is, in effect, a dynamically built subview.

The following is an example of using the ViewBuilder attribute to implement our custom MyVStack view:

```
struct MyVStack<Content: View>: View {
  let content: () -> Content
  init(@ViewBuilder content: @escaping () -> Content) {
    self.content = content
  }

  var body: some View {
    VStack(spacing: 10) {
      content()
```

```
    }
    .font(.largeTitle)
    }
}
```

Note that this declaration still returns an instance that complies with the View protocol and that the body contains the VStack declaration from the previous subview. Instead of including static views to be included in the stack, however, the child views of the stack will be passed to the initializer, handled by ViewBuilder and embedded into the VStack as child views. The custom MyVStack view can now be initialized with different child views wherever it is used in a layout, for example:

```
MyVStack {
    Text("Text 1")
    Text("Text 2")
    HStack {
        Image(systemName: "star.fill")
        Image(systemName: "star.fill")
        Image(systemName: "star")
    }
}
```

19.13 Summary

SwiftUI user interfaces are declared in SwiftUI View files and are composed of components that conform to the View protocol. To conform with the View protocol a structure must contain a property named body which is itself a View.

SwiftUI provides a library of built-in components that can be used to design user interface layouts. The appearance and behavior of a view can be configured by applying modifiers and views can be modified and grouped together to create custom views and subviews. Similarly, custom container views can be created using the ViewBuilder closure property.

When a modifier is applied to a view, a new modified view is returned and subsequent modifiers are then applied to this modified view. This can have significant implications for the order in which modifiers are applied to a view.

![Chapter 20]

20. SwiftUI Stacks and Frames

User interface design is largely a matter of selecting the appropriate interface components, deciding how those views will be positioned on the screen, and then implementing navigation between the different screens and views of the app.

As is to be expected, SwiftUI includes a wide range of user interface components to be used when developing an app such as button, label, slider and toggle views. SwiftUI also provides a set of layout views for the purpose of defining both how the user interface is organized and the way in which the layout responds to changes in screen orientation and size.

This chapter will introduce the Stack container views included with SwiftUI and explain how they can be used to create user interface designs with relative ease.

Once stack views have been explained, this chapter will cover the concept of flexible frames and explain how they can be used to control the sizing behavior of views in a layout.

20.1 SwiftUI Stacks

SwiftUI includes three stack layout views in the form of VStack (vertical), HStack (horizontal) and ZStack (views are layered on top of each other).

A stack is declared by embedding child views into a stack view within the SwiftUI View file. In the following view, for example, three Image views have been embedded within an HStack:

```
struct ContentView: View {
    var body: some View {
        HStack {
            Image(systemName: "goforward.10")
            Image(systemName: "goforward.15")
            Image(systemName: "goforward.30")
        }
    }
}
```

Within the preview canvas, the above layout will appear as illustrated in Figure 20-1:

Figure 20-1

A similarly configured example using a VStack would accomplish the same results with the images stacked vertically:

```
VStack {
    Image(systemName: "goforward.10")
    Image(systemName: "goforward.15")
    Image(systemName: "goforward.30")
}
```

To embed an existing component into a stack, either wrap it manually within a stack declaration, or hover the mouse pointer over the component in the editor so that it highlights, hold down the Command key on the keyboard and left-click on the component. From the resulting menu (Figure 20-2) select the appropriate option:

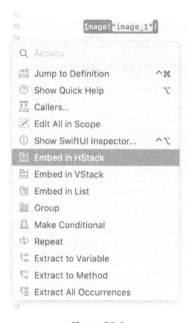

Figure 20-2

Layouts of considerable complexity can be designed simply by embedding stacks within other stacks, for example:

```
VStack {
    Text("Financial Results")
        .font(.title)

    HStack {
        Text("Q1 Sales")
            .font(.headline)

        VStack {
            Text("January")
```

```
            Text("February")
            Text("March")
        }

    VStack {
        Text("$1000")
        Text("$200")
        Text("$3000")
    }
}
}
```

The above layout will appear as shown in Figure 20-3:

Financial Results
January $1000
Q1 Sales February $200
March $3000

Figure 20-3

As currently configured the layout clearly needs some additional work, particularly in terms of alignment and spacing. The layout can be improved in this regard using a combination of alignment settings, the Spacer component and the padding modifier.

20.2 Spacers, Alignment and Padding

To add space between views, SwiftUI includes the Spacer component. When used in a stack layout, the spacer will flexibly expand and contract along the axis of the containing stack (in other words either horizontally or vertically) to provide a gap between views positioned on either side, for example:

```
HStack(alignment: .top) {

    Text("Q1 Sales")
        .font(.headline)
    Spacer()
    VStack(alignment: .leading) {
        Text("January")
        Text("February")
        Text("March")
    }
    Spacer()
```

.

.

In terms of aligning the content of a stack, this can be achieved by specifying an alignment value when the stack is declared, for example:

```
VStack(alignment: .center) {
        Text("Financial Results")
            .font(.title)
```

Alignments may also be specified with a corresponding spacing value:

```
VStack(alignment: .center, spacing: 15) {
        Text("Financial Results")
            .font(.title)
```

Spacing around the sides of any view may also be implemented using the *padding()* modifier. When called without a parameter SwiftUI will automatically use the best padding for the layout, content and screen size (referred to as *adaptable padding*). The following example sets adaptable padding on all four sides of a Text view:

```
Text("Hello World!")
    .padding()
```

Alternatively, a specific amount of padding may be passed as a parameter to the modifier as follows:

```
Text("Hello World!")
    .padding(15)
```

Padding may also be applied to a specific side of a view with or without a specific value. In the following example a specific padding size is applied to the top edge of a Text view:

```
Text("Hello World!")
    .padding(.top, 10)
```

Making use of these options, the example layout created earlier in the chapter can be modified as follows:

```
VStack(alignment: .center, spacing: 15) {
        Text("Financial Results")
            .font(.title)

        HStack(alignment: .top) {
            Text("Q1 Sales")
                .font(.headline)
            Spacer()
            VStack(alignment: .leading) {
                Text("January")
                Text("February")
```

```
            Text("March")
        }
        Spacer()
        VStack(alignment: .leading) {
            Text("$10000")
            Text("$200")
            Text("$3000")
        }
        .padding(5)
    }
    .padding(5)
}
.padding(5)
}
```

With the alignments, spacers and padding modifiers added, the layout should now resemble the following figure:

Financial Results

Q1 Sales	January	$10000
	February	$200
	March	$3000

Figure 20-4

More advanced stack alignment topics will be covered in a later chapter entitled *SwiftUI Stack Alignment and Alignment Guides*.

20.3 Container Child Limit

Container views are limited to 10 direct descendent views. If a stack contains more than 10 direct children, Xcode will likely display the following syntax error:

```
Argument passed to call that takes no arguments
```

If a stack exceeds the 10 direct children limit, the views will need to be embedded into multiple containers. This can, of course, be achieved by adding stacks as subviews, but another useful container is the Group view. In the following example, a VStack can contain 12 Text views by splitting the views between Group containers giving the VStack only two direct descendants:

```
VStack {

    Group {
```

```
            Text("Sample Text")
            Text("Sample Text")
            Text("Sample Text")
            Text("Sample Text")
            Text("Sample Text")
            Text("Sample Text")
        }

        Group {
            Text("Sample Text")
            Text("Sample Text")
            Text("Sample Text")
            Text("Sample Text")
            Text("Sample Text")
            Text("Sample Text")
        }
    }
}
```

In addition to providing a way to avoid the 10-view limit, groups are also useful when performing an operation on multiple views (for example, a set of related views can all be hidden in a single operation by embedding them in a Group and hiding that view).

20.4 Text Line Limits and Layout Priority

By default, an HStack will attempt to display the text within its Text view children on a single line. Take, for example, the following HStack declaration containing an Image view and two Text views:

```
HStack {
    Image(systemName: "airplane")
    Text("Flight times:")
    Text("London")
}
.font(.largeTitle)
```

If the stack has enough room, the above layout will appear as follows:

Figure 20-5

If a stack has insufficient room (for example if it is constrained by a frame or is competing for space with sibling views) the text will automatically wrap onto multiple lines when necessary:

Figure 20-6

While this may work for some situations, it may become an issue if the user interface is required to display this text in a single line. The number of lines over which text can flow can be restricted using the *lineCount()* modifier. The example HStack could, therefore, be limited to 1 line of text with the following change:

```
HStack {
    Image(systemName: "airplane")
    Text("Flight times:")
    Text("London")
}
.font(.largeTitle)
.lineLimit(1)
```

When an HStack has insufficient space to display the full text and is not permitted to wrap the text over enough lines, the view will resort to truncating the text, as is the case in Figure 20-7:

Figure 20-7

In the absence of any priority guidance, the stack view will decide how to truncate the Text views based on the available space and the length of the views. Obviously, the stack has no way of knowing whether the text in one view is more important than the text in another unless the text view declarations include some priority information. This is achieved by making use of the *layoutPriority()* modifier. This modifier can be added to the views in the stack and passed values indicating the level of priority for the corresponding view. The higher the number, the greater the layout priority and the less the view will be subjected to truncation.

Assuming the flight destination city name is more important than the "Flight times:" text, the example stack could be modified as follows:

```
HStack {
    Image(systemName: "airplane")
```

```
    Text("Flight times:")
    Text("London").layoutPriority(1)
}
.font(.largeTitle)
.lineLimit(1)
```

With a higher priority assigned to the city Text view (in the absence of a layout priority the other text view defaults to a priority of 0) the layout will now appear as illustrated in Figure 20-8:

Figure 20-8

20.5 SwiftUI Frames

By default, a view will be sized automatically based on its content and the requirements of any layout in which it may be embedded. Although much can be achieved using the stack layouts to control the size and positioning of a view, sometimes a view is required to be a specific size or to fit within a range of size dimensions. To address this need, SwiftUI includes the flexible frame modifier.

Consider the following Text view which has been modified to display a border:

```
Text("Hello World")
    .font(.largeTitle)
    .border(Color.black)
```

Within the preview canvas, the above text view will appear as follows:

Figure 20-9

In the absence of a frame, the text view has been sized to accommodate its content. If the Text view was required to have height and width dimensions of 100, however, a frame could be applied as follows:

```
Text("Hello World")
    .font(.largeTitle)
    .border(Color.black)
    .frame(width: 100, height: 100, alignment: .center)
```

Now that the Text view is constrained within a frame, the view will appear as follows:

Figure 20-10

In many cases, fixed dimensions will provide the required behavior. In other cases, such as when the content of a view changes dynamically, this can cause problems. Increasing the length of the text, for example, might cause the content to be truncated:

Figure 20-11

This can be resolved by creating a frame with minimum and maximum dimensions:

```
Text("Hello World, how are you?")
        .font(.largeTitle)
        .border(Color.black)
        .frame(minWidth: 100, maxWidth: 300, minHeight: 100,
            maxHeight: 100, alignment: .center)
```

Now that the frame has some flexibility, the view will be sized to accommodate the content within the defined minimum and maximum limits. When the text is short enough, the view will appear as shown in Figure 20-10 above. Longer text, however, will be displayed as follows:

Hello World, how are you?

Figure 20-12

Frames may also be configured to take up all the available space by setting the minimum and maximum values to 0 and infinity respectively:

```
.frame(minWidth: 0, maxWidth: .infinity, minHeight: 0,
        maxHeight: .infinity)
```

Remember that the order in which modifiers are chained often impacts the appearance of a view. In this case, if the border is to be drawn at the edges of the available space it will need to be applied to the frame:

```
Text("Hello World, how are you?")
    .font(.largeTitle)
    .frame(minWidth: 0, maxWidth: .infinity, minHeight: 0,
            maxHeight: .infinity)
    .border(Color.black, width: 5)
```

By default, the frame will honor the safe areas on the screen when filling the display. Areas considered to be outside the safe area include those occupied by the camera notch on some device models and the bar across the top of the screen displaying the time and Wi-Fi and cellular signal strength icons. To configure the frame to extend beyond the safe area, simply use the *edgesIgnoringSafeArea()* modifier, specifying the safe area edges to ignore:

```
.edgesIgnoringSafeArea(.all)
```

20.6 Frames and the Geometry Reader

Frames can also be implemented so that they are sized relative to the size of the container within which the corresponding view is embedded. This is achieved by wrapping the view in a GeometryReader and using the reader to identify the container dimensions. These dimensions can then be used to calculate the frame size. The following example uses a frame to set the dimensions of two Text views relative to the size of the containing VStack:

```
GeometryReader { geometry in
    VStack {
        Text("Hello World, how are you?")
            .font(.largeTitle)
```

```
        .frame(width: geometry.size.width / 2,
            height: (geometry.size.height / 4) * 3)
    Text("Goodbye World")
        .font(.largeTitle)
        .frame(width: geometry.size.width / 3,
            height: geometry.size.height / 4)
    }
}
```

The topmost Text view is configured to occupy half the width and three quarters of the height of the VStack while the lower Text view occupies one third of the width and one quarter of the height.

20.7 **Summary**

User interface design mostly involves gathering together components and laying them out on the screen in a way that provides a pleasant and intuitive user experience. User interface layouts must also be responsive so that they appear correctly on any device regardless of screen size and, ideally, device orientation. To ease the process of user interface layout design, SwiftUI provides several layout views and components. In this chapter we have looked at layout stack views and the flexible frame.

By default, a view will be sized according to its content and the restrictions imposed on it by any view in which it may be contained. When insufficient space is available, a view may be restricted in size resulting in truncated content. Priority settings can be used to control the amount by which views are reduced in size relative to container sibling views.

For greater control of the space allocated to a view, a flexible frame can be applied to the view. The frame can be fixed in size, constrained within a range of minimum and maximum values or, using a Geometry Reader, sized relative to the containing view.

21. Working with SwiftUI State, Observable and Environment Objects

Earlier chapters have described how SwiftUI emphasizes a data driven approach to app development whereby the views in the user interface are updated in response to changes in the underlying data without the need to write handling code. This approach is achieved by establishing a publisher and subscriber binding between the data and the views in the user interface.

SwiftUI offers three options for implementing this behavior in the form of *state properties*, *observable objects* and *environment objects*, all of which provide the *state* that drives the way the user interface appears and behaves. In SwiftUI, the views that make up a user interface layout are never updated directly within code. Instead, the views are updated automatically based on the state objects to which they have been bound as they change over time.

This chapter will describe these three options and outline when they should be used. Later chapters (*A SwiftUI Example Tutorial* and *SwiftUI Observable and Environment Objects – A Tutorial*) will provide practical examples that demonstrates their use.

21.1 State Properties

The most basic form of state is the state property. State properties are used exclusively to store state that is local to a view layout such as whether a toggle button is enabled, the text being entered into a text field or the current selection in a Picker view. State properties are used for storing simple data types such as a String or Int value and are declared using the *@State* property wrapper, for example:

```
struct ContentView: View {

    @State private var wifiEnabled = true
    @State private var userName = ""


  var body: some View {
.

.
```

Note that since state values are local to the enclosing view they should be declared as private properties.

Every change to a state property value is a signal to SwiftUI that the view hierarchy within which the property is declared needs to be re-rendered. This involves rapidly recreating and displaying all of the views in the hierarchy. This, in turn, has the effect of ensuring that any views that rely on the property in some way are updated to reflect the latest value.

Once declared, bindings can be established between state properties and the views contained in the layout. Changes within views that reference the binding are then automatically reflected in the corresponding state property. A binding could, for example, be established between a Toggle view and the Boolean wifiEnabled property declared above. Whenever the user switches the toggle, SwiftUI will automatically update the state property to match the new toggle setting.

A binding to a state property is implemented by prefixing the property name with a '$' sign. In the following example, a TextField view establishes a binding to the userName state property to use as the storage for text entered by the user:

```
struct ContentView: View {

    @State private var wifiEnabled = true
    @State private var userName = ""

    var body: some View {
        VStack {
            TextField("Enter user name", text: $userName)
        }
    }
}
```

With each keystroke performed as the user types into the TextField the binding will store the current text into the userName property. Each change to the state property will, in turn, cause the view hierarchy to be re-rendered by SwiftUI.

Of course, storing something in a state property is only one side of the process. As previously discussed, a change of state usually results in a change to other views in the layout. In this case, a Text view might need to be updated to reflect the user's name as it is being typed. This can be achieved by declaring the userName state property value as the content for a Text view:

```
var body: some View {
    VStack {
        TextField("Enter user name", text: $userName)
        Text(userName)
    }
}
```

As the user types, the Text view will automatically update to reflect the user's input. Note that in this case the userName property is declared without the '$' prefix. This is because we are now referencing the value assigned to the state property (i.e. the String value being typed by the user) instead of a binding to the property.

Similarly, the hypothetical binding between a Toggle view and the wifiEnabled state property described above could be implemented as follows:

```
var body: some View {

    VStack {
        Toggle(isOn: $wifiEnabled) {
            Text("Enable Wi-Fi")
        }
        TextField("Enter user name", text: $userName)
        Text(userName)
        Image(systemName: wifiEnabled ? "wifi" : "wifi.slash")
    }
}
```

In the above declaration, a binding is established between the Toggle view and the state property. The value assigned to the property is then used to decide which image is to be displayed on an Image view.

Note that the Image view in the previous example uses systemName image references. This provides access to the built-in library of SF Symbol drawings. SF Symbols is a collection of 1500 scalable vector drawings available for use when developing apps for Apple platforms and designed to complement Apple's San Francisco system font.

The full set of symbols can be searched and browsed by installing the SF Symbols macOS app available from the following URL:

https://developer.apple.com/design/downloads/SF-Symbols.dmg

21.2 State Binding

A state property is local to the view in which it is declared and any child views. Situations may occur, however, where a view contains one or more subviews which may also need access to the same state properties. Consider, for example, a situation whereby the Wi-Fi Image view in the above example has been extracted into a subview:

```
    .
    .
    VStack {
        Toggle(isOn: $wifiEnabled) {
            Text("Enable WiFi")
        }
        TextField("Enter user name", text: $userName)
        WifiImageView()
    }
}
    .
```

```
.
struct WifiImageView: View {

    var body: some View {
        Image(systemName: wifiEnabled ? "wifi" : "wifi.slash")
    }
}
```

Clearly the WifiImageView subview still needs access to the wifiEnabled state property. As an element of a separate subview, however, the Image view is now out of the scope of the main view. Within the scope of WifiImageView, the wifiEnabled property is an undefined variable.

This problem can be resolved by declaring the property using the *@Binding* property wrapper as follows:

```
struct WifiImageView: View {

    @Binding var wifiEnabled : Bool

    var body: some View {
        Image(systemName: wifiEnabled ? "wifi" : "wifi.slash")
    }
}
```

Now, when the subview is called, it simply needs to be passed a binding to the state property:

```
WifiImageView(wifiEnabled: $wifiEnabled)
```

21.3 Observable Objects

State properties provide a way to locally store the state of a view, are available only to the local view and, as such, cannot be accessed by other views unless they are subviews and state binding is implemented. State properties are also transient in that when the parent view goes away the state is also lost. Observable objects, on the other hand are used to represent persistent data that is both external and accessible to multiple views.

An Observable object takes the form of a class or structure that conforms to the ObservableObject protocol. Though the implementation of an observable object will be application specific depending on the nature and source of the data, it will typically be responsible for gathering and managing one or more data values that are known to change over time. Observable objects can also be used to handle events such as timers and notifications.

The observable object *publishes* the data values for which it is responsible as *published properties*. Observer objects then *subscribe* to the publisher and receive updates whenever changes to the published properties occur. As with the state properties outlined above, by binding to these published properties SwiftUI views will automatically update to reflect changes in the data stored in the observable object.

Observable objects are part of the Combine framework, which was introduced with iOS 13 to make it easier to establish relationships between publishers and subscribers.

The Combine framework provides a platform for building custom publishers for performing a variety of tasks from the merging of multiple publishers into a single stream to transforming published data to match subscriber requirements. This allows for complex, enterprise level data processing chains to be implemented between the original publisher and resulting subscriber. That being said, one of the built-in publisher types will typically be all that is needed for most requirements. In fact, the easiest way to implement a published property within an observable object is to simply use the *@Published* property wrapper when declaring a property. This wrapper simply sends updates to all subscribers each time the wrapped property value changes.

The following structure declaration shows a simple observable object declaration with two published properties:

```
import Foundation
import Combine

class DemoData : ObservableObject {

    @Published var userCount = 0
    @Published var currentUser = ""

    init() {
        // Code here to initialize data
        updateData()
    }

    func updateData() {
        // Code here to keep data up to date
    }
}
```

A subscriber uses the @ObservedObject property wrapper to subscribe to the observable object. Once subscribed, that view and any of its child views access the published properties using the same techniques used with state properties earlier in the chapter. A sample SwiftUI view designed to subscribe to an instance of the above DemoData class might read as follows:

```
import SwiftUI

struct ContentView: View {

    @ObservedObject var demoData : DemoData = DemoData()

    var body: some View {
```

```
        Text("\(demoData.currentUser), you are user number
\(demoData.userCount)")
    }
}

struct ContentView_Previews: PreviewProvider {
    static var previews: some View {
        ContentView()
    }
}
```

As the published data changes, SwiftUI will automatically re-render the view layout to reflect the new state.

21.4 Environment Objects

Observed objects are best used when a particular state needs to be used by a few SwiftUI views within an app. When one view navigates to another view which needs access to the same observed object, the originating view will need to pass a reference to the observed object to the destination view during the navigation (navigation will be covered in the chapter entitled *SwiftUI Lists and Navigation*). Consider, for example, the following code:

```
.
.
@ObservedObject var demoData : DemoData = DemoData()
.
.
NavigationLink(destination: SecondView(demoData)) {
    Text("Next Screen")
}
```

In the above declaration, a navigation link is used to navigate to another view named SecondView, passing through a reference to the demoData observed object.

While this technique is acceptable for many situations, it can become complex when many views within an app need access to the same observed object. In this situation, it may make more sense to use an environment object.

An environment object is declared in the same way as an observable object (in that it must conform to the ObservableObject protocol and appropriate properties must be published). The key difference, however, is that the object is stored in the SwiftUI environment and can be accessed by all views without needing to be passed from view to view.

Objects needing to subscribe to an environment object simply reference the object using the @EnvironmentObject property wrapper instead of the @ObservedObject wrapper:

```
@EnvironmentObject var demoData: DemoData
```

Environment objects cannot be initialized within an observer so must be configured during the setup of the scene in which the accessing views reside. This involves making some changes to the willConnectTo method of the project's *SceneDelegate.swift* file. By default, this method will contain code that reads as follows:

```
let contentView = ContentView()

if let windowScene = scene as? UIWindowScene {
    let window = UIWindow(windowScene: windowScene)
    window.rootViewController =
            UIHostingController(rootView: contentView)
    self.window = window
    window.makeKeyAndVisible()
}
```

To store an instance of our DemoData object in the environment, the above code will need to be changed as follows:

```
let contentView = ContentView()

let demoData = DemoData()

if let windowScene = scene as? UIWindowScene {
    let window = UIWindow(windowScene: windowScene)
    window.rootViewController =
            UIHostingController(rootView:
                contentView.environmentObject(demoData))
    self.window = window
    window.makeKeyAndVisible()
}
```

To make use of an environment object in the SwiftUI preview canvas, the preview provider declaration also needs to be modified:

```
struct ContentView_Previews: PreviewProvider {
    static var previews: some View {

        ContentView().environmentObject(DemoData())

    }
}
```

Once these steps have been taken the object will behave in the same way as an observed object, except that it will be accessible to all layout views.

21.5 **Summary**

SwiftUI provides three ways to bind data to the user interface and logic of an app. State properties are used to store the state of the views in a user interface layout and are local to the current content view. These values are transient and are lost when the view goes away.

For data that is external to the user interface and is required only by a subset of the SwiftUI view structures in an app, the observable object protocol should be used. Using this approach, the class or structure which represents the data must conform to the ObservableObject protocol and any properties to which views will bind must be declared using the @Published property wrapper. To bind to an observable object property in a view declaration the property must use the @ObservedObject property wrapper.

For data that is external to the user interface but for which access is required for many views, the environment object provides the best solution. Although declared in the same way as observable objects, environment object bindings are declared in SwiftUI View files using the @EnvironmentObject property wrapper. The environment object must also be initialized when the view scene is added to the app via code within the scene delegate class.

22. A SwiftUI Example Tutorial

Now that many of the fundamentals of SwiftUI development have been covered, this chapter will begin to put this theory into practice through the design and implementation of an example SwiftUI based project.

The objective of this chapter is to demonstrate the use of Xcode to design a simple interactive user interface, making use of views, modifiers, state variables and some basic animation techniques. Throughout the course of this tutorial a variety of different techniques will be used to add and modify views. While this may appear to be inconsistent, the objective is to gain familiarity with the different options available.

22.1 Creating the Example Project

Start Xcode and select the option to create a new project. On the template selection screen, make sure iOS is selected and choose the Single View App option before proceeding to the next screen as shown in Figure 22-1 below:

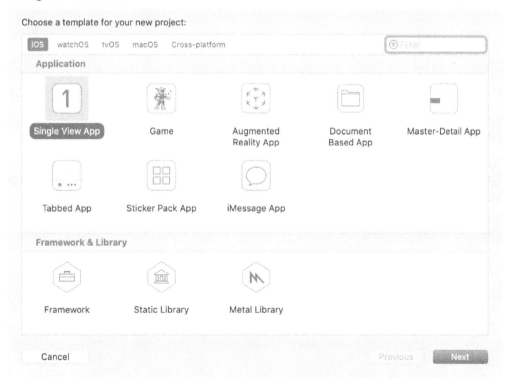

Figure 22-1

On the project options screen, name the project *SwiftUIDemo* and change the User Interface menu to SwiftUI as highlighted in Figure 22-2:

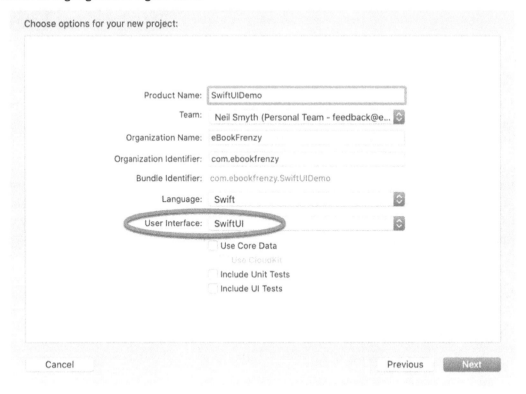

Click Next to proceed to the final screen, choose a suitable filesystem location for the project and click on the Create button.

22.2 Reviewing the Project

Once the project has been created it will contain the standard AppDelegate and SceneDelegate classes along with a SwiftUI View file named *ContentView.swift* which should have loaded into the editor and preview canvas ready for modification (if it has not loaded, simply select it in the project navigator panel). If the preview canvas is in the paused state, click on the Resume button to build the project and display the preview:

Figure 22-3

By default, Xcode has created a single content view and is configured to launch this view as the initial view when the project is run (otherwise known as the *root view controller*). As outlined on the chapter entitled *The Anatomy of a Basic SwiftUI Project*, the code that makes this the root view controller is located in the *willConnectTo* method located in the *SceneDelegate.swift* file and reads as follows:

```
func scene(_ scene: UIScene, willConnectTo session: UISceneSession,
          options connectionOptions: UIScene.ConnectionOptions) {

    let contentView = ContentView()

    if let windowScene = scene as? UIWindowScene {
        let window = UIWindow(windowScene: windowScene)
        window.rootViewController =
                    UIHostingController(rootView: contentView)
        self.window = window
        window.makeKeyAndVisible()
    }
}
```

If you find while developing a project with multiple view files that a different view file needs to serve as the content of the root view controller, simply modify this code accordingly to reference the other view.

22.3 Adding a VStack to the Layout

The view body currently consists of a single Text view of which we will make use in the completed project. A container view now needs to be added so that other views can be included in the layout. For the purposes of this example, the layout will be stacked vertically so a VStack needs to be added to the layout.

Within the code editor, select the Text view entry, hold down the Command key on the keyboard and perform a left-click. From the resulting menu, select the *Embed in VStack* option:

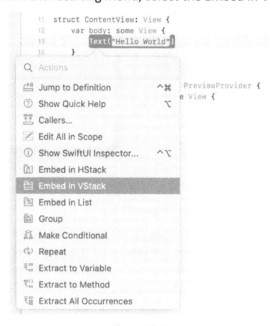

Figure 22-4

Once the Text view has been embedded into the VStack the declaration will read as follows:

```
struct ContentView: View {
    var body: some View {
        VStack {
            Text("Hello World")
        }
    }
}
```

22.4 Adding a Slider View to the Stack

The next item to be added to the layout is a Slider view. Within Xcode, display the Library panel by clicking on the '+' button highlighted in Figure 22-5, locate the Slider in the View list and drag it over the top of the existing Text view within the preview canvas. Make sure the notification panel (also highlighted in Figure 22-5) indicates that the view is going to be inserted into the existing stack (as opposed to being placed in a new vertical stack) before dropping the view into place.

Figure 22-5

Once the slider has been dropped into place, the view implementation should read as follows:

```
struct ContentView: View {
    var body: some View {
        VStack {
            VStack {
                Text("Hello World")
                Slider(value: Value)
            }


        }
    }
}
```

22.5 Adding a State Property

The slider is going to be used to control the amount by which the Text view is to be rotated. As such, a binding needs to be established between the Slider view and a state property into which the current rotation value will be stored. Within the code editor, declare this property and configure the Slider to use a range between 0 and 360 in increments of 0.1:

```
struct ContentView: View {
```

```
@State private var rotation: Double = 0

var body: some View {
    VStack {
        VStack {
            Text("Hello World")
            Slider(value: $rotation, in: 0 ... 360, step: 0.1)
        }


        }
    }
}
```

Note that since we are declaring a binding between the Slider view and the rotation state property it is prefixed by a '$' character.

22.6 Adding Modifiers to the Text View

The next step is to add some modifiers to the Text view to change the font and to adopt the rotation value stored by the Slider view. Begin by displaying the Library panel, switch to the modifier list and drag and drop a font modifier onto the Text view entry in the code editor:

Figure 22-6

Select the modifier line in the editor, refer to the Attributes inspector panel and change the font property from Title to Large Title as shown in Figure 22-7:

Figure 22-7

Note that the modifier added above does not change the font weight. Since modifiers may also be added to a view from within the Attributes inspector, take this opportunity to change the setting of the Weight menu from Inherited to Heavy.

On completion of these steps, the View body should read as follows:

```
var body: some View {
    VStack {
        VStack {
            Text("Hello World")
                .font(.largeTitle)
                .fontWeight(.heavy)
            Slider(value: $rotation, in: 0 ... 360, step: 0.1)
        }

    }
}
```

22.7 Adding Rotation and Animation

The next step is to add the rotation and animation effects to the Text view using the value stored by the Slider (animation is covered in greater detail in the *SwiftUI Animation and Transitions* chapter). This can be implemented using a modifier as follows:

```
.
.
Text("Hello World")
    .font(.largeTitle)
```

```
        .fontWeight(.heavy)
        .rotationEffect(.degrees(self.rotation))
.
.
```

Note that since we are simply reading the value assigned to the rotation state property, as opposed to establishing a binding, the property name is not prefixed with the '$' sign notation.

Click on the Live Preview button (indicated by the arrow in Figure 22-8), wait for the code to compile, then use the slider to rotate the Text view:

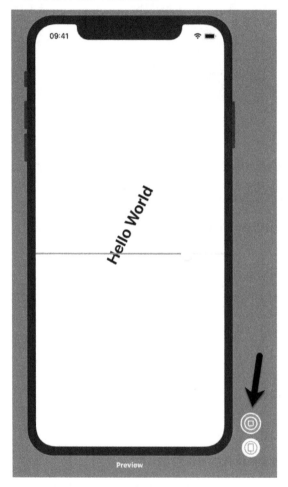

Figure 22-8

Next, add an animation modifier to the Text view to animate the rotation over 5 seconds using the Ease In Out effect:

```
Text("Hello World")
    .font(.largeTitle)
    .fontWeight(.heavy)
```

```
        .rotationEffect(.degrees(self.rotation))
        .animation(.easeInOut(duration: 5))
```

Use the slider once again to rotate the text and note that rotation is now smoothly animated.

22.8 Adding a TextField to the Stack

In addition to supporting text rotation, the app will also allow custom text to be entered and displayed on the Text view. This will require the addition of a TextField view to the project. To achieve this, either directly edit the View structure or use the Library panel to add a TextField so that the structure reads as follows (note also the addition of a state property in which to store the custom text string and the change to the Text view to use this property):

```
struct ContentView: View {

    @State private var rotation: Double = 0
    @State private var text: String = "Welcome to SwiftUI"

    var body: some View {
        VStack {
            VStack {

                Text(text)
                    .font(.largeTitle)
                    .fontWeight(.heavy)
                    .rotationEffect(.degrees(self.rotation))
                    .animation(.easeInOut(duration: 5))

                Slider(value: $rotation, in: 0 ... 360, step: 0.1)

                TextField("Enter text here", text: $text)
                    .textFieldStyle(RoundedBorderTextFieldStyle())
            }
        }
    }
}
```

When the user enters text into the TextField view, that text will be stored in the *text* state property and will automatically appear on the Text view via the binding.

Return to the preview canvas and make sure that the changes work as expected.

22.9 Adding a Color Picker

The final view to be added to the stack before we start to tidy up the layout is a Picker view. The purpose of this view will be to allow the foreground color of the Text view to be chosen by the user from a range of color options. Begin by adding some arrays of color names and Color objects, together with a state property to hold the current array index value as follows:

```
import SwiftUI

struct ContentView: View {

    var colors: [Color] = [.black, .red, .green, .blue]
    var colornames = ["Black", "Red", "Green", "Blue"]

    @State private var colorIndex = 0
    @State private var rotation: Double = 0
    @State private var text: String = "Welcome to SwiftUI"
```

With these variables configured, display the Library panel, locate the Picker in the Views screen and drag and drop it beneath the TextField view in either the code editor or preview canvas so that it is embedded in the existing VStack layout. Once added, the view entry will read as follows:

```
Picker(selection: .constant(1, label: Text("Picker") {
    Text("1").tag(1)
    Text("2").tag(2)
}
```

The Picker view needs to be configured to store the current selection in the *colorIndex* state property and to display an option for each color name in the *colorNames* array. To make the Picker more visually appealing, the background color for each Text view will be changed to the corresponding color in the *colors* array.

For the purposes of iterating through the colorNames array, the code will make use of the SwiftUI *ForEach* construct, the purpose of which is to generate multiple views from a set of data such as an array. Within the editor, modify the Picker view declaration so that it reads as follows:

```
Picker(selection: $colorIndex, label: Text("Color")) {
    ForEach (0 ..< colornames.count) {
        Text(self.colornames[$0])
            .foregroundColor(self.colors[$0])
    }
}
```

Remaining in the code editor, locate the Text view and add a foreground color modifier to set the foreground color based on the current Picker selection value:

```
Text(text)
    .font(.largeTitle)
    .fontWeight(.heavy)
    .rotationEffect(.degrees(self.rotation))
    .animation(.easeInOut(duration: 5))
```

```
.foregroundColor(self.colors[self.colorIndex])
```

Test the app in the preview canvas and confirm that the Picker view appears with all of the color names using the corresponding foreground color and that color selections are reflected in the Text view.

22.10 Tidying the Layout

Up until this point the focus of this tutorial has been on the appearance and functionality of the individual views. Aside from making sure the views are stacked vertically, however, no attention has been paid to the overall appearance of the layout. At this point the layout should resemble that shown in Figure 22-9:

Figure 22-9

The first improvement that is needed is to add some space around the Slider, TextField and Picker views so that they are not so close to the edge of the device display. To achieve this, we will add some padding modifiers to the views:

```
Slider(value: $rotation, in: 0 ... 360, step: 0.1)
```

```
     .padding()

TextField("Enter text here", text: $text)
    .textFieldStyle(RoundedBorderTextFieldStyle())
    .padding()

Picker(selection: $colorIndex, label: Text("Color")) {
    ForEach (0 ..< colornames.count) {
        Text(self.colornames[$0])
            .foregroundColor(self.colors[$0])
    }
}
}
.padding()
```

Next, the layout would probably look better if the Views were evenly spaced. One way to implement this is to add some Spacer views before and after the Text view:

```
VStack {
        Spacer()
        Text(text)
            .font(.largeTitle)
            .fontWeight(.heavy)
            .rotationEffect(.degrees(self.rotation))
            .animation(.easeInOut(duration: 5))
            .foregroundColor(self.colors[self.colorIndex])
        Spacer()
        Slider(value: $rotation, in: 0 ... 360, step: 0.1)
            .padding()
        TextField("Enter text here", text: $text)
            .textFieldStyle(RoundedBorderTextFieldStyle())
            .padding()
        Picker(selection: $colorIndex, label: Text("Color")) {
            ForEach (0 ..< colornames.count) {
                Text(self.colornames[$0])
                    .foregroundColor(self.colors[$0])
            }
        }
        .padding()
}
```

The Spacer view provides a flexible space between views that will expand and contract based on the requirements of the layout. If a Spacer is contained in a stack it will resize along the stack axis. When used outside of a stack container, a Spacer view can resize both horizontally and vertically.

To make the separation between the Text view and the Slider more obvious, also add a Divider view to the layout:

```
.
.
VStack {
    Spacer()
    Text(text)
        .font(.largeTitle)
        .fontWeight(.heavy)
        .rotationEffect(.degrees(self.rotation))
        .animation(.easeInOut(duration: 5))
        .foregroundColor(self.colors[self.colorIndex])
    Spacer()
    Divider()
.
.
```

The Divider view draws a line to indicate separation between two views in a stack container.

With these changes made, the layout should now appear in the preview canvas as shown in Figure 22-10:

Figure 22-10

22.11 **Summary**

The goal of this chapter has been to put into practice some of the theory covered in the previous chapters through the creation of an example app project. In particular, the tutorial made use of a variety of techniques for adding views to a layout in addition to the use of modifiers and state property bindings. The chapter also introduced the Spacer and Divider views and made use of the ForEach structure to dynamically generate views from a data array.

23. SwiftUI Observable and Environment Objects – A Tutorial

The chapter entitled *Working with SwiftUI State, Observable and Environment Objects* introduced the concept of observable and environment objects and explained how these are used to implement a data driven approach to app development in SwiftUI.

This chapter will build on the knowledge from the earlier chapter by creating a simple example project that makes use of both observable and environment objects.

23.1 About the ObservableDemo Project

Observable objects are particularly powerful when used to wrap dynamic data (in other words, data values that change repeatedly). To simulate data of this type, an observable data object will be created which makes use of the Foundation framework Timer object configured to update a counter once every second. This counter will be published so that it can be observed by views within the app project.

Initially, the data will be treated as an observable object and passed from one view to another. Later in the chapter, the data will be converted to an environment object so that it can be accessed by multiple views without being passed from one to the other.

23.2 Creating the Project

Launch Xcode and select the option to create a new Single View App named ObservableDemo with the User Interface option set to SwiftUI.

23.3 Adding the Observable Object

The first step after creating the new project is to add a data class implementing the ObservableObject protocol. Within Xcode, select the *File -> New -> File...* menu option and, in the resulting template dialog, select the Swift File option. Click the Next button and name the file *TimerData* before clicking the Create button.

With the *TimerData.swift* file loaded into the code editor, implement the TimerData class as follows:

```
import Foundation
import Combine

class TimerData : ObservableObject {

    @Published var timeCount = 0
```

```
    var timer : Timer?

    init() {
        timer = Timer.scheduledTimer(timeInterval: 1.0, target: self,
selector: #selector(timerDidFire), userInfo: nil, repeats: true)
    }

    @objc func timerDidFire() {
        timeCount += 1
    }

    func resetCount() {
        timeCount = 0
    }
}
```

The class is declared as implementing the ObservableObject protocol and contains an initializer which simply configures a Timer instance to call a function named *timerDidFire()* once every second. The *timerDidFire()* function, in turn, increments the value assigned to the timeCount variable. The timeCount variable is declared using the @Published property wrapper so that it can be observed from within views elsewhere in the project. The class also includes a method named *resetCount()* to reset the counter to zero.

23.4 Designing the ContentView Layout

The user interface for the app will consist of two screens, the first of which will be represented by the *ContentView.Swift* file. Select this file to load it into the code editor and modify it so that it reads as follows:

```
import SwiftUI

struct ContentView: View {

    @ObservedObject var timerData: TimerData = TimerData()

    var body: some View {

        NavigationView {
            VStack {
                Text("Timer count = \(timerData.timeCount)")

                    .font(.largeTitle)
                    .fontWeight(.bold)
                    .padding()
```

```
            Button(action: resetCount) {
                Text("Reset Counter")
            }
        }
    }
}

    func resetCount() {
        timerData.resetCount()
    }
}

struct ContentView_Previews: PreviewProvider {
    static var previews: some View {
        ContentView()
    }
}
```

With the changes made, use the Live Preview button to test the view. Once the live preview starts, the counter should begin incrementing:

Figure 23-1

Next, click on the Reset Counter button and verify that the counter restarts counting from zero. Now that the initial implementation is working, the next step is to add a second view which will also need access to the same observable object.

23.5 Adding the Second View

Select the *File -> New -> File...* menu option, this time choosing the SwiftUI View template option and naming the view SecondView. Edit the SecondView declaration so that it reads as follows:

```
import SwiftUI

struct SecondView: View {

    @ObservedObject var timerData: TimerData

    var body: some View {

        VStack {
            Text("Second View")
                .font(.largeTitle)
            Text("Timer Count = \(timerData.timeCount)")
                .font(.headline)
        }
        .padding()
    }
}

struct SecondView_Previews: PreviewProvider {
    static var previews: some View {
        SecondView(timerData: TimerData())
    }
}
```

Use live preview to test that the layout matches Figure 23-2 and that the timer begins counting.

In the live preview, the view has its own instance of TimerData which was configured in the SecondView_Previews declaration. To make sure that both ContentView and SecondView are using the same TimerData instance, the observed object needs to be passed to the SecondView when the user navigates to the second screen.

Figure 23-2

23.6 Adding Navigation

A navigation link now needs to be added to ContentView configured to navigate to the second view. Open the *ContentView.swift* file in the code editor and add this link as follows:

```
var body: some View {

    NavigationView {
        VStack {
            Text("Timer count = \(timerData.timeCount)")

                .font(.largeTitle)
                .fontWeight(.bold)
                .padding()

            Button(action: resetCount) {
                Text("Reset Counter")
            }

            NavigationLink(destination:
```

```
                            SecondView(timerData: timerData)) {
                Text("Next Screen")
            }
            .padding()
        }
    }
}
```

Once again using live preview, test the ContentView and check that the counter increments. Taking note of the current counter value, click on the Next Screen link to display the second view and verify that counting continues from the same number. This confirms that both views are subscribed to the same observable object instance.

23.7 Using an Environment Object

The final step in this tutorial is to convert the observable object to an environment object. This will allow both views to access the same TimerData object without the need for a reference to be passed from one view to the other.

This change does not require any modifications to the *TimerData.swift* class declaration and only minor changes are needed within the two SwiftUI view files. Starting with the *ContentView.swift* file, change the @ObservedObject property wrapper to @EnvironmentObject and modify the ContentView_Previews declaration to add an instance of the timer to the environment when previewing the layout:

```
import SwiftUI

struct ContentView: View {

    @EnvironmentObject var timerData: TimerData = TimerData()

    var body: some View {

        NavigationView {
.

.


            NavigationLink(destination: SecondView(timerData:
timerData)) {
                Text("Next Screen")
            }
            .padding()
        }
    }
.
```

```
struct ContentView_Previews: PreviewProvider {
    static var previews: some View {
        ContentView().environmentObject(TimerData())
    }
}
```

Next, modify the *SecondView.swift* file so that it reads as follows:

```
import SwiftUI

struct SecondView: View {

    @EnvironmentObject var timerData: TimerData

    var body: some View {

        VStack {
            Text("Second View")
                .font(.largeTitle)
            Text("Timer Count = \(timerData.timeCount)")
                .font(.headline)
        }.padding()
    }
}

struct SecondView_Previews: PreviewProvider {
    static var previews: some View {
        SecondView().environmentObject(TimerData())
    }
}
```

Finally, modify the *SceneDelegate.swift* file so that a TimerData object is added to the environment when the root scene is created:

```
func scene(_ scene: UIScene, willConnectTo session: UISceneSession,
            options connectionOptions: UIScene.ConnectionOptions) {

    let contentView = ContentView()

    let timerData = TimerData()

    if let windowScene = scene as? UIWindowScene {
        let window = UIWindow(windowScene: windowScene)
        window.rootViewController =
```

```
            UIHostingController(rootView:
                contentView.environmentObject(timerData))
    self.window = window
    window.makeKeyAndVisible()
    }
}
```

Test the project one last time, either using live preview or by running on a physical device or simulator and check that both screens are accessing the same counter data via the environment.

23.8 Summary

This chapter has worked through a tutorial that demonstrates the use of observed and environment objects to bind dynamic data to the views in a user interface, including implementing an observable object, publishing a property, subscribing to an observable object and the use of environment objects.

24. SwiftUI Stack Alignment and Alignment Guides

The chapter entitled *SwiftUI Stacks and Frames* touched on the basics of alignment in the context of stack container views. Inevitably, when it comes to designing complex user interface layouts, it will be necessary to move beyond the standard alignment options provided with SwiftUI stack views. With this in mind, this chapter will introduce more advanced stack alignment techniques including container alignment, alignment guides, custom alignments and the implementation of alignments between different stacks.

24.1 Container Alignment

The most basic of alignment options when working with SwiftUI stacks is container alignment. These settings define how the child views contained within a stack are aligned in relation to each other and the containing stack. This alignment value applies to all the contained child views unless different alignment guides have been applied on individual views. Views that do not have their own alignment guide are said to be *implicitly aligned*.

When working with alignments it is important to remember that horizontal stacks (HStack) align child views vertically, while vertical stacks (VStack) align their children horizontally. In the case of the ZStack, both horizontal and vertical alignment values are used.

The following VStack declaration consists of a simple VStack configuration containing three child views:

```
VStack {
    Text("This is some text")
    Text("This is some longer text")
    Text("This is short")
}
```

In the absence of a specific container alignment value, the VStack will default to aligning the centers (.center) of the contained views as shown in Figure 24-1:

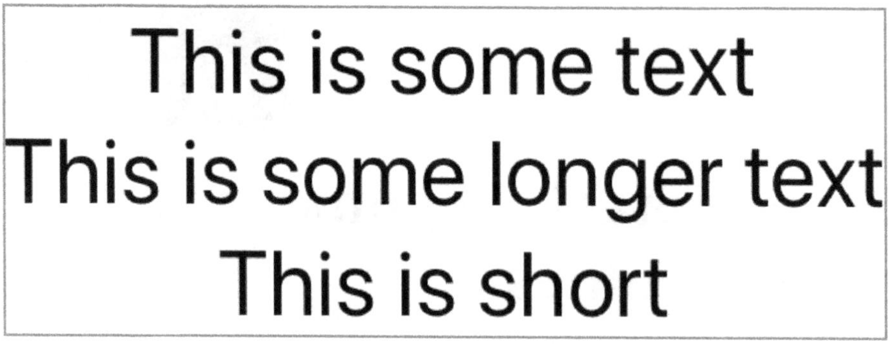

This is some text
This is some longer text
This is short

Figure 24-1

In addition to the default center alignment, a VStack can be configured using .leading or .trailing alignment, for example:

```
VStack(alignment: .trailing) {
    Text("This is some text")
    Text("This is some longer text")
    Text("This is short")
}
```

When rendered, the above VStack layout will appear with the child views aligned along the trailing edges of the views and the container:

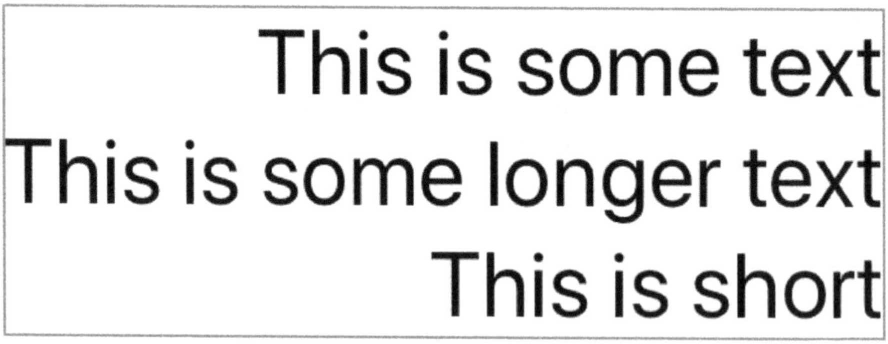

This is some text
This is some longer text
This is short

Figure 24-2

Horizontal stacks also default to center alignment in the absence of a specific setting, but also provide top and bottom alignment options in addition to values for aligning text baselines. It is also possible to include spacing values when specifying an alignment. The following HStack uses the default center alignment with spacing and contains three Text view child views, each using a different font size.

```
HStack(spacing: 20) {
    Text("This is some text")
        .font(.largeTitle)
    Text("This is some much longer text")
        .font(.body)
```

```
Text("This is short")
    .font(.headline)
}
```

The above stack will appear as follows when previewed:

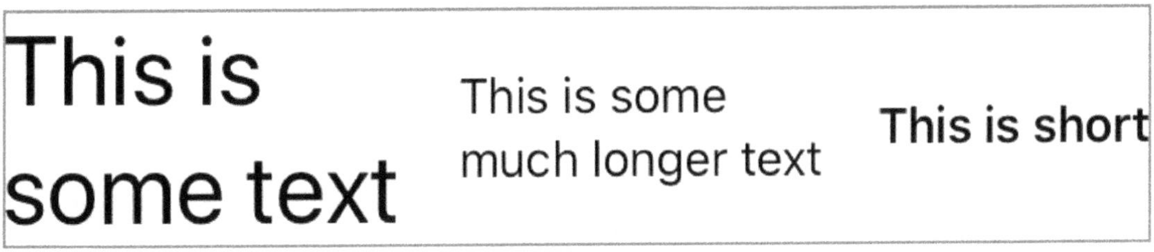

Figure 24-3

Text baseline alignment can be applied based on the baseline of either the first (.firstTextBaseline) or last (.lastTextBaseline) text-based view, for example:

```
HStack(alignment: .lastTextBaseline, spacing: 20) {
    Text("This is some text")
        .font(.largeTitle)
    Text("This is some much longer text")
        .font(.body)
    Text("This is short")
        .font(.headline)
}
```

Now the three Text views will align with the baseline of the last view:

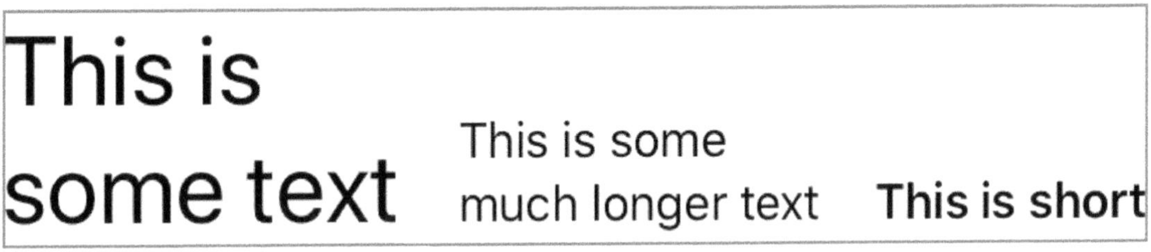

Figure 24-4

24.2 Alignment Guides

An alignment guide is used to define a custom position within a view that is to be used when that view is aligned with other views contained in a stack. This allows more complex alignments to be implemented than those offered by the standard alignment types such as center, leading and top, though these standard types may still be used when defining an alignment guide. An alignment guide could, for example, be used to align a view based on a position two thirds along its length or 20 points from the top edge.

Alignment guides are applied to views using the *alignmentGuide()* modifier which takes as arguments a standard alignment type and a closure which must calculate and return a value indicating the point within the view on which the alignment is to be based. To assist in calculating the alignment position within the view, the closure is passed a ViewDimensions object which can be used to obtain the width and height of the view and also the view's standard alignment positions (.top, .bottom, .leading and so on).

Consider the following VStack which contains three rectangles of differing lengths and colors, aligned on their leading edges:

```
VStack(alignment: .leading) {
    Rectangle()
        .foregroundColor(Color.green)
        .frame(width: 120, height: 50)
    Rectangle()
        .foregroundColor(Color.red)
        .frame(width: 200, height: 50)
    Rectangle()
        .foregroundColor(Color.blue)
        .frame(width: 180, height: 50)
}
```

The above layout will be rendered as shown in Figure 24-5:

Figure 24-5

Now, suppose that instead of being aligned on the leading edge, the second view needs to be aligned 120 points inside the leading edge. This can be implemented using an alignment guide as follows:

```
VStack(alignment: .leading) {
    Rectangle()
        .foregroundColor(Color.green)
        .frame(width: 120, height: 50)
    Rectangle()
```

```
        .foregroundColor(Color.red)
        .alignmentGuide(.leading, computeValue: { d in 120.0 })
        .frame(width: 200, height: 50)
    Rectangle()
        .foregroundColor(Color.blue)
        .frame(width: 180, height: 50)
}
```

While the first and third rectangles continue to be aligned on their leading edges, the second rectangle is aligned at the specified alignment guide position:

Figure 24-6

When working with alignment guides, it is essential that the alignment type specified in the *alignmentGuide()* modifier matches the alignment type applied to the parent stack as shown in Figure 24-7. If these do not match, the alignment guide will be ignored by SwiftUI when the layout is rendered.

```
VStack(alignment: .leading) {
    Rectangle()
        .foregroundColor(Color.green)
        .frame(width: 120, height: 50)
    Rectangle()
        .foregroundColor(Color.red)
        .alignmentGuide(.leading, computeValue: { d in 120.0 })
        .frame(width: 200, height: 50)
    Rectangle()
        .foregroundColor(Color.blue)
        .frame(width: 180, height: 50)
}
```

Must Match

Figure 24-7

Instead of hardcoding an offset, the properties of the ViewDimensions object passed to the closure can be used in calculating the alignment guide position. Using the width property, for example, the alignment guide could be positioned one third of the way along the view from the leading edge:

```
VStack(alignment: .leading) {
```

```
Rectangle()
    .foregroundColor(Color.green)
    .frame(width: 120, height: 50)
Rectangle()
    .foregroundColor(Color.red)
    .alignmentGuide(.leading,
              computeValue: { d in d.width / 3 })
    .frame(width: 200, height: 50)
Rectangle()
    .foregroundColor(Color.blue)
    .frame(width: 180, height: 50)
}
```

Now when the layout is rendered it will appear as shown in Figure 24-8:

Figure 24-8

The ViewDimensions object also provides access to the HorizontalAlignment and VerticalAlignment properties of the view. In the following example, the trailing edge of the view is identified with an additional 20 points added:

```
.alignmentGuide(.leading, computeValue: {
              d in d[HorizontalAlignment.trailing] + 20
})
```

This will cause the trailing edge of the view to be aligned 20 points from the leading edges of the other views:

Figure 24-9

24.3 **Using the Alignment Guides Tool**

The best way to gain familiarity with alignment guides is to experiment with the various settings and options. Fortunately, the SwiftUI Lab has created a useful learning tool for trying out the various alignment settings. To use the tool, begin by creating a new Xcode SwiftUI project named AlignmentTool, open the *ContentView.swift* file and remove all the existing contents.

Next, open a web browser and navigate to the following URL:

http://bit.ly/2MCioyl

This page contains the source code for a tool in a file named *alignment-guides-tool.swift*. Select and copy the entire source code from the file and paste it into the *ContentView.swift* file in Xcode. Once loaded, compile and run the app on an iPad device or simulator in landscape mode where it will appear as shown in Figure 24-10:

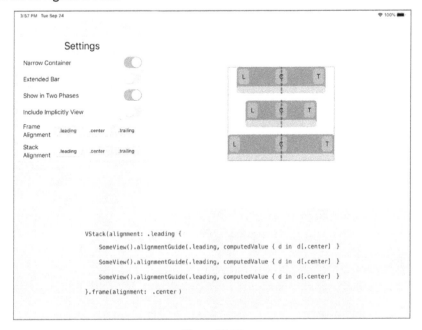

Figure 24-10

Turn on the *Include Implicitly View* option to see what a view will do without any alignment guides and use the yellow bars under each view together with the green L, C and T buttons and the Stack Alignment options to try different combinations of guide settings. With each selection, the VStack declaration in the bottom section of the screen will change to reflect the current configuration.

24.4 Custom Alignment Types

In the previous examples, changes have been made to view alignments based on the standard alignment types. SwiftUI provides a way for the set of standard types to be extended by declaring custom alignment types. A custom alignment type named *.oneThird* could, for example, be created which would make the point of alignment one third of the distance from a specified edge of a view.

Take, for example, the following HStack configuration consisting of four rectangles centered vertically:

Figure 24-11

The declaration to display the above layout reads as follows:

```
HStack(alignment: .center) {
    Rectangle()
        .foregroundColor(Color.green)
        .frame(width: 50, height: 200)
    Rectangle()
        .foregroundColor(Color.red)
        .frame(width: 50, height: 200)
    Rectangle()
        .foregroundColor(Color.blue)
        .frame(width: 50, height: 200)
    Rectangle()
        .foregroundColor(Color.orange)
        .frame(width: 50, height: 200)
}
```

To change the alignment of one or more of these rectangles, alignment guides could be applied containing the calculations for a computed value. An alternative approach is to create a custom alignment which can be applied to multiple views. This is achieved by extending either VerticalAlignment or HorizontalAlignment to add a new alignment type which returns a calculated value. The following example creates a new vertical alignment type:

```
extension VerticalAlignment {
    private enum OneThird : AlignmentID {
        static func defaultValue(in d: ViewDimensions) -> CGFloat {
            return d.height / 3
        }
    }
    static let oneThird = VerticalAlignment(OneThird.self)
}
```

The extension must contain an enum that conforms to the AlignmentID protocol which, in turn, dictates that a function named *defaultValue()* is implemented. This function must accept a ViewDimensions object for a view and return a CGFloat computed value indicating the alignment guide position. In the above example, a position one third of the height of the view is returned.

Once implemented, the custom alignment can be used as shown in the following HStack declaration:

```
HStack(alignment: .oneThird) {
    Rectangle()
        .foregroundColor(Color.green)
        .frame(width: 50, height: 200)
    Rectangle()
        .foregroundColor(Color.red)
        .alignmentGuide(.oneThird,
            computeValue: { d in d[VerticalAlignment.top] })
        .frame(width: 50, height: 200)

    Rectangle()
        .foregroundColor(Color.blue)

        .frame(width: 50, height: 200)
    Rectangle()
        .foregroundColor(Color.orange)
        .alignmentGuide(.oneThird,
            computeValue: { d in d[VerticalAlignment.top] })
        .frame(width: 50, height: 200)
}
```

In the above example, the new .oneThird custom alignment has been applied to two of the rectangle views, resulting in the following layout:

Figure 24-12

In both cases, the alignment was calculated relative to the top of the view with no additional modifications. In fact, the custom alignment can be used in the same way as a standard alignment type. For example, the following changes align the red rectangle relative to the bottom edge of the view:

```
.alignmentGuide(.oneThird,
            computeValue: { d in d[VerticalAlignment.bottom] })
```

Now when the view is rendered, the alignment guide is set to a position one third of the view height below the bottom edge of the view:

Figure 24-13

24.5 **Cross Stack Alignment**

A typical user interface layout will be created by nesting stacks to multiple levels. A key shortcoming of the standard alignment types is that they do not provide a way for a view in one stack to be aligned with a view in another stack. Consider the following stack configuration consisting of a VStack embedded inside a HStack. In addition to the embedded VStack, the HStack also contains a single additional view:

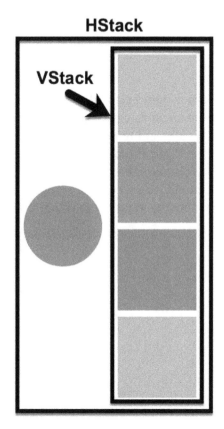

Figure 24-14

The corresponding declaration for the above nested layout reads as follows:

```
HStack(alignment: .center, spacing: 20) {

    Circle()
        .foregroundColor(Color.purple)
        .frame(width: 100, height: 100)

    VStack(alignment: .center) {
        Rectangle()
            .foregroundColor(Color.green)
            .frame(width: 100, height: 100)
```

```
            Rectangle()
                .foregroundColor(Color.red)
                .frame(width: 100, height: 100)
            Rectangle()
                .foregroundColor(Color.blue)
                .frame(width: 100, height: 100)
            Rectangle()
                .foregroundColor(Color.orange)
                .frame(width: 100, height: 100)
        }
    }
```

Currently, both the view represented by the circle and the VStack are centered in the vertical plane within the HStack. If we wanted the circle to align with either the top or bottom squares in the VStack we could change the HStack alignment to .top or .bottom and the view would align with the top or bottom squares respectively. If, on the other hand, the purple circle view needed to be aligned with either the second or third square there would be no way of doing so using the standard alignment types. Fortunately, this can be achieved by creating a custom alignment and applying it to both the circle and the square within the VStack with which it is to be aligned.

A simple custom alignment that returns an alignment value relative to the bottom edge of a view can be implemented as follows:

```
extension VerticalAlignment {
    private enum CrossAlignment : AlignmentID {
        static func defaultValue(in d: ViewDimensions) -> CGFloat {
            return d[.bottom]
        }
    }
    static let crossAlignment = VerticalAlignment(CrossAlignment.self)
}
```

This custom alignment can now be used to align views embedded in different stacks. In the following example, the bottom edge of the circle view is aligned with the third square embedded in the VStack:

```
HStack(alignment: .crossAlignment, spacing: 20) {

    Circle()
        .foregroundColor(Color.purple)
        .alignmentGuide(.crossAlignment,
            computeValue: { d in d[VerticalAlignment.center] })
        .frame(width: 100, height: 100)

    VStack(alignment: .center) {
        Rectangle()
```

```
        .foregroundColor(Color.green)
        .frame(width: 100, height: 100)
    Rectangle()
        .foregroundColor(Color.red)
        .frame(width: 100, height: 100)
    Rectangle()
        .foregroundColor(Color.blue)
        .alignmentGuide(.crossAlignment, computeValue:
                        { d in d[VerticalAlignment.center] })
        .frame(width: 100, height: 100)
    Rectangle()
        .foregroundColor(Color.orange)
        .frame(width: 100, height: 100)
    }

}
```

Note that the alignment of the containing HStack also needs to use the crossAlignment type for the custom alignment to take effect. When rendered, the layout now will appear as illustrated in Figure 24-15 below:

Figure 24-15

24.6 **ZStack Custom Alignment**

By default, the child views of a ZStack are overlaid on top of each other and center aligned. The following figure shows three shape views (circle, square and capsule) stacked on top of each other in a ZStack and center aligned:

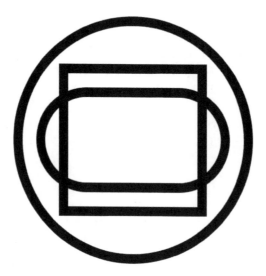

Figure 24-16

Using the standard alignment types, the alignment of all the embedded views can be changed. In Figure 24-17 for example, the ZStack has .leading alignment configured:

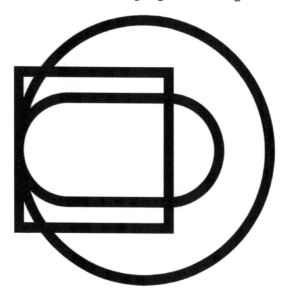

Figure 24-17

To perform more advanced alignment layouts, where each view within the stack has its own alignment, both horizontal and vertical custom alignments must be combined into a single custom alignment, for example:

```
extension HorizontalAlignment {
    enum MyHorizontal: AlignmentID {
        static func defaultValue(in d: ViewDimensions) -> CGFloat
                { d[HorizontalAlignment.center] }
    }
    static let myAlignment =
                HorizontalAlignment(MyHorizontal.self)
}

extension VerticalAlignment {
    enum MyVertical: AlignmentID {
        static func defaultValue(in d: ViewDimensions) -> CGFloat
                { d[VerticalAlignment.center] }
    }
    static let myAlignment = VerticalAlignment(MyVertical.self)
}

extension Alignment {
    static let myAlignment = Alignment(horizontal: .myAlignment,
                                vertical: .myAlignment)
}
```

Once implemented, the custom alignments can be used to position ZStack child views on both the horizontal and vertical axes:

```
ZStack(alignment: .myAlignment) {
    Rectangle()
        .foregroundColor(Color.green)
        .alignmentGuide(HorizontalAlignment.myAlignment)
                    { d in d[.trailing]}
        .alignmentGuide(VerticalAlignment.myAlignment)
                    { d in d[VerticalAlignment.bottom] }
        .frame(width: 100, height: 100)

    Rectangle()
        .foregroundColor(Color.red)
        .alignmentGuide(VerticalAlignment.myAlignment)
                    { d in d[VerticalAlignment.top] }
        .alignmentGuide(HorizontalAlignment.myAlignment)
                    { d in d[HorizontalAlignment.center] }
        .frame(width: 100, height: 100)
```

```
Circle()
    .foregroundColor(Color.orange)
    .alignmentGuide(HorizontalAlignment.myAlignment)
                     { d in d[.leading] }
    .alignmentGuide(VerticalAlignment.myAlignment)
                     { d in d[.bottom] }
    .frame(width: 100, height: 100)
}
```

The above ZStack will appear as shown in Figure 24-18 when rendered:

Figure 24-18

Take some time to experiment with the alignment settings on each view to gain an understanding of how ZStack custom alignment works. Begin, for example, with the following changes:

```
ZStack(alignment: .myAlignment) {
    Rectangle()
        .foregroundColor(Color.green)
        .alignmentGuide(HorizontalAlignment.myAlignment)
                         { d in d[.leading]}
        .alignmentGuide(VerticalAlignment.myAlignment)
                         { d in d[VerticalAlignment.bottom] }
        .frame(width: 100, height: 100)

    Rectangle()
        .foregroundColor(Color.red)
        .alignmentGuide(VerticalAlignment.myAlignment)
```

```
                          { d in d[VerticalAlignment.center] }
         .alignmentGuide(HorizontalAlignment.myAlignment)
                          { d in d[HorizontalAlignment.trailing] }
         .frame(width: 100, height: 100)

    Circle()
        .foregroundColor(Color.orange)
        .alignmentGuide(HorizontalAlignment.myAlignment)
                          { d in d[.leading] }
        .alignmentGuide(VerticalAlignment.myAlignment)
                          { d in d[.top] }
        .frame(width: 100, height: 100)
}
```

With these changes made, check the preview canvas and verify that the layout now matches Figure 24-19:

Figure 24-19

24.7 **Summary**

The SwiftUI stack container views can be configured using basic alignment settings that control the positioning of all child views relative to the container. Alignment of individual views within a stack may be configured using alignment guides. An alignment guide includes a closure which is passed a ViewDimensions object which can be used to compute the alignment position for the view based on the view's height and width. These alignment guides can be implemented as custom alignments which can be reused in the same way as standard alignments when declaring a stack view layout. Custom alignments are also a useful tool when views contained in different stacks need to be aligned with each other. Custom alignment of ZStack child views requires both horizontal and vertical alignment guides.

25. SwiftUI Lists and Navigation

The SwiftUI List view provides a way to present information to the user in the form of a vertical list of rows. Often the items within a list will navigate to another area of the app when tapped by the user. Behavior of this type is implemented in SwiftUI using the NavigationView and NavigationLink components.

The List view can present both static and dynamic data and may also be extended to allow for the addition, removal and reordering of row entries.

This chapter will provide an overview of the List View used in conjunction with NavigationView and NavigationLink in preparation for the tutorial in the next chapter entitled *A SwiftUI List and Navigation Tutorial*.

25.1 SwiftUI Lists

The SwiftUI List control provides similar functionality to the UIKit TableView class in that it presents information in a vertical list of rows with each row containing one or more views contained within a cell. Consider, for example, the following List implementation:

```
struct ContentView: View {
    var body: some View {

        List {
            Text("Wash the car")
            Text("Vacuum house")
            Text("Pick up kids from school bus @ 3pm")
            Text("Auction the kids on eBay")
            Text("Order Pizza for dinner")
        }
    }
}
```

When displayed in the preview, the above list will appear as shown in Figure 25-1:

Figure 25-1

A list cell is not restricted to containing a single component. In fact, any combination of components can be displayed in a list cell. Each row of the list in the following example consists of an image and text component within an HStack:

```
List {
    HStack {
        Image(systemName: "trash.circle.fill")
        Text("Take out the trash")
    }
    HStack {
        Image(systemName: "person.2.fill")
        Text("Pick up the kids") }
    HStack {
        Image(systemName: "car.fill")
        Text("Wash the car")
    }
}
```

The preview canvas for the above view structure will appear as shown in Figure 25-2 below:

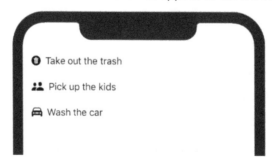

Figure 25-2

The above examples demonstrate the use of a List to display static information. To display a dynamic list of items a few additional steps are required.

25.2 **SwiftUI Dynamic Lists**

A list is considered to be dynamic when it contains a set of items that can change over time. In other words, items can be added, edited and deleted and the list updates dynamically to reflect those changes.

To support a list of this type, the data to be displayed must be contained within a class or structure that conforms to the Identifiable protocol. The Identifiable protocol requires that the instance contain a property named *id* which can be used to uniquely identify each item in the list. The id property can be any Swift or custom type that conforms to the Hashable protocol which includes the String, Int and UUID types in addition to several hundred other standard Swift types. If you opt to use UUID as the type for the property, the *UUID()* method can be used to automatically generate a unique ID for each list item.

The following code implements a simple structure for the To Do list example that conforms to the Identifiable protocol. In this case, the id is generated automatically via a call to *UUID()*:

```
struct ToDoItem : Identifiable {
    var id = UUID()
    var task: String
    var imageName: String
}
```

For the purposes of an example, an array of ToDoItem objects can be used to simulate the supply of data to the list which can now be implemented as follows:

```
struct ContentView: View {

    var listData: [ToDoItem] = [
        ToDoItem(task: "Take out trash", imageName: "trash.circle.fill"),
        ToDoItem(task: "Pick up the kids", imageName: "person.2.fill"),
        ToDoItem(task: "Wash the car", imageName: "car.fill")
        ]

    var body: some View {

        List(listData) { item in
            HStack {
                Image(systemName: item.imageName)
                Text(item.task)
            }
        }
    }
}
.
.
```

Now the list no longer needs a view for each cell. Instead, the list iterates through the data array and reuses the same HStack declaration, simply plugging in the appropriate data for each array element.

In situations where dynamic and static content need to be displayed together within a list, the ForEach statement can be used within the body of the list to iterate through the dynamic data while also declaring static entries. The following example includes a static toggle button together with a ForEach loop for the dynamic content:

```
struct ContentView: View {

    @State var toggleStatus = true
    .
    .
    var body: some View {

        List {

            Toggle(isOn: $toggleStatus) {
                Text("Allow Notifications")
            }

            ForEach (listData) { item in
                HStack {
                    Image(systemName: item.imageName)
                    Text(item.task)
                }
            }
        }
    }
}
```

Note the appearance of the toggle button and the dynamic list items in Figure 25-3:

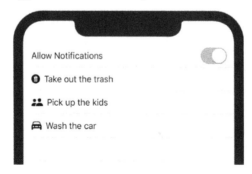

Figure 25-3

A SwiftUI List implementation may also be divided into sections using the Section view, including headers and footers if required. Figure 25-4 shows the list divided into two sections, each with a header:

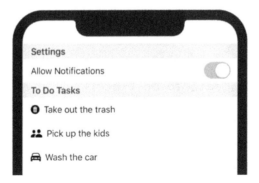

Figure 25-4

The changes to the view declaration to implement these sections are as follows:

```
List {
    Section(header: Text("Settings")) {
        Toggle(isOn: $toggleStatus) {
            Text("Allow Notifications")
        }
    }

    Section(header: Text("To Do Tasks")) {
        ForEach (listData) { item in
            HStack {
                Image(systemName: item.imageName)
                Text(item.task)
            }
        }
    }
}
```

Often the items within a list will navigate to another area of the app when tapped by the user. Behavior of this type is implemented in SwiftUI using the NavigationView and NavigationLink views.

25.3 SwiftUI NavigationView and NavigationLink

To make items in a list navigable, the first step is to embed the list within a NavigationView. Once the list is embedded, the individual rows must be wrapped in a NavigationLink control which is, in turn, configured with the destination view to which the user is to be taken when the row is tapped.

The NavigationView title bar may also be customized using modifiers on the List component to set the title and to add buttons to perform additional tasks. In the following code fragment the title is set to "To Do List" and a button labelled "Add" is added as a bar item and configured to call a hypothetical method named *addTask()*:

```
NavigationView {
    List {
    .
    .
    }
    .navigationBarTitle(Text("To Do List"))
    .navigationBarItems(trailing: Button(action: addTask) {
        Text("Add")
    })
    .
    .
}
```

Remaining with the To Do list example, the following changes are necessary to implement navigation and add a navigation bar title:

```
var body: some View {
    NavigationView {
        List {
            Section(header: Text("Settings")) {
                Toggle(isOn: $toggleStatus) {
                    Text("Allow Notifications")
                }
            }

            Section(header: Text("To Do Tasks")) {
                ForEach (listData) { item in
                    HStack {
                        NavigationLink(destination: Text(item.task)) {
                            Image(systemName: item.imageName)
                            Text(item.task)
                        }
                    }
                }
            }
        }
        .navigationBarTitle(Text("To Do List"))
    }
}
```

In this example, the navigation link will simply display a new screen containing a Text view displaying the task string value. When tested in the canvas using live preview, the finished list will appear as shown in Figure 25-5 with the title and chevrons on the far right of each row now visible. Tapping the links will navigate to the text view.

Figure 25-5

25.4 Making the List Editable

It is common for an app to allow the user to delete items from a list and, in some cases, even move an item from one position to another. Deletion can be enabled by adding an *onDelete()* modifier to each list cell, specifying a method to be called which will delete the item from the data source. When this method is called it will be passed an IndexSet object containing the offsets of the rows being deleted. Once implemented, the user will be able to swipe left on rows in the list to reveal the Delete button as shown in Figure 25-6:

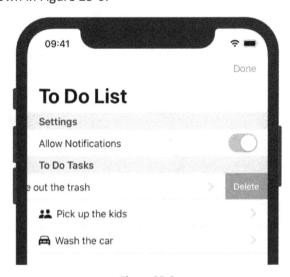

Figure 25-6

The changes to the example List to implement this behavior might read as follows:

```
    .
    .
List {
        Section(header: Text("Settings")) {
            Toggle(isOn: $toggleStatus) {
                Text("Allow Notifications")
            }
        }

        Section(header: Text("To Do Tasks")) {
            ForEach (listData) { item in
                HStack {
                    NavigationLink(destination: Text(item.task)) {
                        Image(systemName: item.imageName)
                        Text(item.task)
                    }
                }
            }
            .onDelete(perform: deleteItem)
        }
    }
    .navigationBarTitle(Text("To Do List"))
}
    .
    .

func deleteItem(at offsets: IndexSet) {
    // Delete items from data source here
}
```

To allow the user to move items up and down in the list the *onMove()* modifier must be applied to the cell, once again specifying a method to be called to modify the ordering of the source data. In this case, the method will be passed an IndexSet object containing the positions of the rows being moved and an integer indicating the destination position.

In addition to adding the *onMove()* modifier, an EditButton instance needs to be added to the List. When tapped, this button automatically switches the list into editable mode and allows items to be moved and deleted by the user. This edit button is added as a navigation bar item which can be added to a list by applying the *navigationBarItems()* modifier. The List declaration can be modified as follows to add this functionality:

```
List {
        Section(header: Text("Settings")) {
            Toggle(isOn: $toggleStatus) {
                Text("Allow Notifications")
            }
```

```
            }

        Section(header: Text("To Do Tasks")) {
            ForEach (listData) { item in
                HStack {
                    NavigationLink(destination: Text(item.task)) {
                        Image(systemName: item.imageName)
                        Text(item.task)
                    }
                }
            }
            .onDelete(perform: deleteItem)
            .onMove(perform: moveItem)
        }
    }
    .navigationBarTitle(Text("To Do List"))
    .navigationBarItems(trailing: EditButton())
}
.
.
.
func moveItem(from source: IndexSet, to destination: Int) {
    // Reorder items is source data here
}
```

Viewed within the preview canvas, the list will appear as shown in Figure 25-7 when the Edit button is tapped by the user. Clicking and dragging the three lines on the right side of each row allows the row to be moved to a different list position (in the figure below the "Pick up the kids" entry is in the process of being moved):

Figure 25-7

25.5 **Summary**

The SwiftUI List view provides a way to order items in a single column of rows, each containing a cell. Each cell, in turn, can contain multiple views when those views are encapsulated in a container view such as a stack layout. The List view provides support for displaying both static and dynamic items or a combination of both.

List views are usually used as a way to allow the user to navigate to other screens. This navigation is implemented by wrapping the List declaration in a NavigationView and each row in a NavigationLink.

Lists can be divided into titled sections and assigned a navigation bar containing a title and buttons. Lists may also be configured to allow rows to be added, deleted and moved.

26. A SwiftUI List and Navigation Tutorial

The previous chapter introduced the List, NavigationView and NavigationLink views and explained how these can be used to present a navigable and editable list of items to the user. This chapter will work through the creation of a project intended to provide a practical example of these concepts.

26.1 About the ListNavDemo Project

When completed, the project will consist of a List view in which each row contains a cell displaying image and text information. Selecting a row within the list will navigate to a details screen containing more information about the selected item. In addition, the List view will include options to add and remove entries and to change the ordering of rows in the list.

The project will also make extensive use of state properties and observable objects to keep the user interface synchronized with the data model.

26.2 Creating the ListNavDemo Project

Launch Xcode and select the option to create a new Single View App named ListNavDemo with the User Interface option set to SwiftUI.

26.3 Preparing the Project

Before beginning development of the app project, some preparatory work needs to be performed involving the addition of image and data assets which will be needed later in the chapter.

The assets to be used in the project are included in the source code sample download provided with the book available from the following URL:

https://www.ebookfrenzy.com/retail/swiftui/

Once the code samples have been downloaded and unpacked, open a Finder window, locate the *CarAssets.xcassets* folder and drag and drop it onto the project navigator panel as illustrated in Figure 26-1:

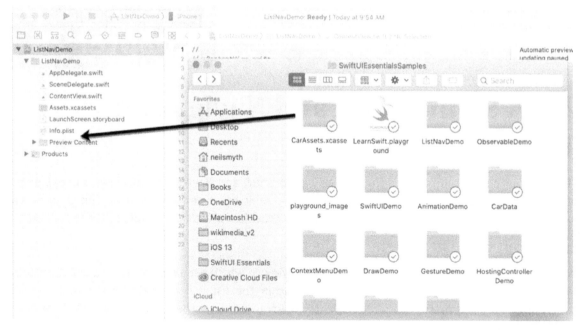

Figure 26-1

When the options dialog appears, enable the *Copy items if needed* option so that the assets are included within the project folder before clicking on the Finish button. With the image assets added, find the *carData.json* file located in the CarData folder and drag and drop it onto the Project navigator panel to also add it to the project.

This JSON file contains entries for different hybrid and electric cars including a unique id, model, description, a Boolean property indicating whether or not it is a hybrid vehicle and the filename of the corresponding image of the car in the asset catalog. The following, for example, is the JSON entry for the Tesla Model 3:

```
{
    "id": "aa32jj887hhg55",
    "name": "Tesla Model 3",
    "description": "Luxury 4-door all-electric car. Range of 310 miles.
0-60mph in 3.2 seconds ",
    "isHybrid": false,
    "imageName": "tesla_model_3"
}
```

26.4 Adding the Car Structure

Now that the JSON file has been added to the project, a structure needs to be declared to represent each car model. Add a new Swift file to the project by selecting the *File -> New -> File...* menu option, selecting Swift File in the template dialog and clicking on the Next button. On the subsequent screen, name the file *Car.swift* before clicking on the Create button.

Once created, the new file will load into the code editor where it needs to be modified so that it reads as follows:

```
import SwiftUI

struct Car : Codable, Identifiable {
    var id: String
    var name: String

    var description: String
    var isHybrid: Bool

    var imageName: String

}
```

As we can see, the structure contains a property for each field in the JSON file and is declared as conforming to the Identifiable protocol so that each instance can be uniquely identified within the List view.

26.5 Loading the JSON Data

The project is also going to need a way to load the *carData.json* file and translate the car entries into an array of Car objects. For this we will add another Swift file containing a convenience function that reads the JSON file and initializes an array which can be accessed elsewhere in the project.

Using the steps outlined previously, add another Swift file named *CarData.swift* to the project and modify it as follows:

```
import UIKit
import SwiftUI

var carData: [Car] = loadJson("carData.json")

func loadJson<T: Decodable>(_ filename: String) -> T {
    let data: Data

    guard let file = Bundle.main.url(forResource: filename,
                                            withExtension: nil)
    else {
        fatalError("\(filename) not found.")
    }

    do {
        data = try Data(contentsOf: file)
    } catch {
```

```
            fatalError("Could not load \(filename): (error)")
    }

    do {
        return try JSONDecoder().decode(T.self, from: data)
    } catch {
        fatalError("Unable to parse \(filename): (error)")
    }
}
```

The file contains a variable referencing an array of Car objects which is initialized by a call to the *loadJson()* function. The *loadJson()* function is a standard example of how to load a JSON file and can be used in your own apps.

26.6 Adding the Data Store

When the user interface has been designed, the List view will rely on an observable object to ensure that the latest data is always displayed to the user. So far, we have a Car structure and an array of Car objects loaded from the JSON file to act as a data source for the project. The last step in getting the data ready for use in the app is to add a data store structure. This structure will need to contain a published property that can be observed by the user interface to keep the List view up to date. Add another Swift file to the project, this time named *CarStore.swift*, and implement the class as follows:

```
import SwiftUI
import Combine

class CarStore : ObservableObject {

    @Published var cars: [Car]

    init (cars: [Car] = []) {
        self.cars = cars
    }
}
```

This file contains a published property in the form of an array of Car objects and an initializer which is passed the array to be published.

With the data side of the project complete, it is now time to begin designing the user interface.

26.7 Designing the Content View

Select the *ContentView.swift* file and modify it as follows to add an observed object binding to an instance of CarStore, passing through to its initializer the carData array created in the *CarData.swift* file:

```
import SwiftUI

struct ContentView: View {

    @ObservedObject var carStore : CarStore = CarStore(cars: carData)
    .
    .
```

The content view is going to require a List view to display information about each car. Now that we have access to the array of cars via the carStore property, we can use a ForEach loop to display a row for each car model. The cell for each row will be implemented as an HStack containing an Image and a Text view, the content of which will be extracted from the carData array elements. Remaining in the *ContentView.swift* file, delete the existing "Hello World!" Text view and implement the list as follows:

```
    .
    .
var body: some View {

        List {
            ForEach (carStore.cars) { car in

                HStack {
                    Image(car.imageName)
                        .resizable()
                        .aspectRatio(contentMode: .fit)
                        .frame(width: 100, height: 60)
                    Text(car.name)
                }
            }
        }
    }
}
    .
    .
```

With the change made to the view, use the preview canvas to verify that the list populates with content as shown in Figure 26-2:

Figure 26-2

Before moving to the next step in the tutorial, the cell declaration will be extracted to a subview to make the declaration tidier. Within the editor, hover the mouse pointer over the HStack declaration and hold down the keyboard Command key so that the declaration highlights. With the Command key still depressed, left-click and select the *Extract to Subview* menu option:

Figure 26-3

Once the view has been extracted, change the name from the default ExtractedView to ListCell. Because the ListCell subview is used within a ForEach statement, the current car will need to be passed through when it is used. Modify both the ListCell declaration and the reference as follows to remove the syntax errors:

```
    var body: some View {

        List {
            ForEach (carStore.cars) { car in

                ListCell(car: car)
            }
        }
    }
}
struct ListCell: View {

    var car: Car

    var body: some View {
        HStack {
            Image(car.imageName)
                .resizable()
                .aspectRatio(contentMode: .fit)
                .frame(width: 100, height: 60)
            Text(car.name)
        }
    }
}
```

Use the preview canvas to confirm that the extraction of the cell as a subview has worked successfully.

26.8 Designing the Detail View

When a user taps a row in the list, a detail screen will appear showing additional information about the selected car. The layout for this screen will be declared in a separate SwiftUI View file which now needs to be added to the project. Use the *File -> New -> File…* menu option once again, this time selecting the SwiftUI View template option and naming the file CarDetail.

When the user navigates to this view from within the List, it will need to be passed the Car instance for the selected car so that the correct details are displayed. Begin by adding a property to the structure and configuring the preview provider to display the details of the first car in the carData array within the preview canvas as follows:

```
import SwiftUI

struct CarDetails: View {

    let selectedCar: Car
```

```
    var body: some View {
        Text"Hello World!")
    }
}


struct CarDetails_Previews: PreviewProvider {
    static var previews: some View {
        CarDetails(selectedCar: carData[0])
    }
}
```

For this layout, a Form container will be used to organize the views. This is a container view that allows views to be grouped together and divided into different sections. The Form also places a line divider between each child view. Within the body of the *CarDetail.swift* file, implement the layout as follows:

```
var body: some View {
        Form {
            Section(header: Text("Car Details")) {
                Image(selectedCar.imageName)
                    .resizable()
                    .cornerRadius(12.0)
                    .aspectRatio(contentMode: .fit)
                    .padding()

                Text(selectedCar.name)
                    .font(.headline)

                Text(selectedCar.description)
                    .font(.body)

                HStack {
                    Text("Hybrid").font(.headline)
                    Spacer()
                    Image(systemName: selectedCar.isHybrid ?
                            "checkmark.circle" : "xmark.circle" )
                }


            }
        }
}
```

Note that the Image view is configured to be resizable and scaled to fit the available space while retaining the aspect ratio. Rounded corners are also applied to make the image more visually appealing and either a circle or checkmark image is displayed in the HStack based on the setting of the isHybrid Boolean setting of the selected car.

When previewed, the screen should match that shown in Figure 26-4:

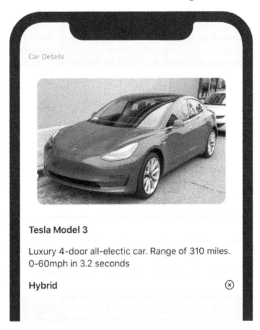

Tesla Model 3

Luxury 4-door all-electic car. Range of 310 miles. 0-60mph in 3.2 seconds

Hybrid

Figure 26-4

26.9 **Adding Navigation to the List**

The next step in this tutorial is to return to the List view in the *ContentView.swift* file and implement navigation so that selecting a row displays the detail screen populated with the corresponding car details.

With the *ContentView.swift* file loaded into the code editor, locate the ListCell subview declaration and embed the HStack in a NavigationLink with the CarDetail view configured as the destination, making sure to pass through the selected car object:

```
struct ListCell: View {

    var car: Car

    var body: some View {

        NavigationLink(destination: CarDetail(selectedCar: car)) {
            HStack {
                Image(car.imageName)
                    .resizable()
                    .aspectRatio(contentMode: .fit)
```

```
                          .frame(width: 100, height: 60)
                Text(car.name)
            }
        }
    }
}
```

For this navigation link to function, the List view must also be embedded in a NavigationView as follows:

```
var body: some View {

    NavigationView {
        List {
            ForEach (carStore.cars) { car in

                ListCell(car: car)
            }
        }
    }
}
```

Test that the navigation works by clicking on the Live Preview button in the preview canvas and selecting different rows, confirming each time that the detail view appears containing information that matches the selected car model.

26.10 Designing the Add Car View

The final view to be added to the project represents the screen to be displayed when the user is adding a new car to the list. Add a new SwiftUI View file to the project named *AddNewCar.swift* including some state properties and a declaration for storing a reference to the carStore binding (this reference will be passed to the view from the ContentView when the user taps an Add button). Also modify the preview provider to pass the carData array into the view for testing purposes:

```
import SwiftUI

struct AddNewCar: View {

    @ObservedObject var carStore : CarStore

    @State var isHybrid = false
    @State var name: String = ""
    @State var description: String = ""

.

.

struct AddNewCar_Previews: PreviewProvider {
```

```
        static var previews: some View {
            AddNewCar(carStore: CarStore(cars: carData))
        }
    }
}
```

Next, add a new subview to the declaration that can be used to display a Text and TextField view pair into which the user will enter details of the new car. This subview will be passed a String value for the text to appear on the Text view and a state property binding into which the user's input is to be stored. As outlined in the chapter entitled *Working with SwiftUI State, Observable and Environment Objects*, a property must be declared using the @Binding property wrapper if the view is being passed a state property. Remaining in the *AddNewCar.swift* file, implement this subview as follows:

```
struct DataInput: View {

    var title: String
    @Binding var userInput: String

    var body: some View {
        VStack(alignment: HorizontalAlignment.leading) {
            Text(title)
                .font(.headline)
            TextField("Enter \(title)", text: $userInput)
                    .textFieldStyle(RoundedBorderTextFieldStyle())
        }
        .padding()
    }
}
```

With the subview added, declare the user interface layout for the main view as follows:

```
var body: some View {

    Form {
        Section(header: Text("Car Details")) {
            Image(systemName: "car.fill")
                .resizable()
                .aspectRatio(contentMode: .fit)
                .padding()

            DataInput(title: "Model", userInput: $name)
            DataInput(title: "Description", userInput: $description)

            Toggle(isOn: $isHybrid) {
                    Text("Hybrid").font(.headline)
```

```
            }.padding()
        }


        Button(action: addNewCar) {
            Text("Add Car")
            }
        }
    }
}
```

Note that two instances of the DataInput subview are included in the layout together with an Image view, a Toggle and a Button. The Button view is configured to call an action method named addNewCar when clicked. Within the body of the ContentView declaration, add this function now so that it reads as follows:

```
.
.
Button(action: addNewCar) {
            Text("Add Car")
            }
        }
    }

    func addNewCar() {
        let newCar = Car(id: UUID().uuidString,
                        name: name, description: description,
                        isHybrid: isHybrid, imageName: "tesla_model_3" )

        carStore.cars.append(newCar)
    }
}
```

The new car function creates a new Car instance using the Swift *UUID()* method to generate a unique identifier for the entry and the content entered by the user. For simplicity, rather than add code to select a photo from the photo library the function simply reuses the tesla_model_3 image for new car entries. Finally, the new Car instance is appended to the carStore car array.

When rendered in the preview canvas, the AddNewCar view should match Figure 26-5 below:

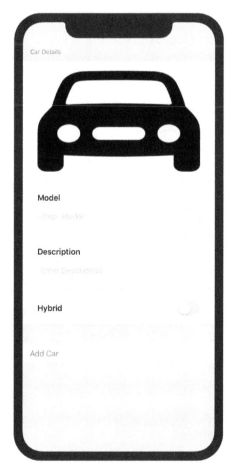

Figure 26-5

With this view completed, the next step is to modify the ContentView layout to include Add and Edit buttons.

26.11 Implementing Add and Edit Buttons

The Add and Edit buttons will be added to a navigation bar applied to the List view in the ContentView layout. The Navigation bar will also be used to display a title at the top of the list. These changes require the use of the *navigationBarTitle()* and *navigationBarItems()* modifiers as follows:

```
var body: some View {

    NavigationView {
        List {
            ForEach (carStore.cars) { car in

                ListCell(car: car)
        }
```

```
        }
        .navigationBarTitle(Text("EV Cars"))
        .navigationBarItems(leading: NavigationLink(destination:
                            AddNewCar(carStore: self.carStore)) {
            Text("Add")
                .foregroundColor(.blue)
        }, trailing: EditButton())
    }
}
```

The Add button is configured to appear at the leading edge of the navigation bar and is implemented as a NavigationLink configured to display the AddNewCar view, passing through a reference to the observable carStore binding.

The Edit button, on the other hand, is positioned on the trailing edge of the navigation bar and is configured to display the built-in EditButton view. A preview of the modified layout at this point should match the following figure:

Figure 26-6

Using Live Preview mode, test that the Add button displays the new car screen and that entering new car details and clicking the Add Car button causes the new entry to appear in the list after returning to the content view screen.

26.12 **Adding the Edit Button Methods**

The final task in this tutorial is to add some action methods to be used by the EditButton view added to the navigation bar in the previous section. Because these actions are to be available for every row in the list, the actions must be applied to the list cells as follows:

```
var body: some View {

    NavigationView {
            List {
                ForEach (carStore.cars) { car in

                        ListCell(car: car)
                }
                .onDelete(perform: deleteItems)
                .onMove(perform: moveItems)
            }
            .navigationBarTitle(Text("EV Cars"))
.
.
```

Next, implement the *deleteItems()* and *moveItems()* functions within the scope of the body declaration:

```
.
.
.navigationBarTitle(Text("EV Cars"))
            .navigationBarItems(leading: NavigationLink(destination:
AddNewCar(carStore: self.carStore)) {
                Text("Add")
                    .foregroundColor(.blue)
            }, trailing: EditButton())
        }
    }

    func deleteItems(at offsets: IndexSet) {
        carStore.cars.remove(atOffsets: offsets)
    }

    func moveItems(from source: IndexSet, to destination: Int) {
        carStore.cars.move(fromOffsets: source, toOffset: destination)
    }
}
```

In the case of the *deleteItems()* function, the offsets of the selected rows are provided and used to remove the corresponding elements from the car store array. The *moveItems()* function, on the other hand, is called when the user moves rows to a different location within the list. This function is passed source and destination values which are used to match the row position in the array.

Using Live Preview, click the Edit button and verify that it is possible to delete rows by tapping the red delete icon next to a row and to move rows by clicking and dragging on the three horizontal lines at the far-right edge of a row. In each case, list contents should update to reflect the changes:

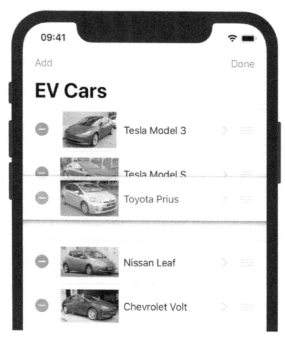

Figure 26-7

26.13 Summary

The main objective of this chapter has been to provide a practical example of using lists, navigation views and navigation links within a SwiftUI project. This included the implementation of dynamic lists and list editing features. The chapter also served to reinforce topics covered in previous chapters including the use of observable objects, state properties and property bindings. The chapter also introduced some additional SwiftUI features including the Form container view, navigation bar items and the TextField view.

27. Building Tabbed Views in SwiftUI

The SwiftUI TabView component allows the user to navigate between different child views by selecting tab items located in a tab bar. This chapter will work through an example project intended to demonstrate how to implement a TabView based interface in a SwiftUI app.

27.1 An Overview of SwiftUI TabView

Tabbed views are created in SwiftUI using the TabView container view and consist of a range of child views which represent the screens through which the user will navigate.

The TabView presents a tab bar at the bottom of the layout which contains the tab items used to navigate between the child views. A tab item is applied to each content view using a modifier and can be customized to contain Text and Image views (other view types are not supported in tab items).

The currently selected tab may also be controlled programmatically by adding tags to the tab items.

Figure 27-1 shows an example TabView layout:

Figure 27-1

27.2 **Creating the TabViewDemo App**

Launch Xcode and select the option to create a new Single View App named TabViewDemo with the User Interface option set to SwiftUI.

27.3 **Adding the TabView Container**

With the *ContentView.swift* file loaded into the code editor, delete the default "Hello World" Text view and add a TabView as follows:

```
import SwiftUI

struct ContentView: View {

    var body: some View {
        TabView {


        }
    }
}
```

27.4 **Adding the Content Views**

Next, add three content views to the layout. For the purposes of this example Text views will be used, but in practice these are likely to be more complex views consisting of stack layouts (note the addition of a font modifier to increase the size of the content text):

```
var body: some View {
    TabView {
        Text("First Content View")
        Text("Second Content View")
        Text("Third Content View")
    }
    .font(.largeTitle)
}
```

27.5 **Adding the Tab Items**

When the layout is now previewed, the first content view will be visible along with the tab bar located along the bottom edge of the screen. Since no tab items have been added, the tab bar is currently empty. Clearly the next step is to apply a tab item to each content view using the *tabItem()* modifier. In this example, each tab item will contain a Text and an Image view:

```
var body: some View {
    TabView {
        Text("First Content View")
            .tabItem {
                Image(systemName: "1.circle")
```

```
                Text("Screen One")
            }
        Text("Second Content View")
            .tabItem {
                Image(systemName: "2.circle")
                Text("Screen Two")
            }
        Text("Third Content View")
            .tabItem {
                Image(systemName: "3.circle")
                Text("Screen Three")
            }
    }
    .font(.largeTitle)
}
```

With the changes made, verify that the tab items now appear in the tab bar before using Live Preview to test that clicking on a tab item displays the corresponding content view. The completed app should resemble that illustrated in Figure 27-1 above.

27.6 Adding Tab Item Tags

To control the currently selected tab in code, a tag needs to be added to each tab item and a state property declared to store the current selection as follows:

```
struct ContentView: View {

    @State private var selection = 1

    var body: some View {
        TabView() {
            Text("First Content View")
                .tabItem {
                    Image(systemName: "1.circle")
                    Text("Screen One")
                }.tag(1)
            Text("Second Content View")
                .tabItem {
                    Image(systemName: "2.circle")
                    Text("Screen Two")
                }.tag(2)
            Text("Third Content View")
                .tabItem {
                    Image(systemName: "3.circle")
                    Text("Screen Three")
```

```
                }.tag(3)
            }
        .font(.largeTitle)
    }
}
```

Next, bind the current selection value of the TabView to the selection state property:

```
var body: some View {
    TabView(selection: $selection) {
        Text("First Content View")
            .tabItem {
.
.
```

Any changes to the selection state property to a different value within the tag range (in this case a value between 1 and 3) elsewhere in the view will now cause the tabbed view to switch to the corresponding content view.

Test this behavior by changing the value assigned to the selection state property while the app is running in live preview mode.

27.7 **Summary**

The SwiftUI TabView container provides a mechanism via which the user can navigate between content views by selecting tabs in a tab bar. The TabView is implemented by declaring child content views and assigning a tab item to each view. The tab items appear in the tab bar and can be constructed from a Text view, an Image view or a combination of Text and Image views.

To control the current selection of a TabView programmatically, each tab item must be assigned a tag containing a unique value, binding the TabView current selection value to a state property.

28. Building Context Menus in SwiftUI

A context menu in SwiftUI is a menu of options that appears when the user performs a long press over a view on which a menu has been configured. Each menu item will typically contain a Button view configured to perform an action when selected, together with a Text view and an optional Image view.

This chapter will work through the creation of an example app that makes use of a context menu to perform color changes on a view.

28.1 Creating the ContextMenuDemo Project

Launch Xcode and select the option to create a new Single View App named ContextMenuDemo with the User Interface option set to SwiftUI.

28.2 Preparing the Content View

A context menu may be added to any view within a layout, but for the purposes of this example, the default "Hello World" Text view will be used. Within Xcode, load the *ContentView.swift* file into the editor, add some state properties to store the foreground and background color values, and use these to control the color settings of the Text view. Also use the *font()* modifier to increase the text font size:

```
import SwiftUI

struct ContentView: View {

    @State private var foregroundColor: Color = Color.black
    @State private var backgroundColor: Color = Color.white

    var body: some View {

        Text("Hello World")
            .font(.largeTitle)
            .padding()
            .foregroundColor(foregroundColor)
            .background(backgroundColor)
```

.

.

28.3 **Adding the Context Menu**

Context menus are added to views in SwiftUI using the *contextMenu()* modifier and declaring the views that are to serve as menu items. Add menu items to the context menu by making the following changes to the body view of the *ContentView.swift* file:

```
var body: some View {


    Text("Hello World")
        .font(.largeTitle)
        .padding()
        .foregroundColor(foregroundColor)
        .background(backgroundColor)
        .contextMenu {
            Button(action: {

            }) {
                Text("Normal Colors")
                Image(systemName: "paintbrush")
            }

            Button(action: {

            }) {
                Text("Inverted Colors")
                Image(systemName: "paintbrush.fill")
            }
        }
    }
}
```

Finally, add code to the two button actions to change the values assigned to the foreground and background state properties:

```
var body: some View {

    Text("Hello World")
        .font(.largeTitle)
        .padding()
        .foregroundColor(foregroundColor)
        .background(backgroundColor)

        .contextMenu {
            Button(action: {
                self.foregroundColor = .black
```

```
            self.backgroundColor = .white
        }) {
            Text("Normal Colors")
            Image(systemName: "paintbrush")
        }

        Button(action: {
            self.foregroundColor = .white
            self.backgroundColor = .black
        }) {
            Text("Inverted Colors")
            Image(systemName: "paintbrush.fill")
        }
    }
}
```

28.4 Testing the Context Menu

Use live preview mode to test the view and perform a long press on the Text view. After a short delay the context menu should appear resembling Figure 28-1 below:

Figure 28-1

Select the Inverted Colors option to dismiss the menu and invert the colors on the Text view:

Figure 28-2

28.5 **Summary**

Context menus appear when a long press gesture is performed over a view in a layout. A context menu can be added to any view type and is implemented using the *contextMenu()* modifier. The menu is comprised of menu items which usually take the form of Button views configured with an action together with a text view and an optional Image view.

29. Basic SwiftUI Graphics Drawing

The goal of this chapter is to introduce SwiftUI 2D drawing techniques. In addition to a group of built-in shape and gradient drawing options, SwiftUI also allows custom drawing to be performed by creating entirely new views that conform to the Shape and Path protocols.

29.1 Creating the DrawDemo Project

Launch Xcode and select the option to create a new Single View App named DrawDemo with the User Interface option set to SwiftUI.

29.2 SwiftUI Shapes

SwiftUI includes a set of five pre-defined shapes that conform to the Shape protocol which can be used to draw circles, rectangles, rounded rectangles and ellipses. Within the DrawDemo project, open the *ContentView.swift* file and add a single rectangle:

```
struct ContentView: View {
    var body: some View {
        Rectangle()
}
```

By default, a shape will occupy all the space available to it within the containing view and will be filled with the foreground color of the parent view (by default this will be black). Within the preview canvas, a black rectangle will fill the entire safe area of the screen.

The color and size of the shape may be adjusted using the *fill()* modifier and by wrapping it in a frame. Delete the Rectangle view and replace it with the declaration which draws a red filled 200x200 circle:

```
Circle()
    .fill(Color.red)
    .frame(width: 200, height: 200)
```

When previewed, the above circle will appear as illustrated in Figure 29-1:

Figure 29-1

To draw an unfilled shape with a stroked outline, the *stroke()* modifier can be applied, passing through an optional line width value. By default, a stroked shape will be drawn using the default foreground color which may be altered using the *foregroundColor()* modifier. Remaining in the *ContentView.swift* file, replace the circle with the following:

```
Capsule()
    .stroke(lineWidth: 10)
    .foregroundColor(.blue)
    .frame(width: 200, height: 100)
```

Note that the frame for the above Capsule shape is rectangular. A Capsule contained in a square frame simply draws a circle. The above capsule declaration appears as follows when rendered:

Figure 29-2

The stroke modifier also supports different style types using a StrokeStyle instance. The following declaration, for example, draws a rounded rectangle using a dashed line:

```
RoundedRectangle(cornerRadius: CGFloat(20))
    .stroke(style: StrokeStyle(lineWidth: 8, dash: [CGFloat(10)]))
    .foregroundColor(.blue)
```

```
.frame(width: 200, height: 100)
```

The above shape will be rendered as follows:

Figure 29-3

By providing additional dash values to a *StrokeStyle()* instance and adding a dash phase value, a range of different dash effects can be achieved, for example:

```
Ellipse()
    .stroke(style: StrokeStyle(lineWidth: 20,
            dash: [CGFloat(10), CGFloat(5), CGFloat(2)],
            dashPhase: CGFloat(10)))
    .foregroundColor(.blue)
    .frame(width: 250, height: 150)
```

When run or previewed, the above declaration will draw the following ellipse:

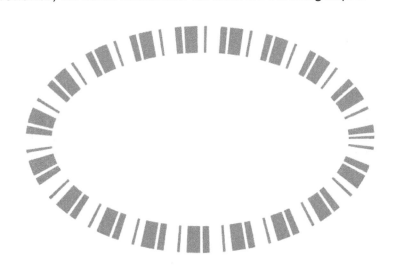

Figure 29-4

29.3 **Using Overlays**

When drawing a shape, it is not possible to combine the fill and stroke modifiers to render a filled shape with a stroked outline. This effect can, however, be achieved by overlaying a stroked view on top of the filled shape, for example:

```
Ellipse()
    .fill(Color.red)
    .overlay(Ellipse()
        .stroke(Color.blue, lineWidth: 10))
    .frame(width: 250, height: 150)
```

The above example draws a blue filled ellipse with a red stroked outlined as illustrated in Figure 29-5:

Figure 29-5

29.4 **Drawing Custom Paths and Shapes**

The shapes used so far in this chapter are essentially structure objects that conform to the Shape protocol. To conform with the shape protocol, a structure must implement a function named *path()* which accepts a rectangle in the form of a CGRect value and returns a Path object that defines what is to be drawn in that rectangle.

A Path instance provides the outline of a 2D shape by specifying coordinates between points and defining the lines drawn between those points. Lines between points in a path can be drawn using straight lines, cubic and quadratic Bézier curves, arcs, ellipses and rectangles.

In addition to being used in a custom shape implementation, paths may also be drawn directly within a view. Try modifying the *ContentView.swift* file so that it reads as follows:

```
struct ContentView: View {
    var body: some View {
```

```
Path { path in
    path.move(to: CGPoint(x: 10, y: 0))
    path.addLine(to: CGPoint(x: 10, y: 350))
    path.addLine(to: CGPoint(x: 300, y: 300))
    path.closeSubpath()
}
}
}
```

A path begins with the coordinates of the start point using the *move()* method. Methods are then called to add additional lines between coordinates. In this case, the *addLine()* method is used to add straight lines. Lines may be drawn in a path using the following methods. In each case, the drawing starts at the current point in the path and ends at the specified end point:

- **addArc** – Adds an arc based on radius and angle values.
- **addCurve** – Adds a cubic Bézier curve using the provided end and control points.
- **addLine** – Adds a straight line ending at the specified point.
- **addLines** – Adds straight lines between the provided array of end points.
- **addQuadCurve** – Adds a quadratic Bézier curve using the specified control and end points.
- **closeSubPath** – Closes the path by connecting the end point to the start point.

A full listing of the line drawing methods and supported arguments can be found online at:

https://developer.apple.com/documentation/swiftui/path

When rendered in the preview canvas, the above path will appear as shown in Figure 29-6:

Figure 29-6

The custom drawing may also be adapted by applying modifiers, for example with a green fill color:

```
Path { path in
    path.move(to: CGPoint(x: 10, y: 0))
    path.addLine(to: CGPoint(x: 10, y: 350))
    path.addLine(to: CGPoint(x: 300, y: 300))
    path.closeSubpath()
}
.fill(Color.green)
```

Although it is possible to draw directly within a view, it generally makes more sense to implement custom shapes as reusable components. Within the *ContentView.swift* file, implement a custom shape as follows:

```
struct MyShape: Shape {
    func path(in rect: CGRect) -> Path {
        var path = Path()

        path.move(to: CGPoint(x: rect.minX, y: rect.minY))
        path.addQuadCurve(to: CGPoint(x: rect.minX, y: rect.maxY),
            control: CGPoint(x: rect.midX, y: rect.midY))
        path.addLine(to: CGPoint(x: rect.minX, y: rect.maxY))
        path.addLine(to: CGPoint(x: rect.maxX, y: rect.maxY))
        path.closeSubpath()
        return path
    }
}
```

The custom shape structure conforms to the Shape protocol by implementing the required *path()* function. The CGRect value passed to the function is used to define the boundaries into which a triangle shape is drawn, with one of the sides drawn using a quadratic curve.

Now that the custom shape has been declared, it can be used in the same way as the built-in SwiftUI shapes, including the use of modifiers. To see this in action, change the body of the main view to read as follows:

```
struct ContentView: View {
    var body: some View {

        MyShape()
            .fill(Color.red)
            .frame(width: 360, height: 350)
    }
}
```

When rendered, the custom shape will appear in the designated frame as illustrated in Figure 29-7 below:

Figure 29-7

29.5 Drawing Gradients

SwiftUI provides support for drawing gradients including linear, angular (conic) and radial gradients. In each case, the gradient is provided with a Gradient object initialized with an array of colors to be included in the gradient and values that control the way in which the gradient is rendered.

The following declaration, for example, generates a radial gradient consisting of five colors applied as the fill pattern for a Circle:

```
struct ContentView: View {

    let colors = Gradient(colors: [Color.red, Color.yellow,
            Color.green, Color.blue, Color.purple])

    var body: some View {

        Circle()
            .fill(RadialGradient(gradient: colors,
                center: .center,
                startRadius: CGFloat(0),
                endRadius: CGFloat(300)))
    }
}
```

When rendered the above gradient will appear as follows:

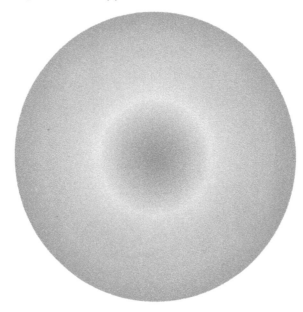

Figure 29-8

The following declaration, on the other hand, generates an angular gradient with the same color range:

```
Circle()
    .fill(AngularGradient(gradient: colors, center: .center))
```

The angular gradient will appear as illustrated in the following figure:

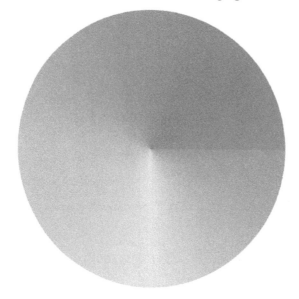

Figure 29-9

Similarly, a LinearGradient running diagonally would be implemented as follows:

```
Rectangle()
    .fill(LinearGradient(gradient: colors,
                      startPoint: .topLeading,
                       endPoint: .bottomTrailing))
    .frame(width: 360, height: 350)
```

The linear gradient will be rendered as follows:

Figure 29-10

The final step in the DrawingDemo project is to apply gradients for the fill and background modifiers for our MyShape instance as follows:

```
MyShape()
    .fill(RadialGradient(gradient: colors,
                        center: .center,
                   startRadius: CGFloat(0),
                     endRadius: CGFloat(300)))
    .background(LinearGradient(gradient: Gradient(colors:
                           [Color.black, Color.white]),
                     startPoint: .topLeading,
                      endPoint: .bottomTrailing))
    .frame(width: 360, height: 350)
```

With the gradients added, the MyShape rendering should match figure below:

Figure 29-11

29.6 **Summary**

SwiftUI includes a built-in set of views that conform to the Shape protocol for drawing standard shapes such as rectangles, circles and ellipses. Modifiers can be applied to these views to control stroke, fill and color properties.

Custom shapes are created by specifying paths which consist of sets of points joined by straight or curved lines. SwiftUI also includes support for drawing radial, linear and angular gradient patterns.

30. SwiftUI Animation and Transitions

This chapter is intended to provide an overview and examples of animating views and implementing transitions within a SwiftUI app. Animation can take a variety of forms including the rotation, scaling and motion of a view on the screen.

Transitions, on the other hand, define how a view will appear as it is added to or removed from a layout, for example whether a view slides into place when it is added, or shrinks from view when it is removed.

30.1 Creating the AnimationDemo Example Project

To try out the examples in this chapter, create a new Single View App Xcode project named AnimationDemo with SwiftUI enabled.

30.2 Implicit Animation

Many of the built-in view types included with SwiftUI contain properties that control the appearance of the view such as scale, opacity, color and rotation angle. Properties of this type are *animatable*, in that the change from one property state to another can be animated instead of occurring instantly. One way to animate these changes to a view is to use the *.animation()* modifier (a concept referred to as *implicit animation* because the animation is implied for any modifiers applied to the view that precede the animation modifier).

To experience basic animation using this technique, modify the *ContentView.swift* file in the AnimationDemo project so that it contains a Button view configured to rotate in 60 degree increments each time it is tapped:

```
struct ContentView : View {

    @State private var rotation: Double = 0

    var body: some View {
        Button(action: {
            self.rotation =
                    (self.rotation < 360 ? self.rotation + 60 : 0)
        }) {
            Text("Click to animate")
                .rotationEffect(.degrees(rotation))
        }
    }
}
```

```
}
```

When tested using live preview, each click causes the Button view to rotate as expected, but the rotation is immediate. Similarly, when the rotation reaches a full 360 degrees, the view actually rotates counter-clockwise 360 degrees, but so quickly the effect is not visible. These effects can be slowed down and smoothed out by adding the *animation()* modifier with an optional animation curve to control the timing of the animation:

```
var body: some View {
    Button(action: {
        self.rotation =
                (self.rotation < 360 ? self.rotation + 60 : 0)
    }) {
        Text("Click to Animate")
            .rotationEffect(.degrees(rotation))
            .animation(.linear)
    }
}
```

The optional animation curve defines the linearity of the animation timeline. This setting controls whether the animation is performed at a constant speed or whether it starts out slow and speeds up. SwiftUI provides the following basic animation curves:

- **.linear** – The animation is performed at constant speed for the specified duration and is the option declared in the above code example.
- **.easeOut** – The animation starts out fast and slows as the end of the sequence approaches.
- **.easeIn** – The animation sequence starts out slow and speeds up as the end approaches.
- **.easeInOut** – The animation starts slow, speeds up and then slows down again.

Preview the animation once again and note that the rotation now animates smoothly. When defining an animation, the duration may also be specified. Change the animation modifier so that it reads as follows:

```
.animation(.linear(duration: 1))
```

Now the animation will be performed more slowly each time the Button is clicked.

As previously mentioned, an animation can apply to more than one modifier. The following changes, for example, animate both rotation and scaling effects:

```
.
.
@State private var scale: CGFloat = 1

var body: some View {
    Button(action: {
        self.rotation =
```

```
            (self.rotation < 360 ? self.rotation + 60 : 0)
        self.scale = (self.scale < 2.8 ? self.scale + 0.3 : 1)
    }) {

        Text("Click to Animate")
          .scaleEffect(scale)
          .rotationEffect(.degrees(rotation))
          .animation(.linear(duration: 1))
    }
}
```

These changes will cause the button to increase in size with each rotation, then scale back to its original size during the return rotation.

Figure 30-1

A variety of spring effects may also be added to the animation using the *spring()* modifier, for example:

```
Text("Click to Animate")
      .scaleEffect(scale)
      .rotationEffect(.degrees(rotation))
      .animation(.spring(response: 1, dampingFraction: 0.2, blendDuration:
0))
```

This will cause the rotation and scale effects to go slightly beyond the designated setting, then bounce back and forth before coming to rest at the target angle and scale.

When working with the *animation()* modifier, it is important to be aware that the animation is only implicit for modifiers that are applied before the animation modifier itself. In the following implementation, for example, only the rotation effect is animated since the scale effect is applied after the animation modifier:

```
Text("Click to Animate")
    .rotationEffect(.degrees(rotation))
    .scaleEffect(scale)
    .animation(.spring(response: 1, dampingFraction: 0.2, blendDuration:
0))
    .scaleEffect(scale)
```

30.3 Repeating an Animation

By default, an animation will be performed once each time it is initiated. An animation may, however, be configured to repeat one or more times. In the following example, the animation is configured to repeat a specific number of times:

```
.animation(Animation.linear(duration: 1).repeatCount(10))
```

Each time an animation repeats, it will perform the animation in reverse as the view returns to its original state. If the view is required to instantly revert to its original appearance before repeating the animation, the autoreverses parameter must be set to false:

```
.animation(Animation.linear(duration: 1).repeatCount(10,
        autoreverses: false))
```

An animation may also be configured to repeat indefinitely using the *repeatForever()* modifier as follows:

```
.repeatForever(autoreverses: true))
```

30.4 Explicit Animation

As previously discussed, implicit animation using the *animation()* modifier implements animation on any of the animatable properties on a view that appear before the animation modifier. SwiftUI provides an alternative approach referred to as *explicit animation* which is implemented using the *withAnimation()* closure. When using explicit animation, only the property changes that take place within the *withAnimation()* closure will be animated. To experience this in action, modify the example so that the rotation effect is performed within a *withAnimation()* closure and remove the *animation()* modifier:

```
var body: some View {
    Button(action: { withAnimation(.linear (duration: 2)) {
            self.rotation =
                (self.rotation < 360 ? self.rotation + 60 : 0)
        }
        self.scale = (self.scale < 2.8 ? self.scale + 0.3 : 1)
    }) {

        Text("Click to Animate")
            .rotationEffect(.degrees(rotation))
            .scaleEffect(scale)
```

~~.animation(.linear(duration: 1))~~

```
        }
    }
```

With the changes made, preview the layout and note that only the rotation is now animated. By using explicit animation, animation can be limited to specific properties of a view without having to worry about the ordering of modifiers.

30.5 **Animation and State Bindings**

Animations may also be applied to state property bindings such that any view changes that occur as a result of that state value changing will be animated. If the state of a Toggle view causes one or more other views to become visible to the user, for example, applying an animation to the binding will cause the appearance and disappearance of all those views to be animated.

Within the *ContentView.swift* file, implement the following layout which consists of a VStack, Toggle view and two Text views. The Toggle view is bound to a state property named *visible*, the value of which is used to control which of the two Text views is visible at one time:

```
.
.
.
@State private var visibility = false

var body: some View {
    VStack {
        Toggle(isOn: $visibility) {
            Text("Toggle Text Views")
        }
        .padding()

        if visibility {
            Text("Hello World")
                .font(.largeTitle)
        }

        if !visibility {
            Text("Goodbye World")
                .font(.largeTitle)
        }
    }
}
.
.
```

When previewed, switching the toggle on and off will cause one or other of the Text views to appear instantly. To add an amination to this change, simply apply a modifier to the state binding as follows:

```
.
.
Var body: some View {
    VStack {
        Toggle(isOn: $visibility.animation(.linear(duration: 5))) {
            Text("Toggle Text Views")
        }
        .padding()
.
.
```

Now when the toggle is switched, one Text view will gradually fade from view as the other gradually fades in (unfortunately, at the time of writing this and other transition effects were only working when running on a simulator or physical device). The same animation will also be applied to any other views in the layout where the appearance changes as a result of the current state of the *visibility* property.

30.6 **Automatically Starting an Animation**

So far in this chapter, all the animations have been triggered by an event such as a button click. Often an animation will need to start without user interaction, for example when a view is first displayed to the user. Since an animation is triggered each time an animatable property of a view changes, this can be used to automatically start an animation when a view appears.

To see this technique in action, modify the example *ContentView.swift* file as follows:

```
struct ContentView : View {

    var body: some View {

        ZStack {
            Circle()
                .stroke(lineWidth: 2)
                .foregroundColor(Color.blue)
                .frame(width: 360, height: 360)

            Image(systemName: "forward.fill")
                .font(.largeTitle)
                .offset(y: -180)
        }
    }
}
```

The content view uses a ZStack to overlay an Image view over a circle drawing where the offset of the Image view has been adjusted to position the image on the circumference of the circle. When previewed, the view should match that shown in Figure 30-2:

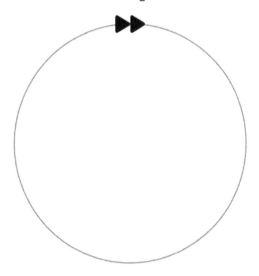

Figure 30-2

Adding a rotation effect to the Image view will give the appearance that the arrows are following the circle. Add this effect and an animation to the Image view as follows:

```
Image(systemName: "forward.fill")
    .font(.largeTitle)
    .offset(y: -180)
    .rotationEffect(.degrees(360))
    .animation(Animation.linear(duration: 5)
                        .repeatForever(autoreverses: false))
```

As currently implemented the animation will not trigger when the view is tested in a live preview. This is because no action is taking place to change an animatable property, thereby initiating the animation.

This can be solved by making the angle of rotation subject to a Boolean state property, and then toggling that property when the ZStack first appears via the *onAppear()* modifier. In terms of implementing this behavior for our circle example, the content view declarations need to read as follows:

```
import SwiftUI

struct ContentView : View {

    @State private var isSpinning: Bool = true
```

```
var body: some View {

    ZStack {
        Circle()
            .stroke(lineWidth: 2)
            .foregroundColor(Color.blue)
            .frame(width: 360, height: 360)

        Image(systemName: "forward.fill")
            .font(.largeTitle)
            .offset(y: -180)
            .rotationEffect(.degrees(isSpinning ? 0 : 360))
            .animation(Animation.linear(duration: 5)
                    .repeatForever(autoreverses: false))
    }
    .onAppear() {
        self.isSpinning.toggle()
    }

    }
}
```

When SwiftUI initializes the content view, but before it appears on the screen, the isSpinning state property will be set to true and, based on the ternary operator, the rotation angle set to zero. After the view has appeared, however, the *onAppear()* modifier will toggle the isSpinning state property to false which will, in turn, cause the ternary operator to change the rotation angle to 360 degrees. As this is an animatable property, the animation modifier will activate and animate the rotation of the Image view through 360 degrees. Since this animation has been configured to repeat indefinitely, the image will continue to animate around the circle.

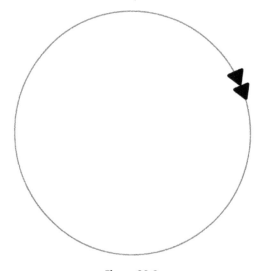

Figure 30-3

30.7 **SwiftUI Transitions**

A transition occurs in SwiftUI whenever a view is made visible or invisible to the user. To make this process more visually appealing than having the view instantly appear and disappear, SwiftUI allows these transitions to be animated in several ways using either individual effects or by combining multiple effects.

Begin by implementing a simple layout consisting of a Toggle button and a Text view. The toggle is bound to a state property which is then used to control whether the text view is visible. To make the transition more noticeable, animation has been applied to the state property binding:

```
struct ContentView : View {

    @State private var isButtonVisible: Bool = true

    var body: some View {
        VStack {
            Toggle(isOn:$isButtonVisible.animation(
                                    .linear(duration: 2))) {
                Text("Show/Hide Button")
            }
            .padding()

            if isButtonVisible {
                Button(action: {}) {
                    Text("Example Button")
                }
                .font(.largeTitle)
            }
        }
    }
}
```

After making the changes, use the live preview to switch the toggle button state and note that the Text view fades in and out of view as the state changes. This fading effect is the default transition used by SwiftUI. This default can be changed by passing a different transition to the *transition()* modifier, for which the following options are available:

- **.scale** – The view increases in size as it is made visible and shrinks as it disappears.
- **.slide** – The view slides in and out of view.
- **.move(edge: edge)** – As the view is added or removed it does so by moving either from or toward direction of the specified edge.
- **.opacity** – The view retains its size and position while fading from view (the default transition behavior).

To configure the Text view to slide into view, change the example as follows:

```
if isButtonVisible {
    Button(action: {}) {
        Text("Hidden Button")
    }
    .font(.largeTitle)
    .transition(.slide)
}
```

Alternatively, the view can be made to shrink from view and then grow in size when inserted and removed:

```
.transition(.scale)
```

The *move()* transition can be used as follows to move the view toward a specified edge of the containing view. In the following example, the view moves from bottom to top when disappearing and from top to bottom when appearing:

```
.transition(.move(edge: .top))
```

When previewing the above move transition, you may have noticed that after completing the move, the Button disappears instantly. This somewhat jarring effect can be improved by combining the move with another transition.

30.8 Combining Transitions

SwiftUI transitions are combined using an instance of AnyTransition together with the *combined(with:)* method. To combine, for example, movement with opacity, a transition could be configured as follows:

```
.transition(AnyTransition.opacity.combined(with: .move(edge: .top)))
```

When the above example is implemented, the Text view will include a fading effect while moving.

To remove clutter from layout bodies and to promote reusability, transitions can be implemented as extensions to the AnyTransition class. The above combined transition, for example, can be implemented as follows:

```
extension AnyTransition {
    static var fadeAndMove: AnyTransition {
        AnyTransition.opacity.combined(with: .move(edge: .top))
    }
}
```

When implemented as an extension, the transition can simply be passed as an argument to the *transition()* modifier, for example:

```
.transition(.fadeAndMove)
```

30.9 **Asymmetrical Transitions**

By default, SwiftUI will simply reverse the specified insertion transition when removing a view. To specify a different transition for adding and removing views, the transition can be declared as being asymmetric. The following transition, for example, uses the scale transition for view insertion and sliding for removal:

```
.transition(.asymmetric(insertion: .scale, removal: .slide))
```

30.10 **Summary**

This chapter has explored the implementation of animation when changes are made to the appearance of a view. In the case of implicit animation, changes to a view caused by modifiers can be animated through the application of the *animated()* modifier. Explicit animation allows only specified properties of a view to be animated in response to appearance changes. Animation may also be applied to state property bindings such that any view changes that occur as a result of that state value changing will be animated.

A transition occurs when a view is inserted into, or removed from, a layout. SwiftUI provides several options for animating these transitions including fading, scaling and sliding. SwiftUI also provides the ability to both combine transitions and define asymmetric transitions where different animation effects are used for insertion and removal of a view.

31. Working with Gesture Recognizers in SwiftUI

The term *gesture* is used to describe an interaction between the touch screen and the user which can be detected and used to trigger an event in the app. Drags, taps, double taps, pinching, rotation motions and long presses are all considered to be gestures in SwiftUI.

The goal of this chapter is to explore the use of SwiftUI gesture recognizers within a SwiftUI based app.

31.1 Creating the GestureDemo Example Project

To try out the examples in this chapter, create a new Single View App Xcode project named GestureDemo with SwiftUI enabled.

31.2 Basic Gestures

Gestures performed within the bounds of a view can be detected by adding a gesture recognizer to that view. SwiftUI provides detectors for tap, long press, rotation, magnification (pinch) and drag gestures.

A gesture recognizer is added to a view using the *gesture()* modifier, passing through the gesture recognizer to be added.

In the simplest form, a recognizer will include one or more action callbacks containing the code to be executed when a matching gesture is detected on the view. The following example adds a tap gesture detector to an Image view and implements the *onEnded* callback containing the code to be performed when the gesture is completed successfully:

```
struct ContentView: View {
    var body: some View {
        Image(systemName: "hand.point.right.fill")
            .gesture(
                TapGesture()
                    .onEnded { _ in
                        print("Tapped")
                    }
            )
    }
}
```

Using live preview in debug mode, test the above view declaration, noting the appearance of the "Tapped" message in the debug console panel when the image is clicked.

When working with gesture recognizers, it is usually preferable to assign the recognizer to a variable and then reference that variable in the modifier. This makes for tidier view body declarations and encourages reuse:

```
var body: some View {

    let tap = TapGesture()
            .onEnded { _ in
            print("Tapped")
        }


    return Image(systemName: "hand.point.right.fill")
        .gesture(tap)
}
```

When using the tap gesture recognizer, the number of taps required to complete the gesture may also be specified. The following, for example, will only detect double taps:

```
let tap = TapGesture(count: 2)
            .onEnded { _ in
            print("Tapped")
        }
```

The long press gesture recognizer is used in a similar way and is designed to detect when a view is touched for an extended length of time. The following declaration detects when a long press is performed on an Image view using the default time duration:

```
var body: some View {

    let longPress = LongPressGesture()
        .onEnded { _ in
            print("Long Press")
        }


    return Image(systemName: "hand.point.right.fill")
        .gesture(longPress)
}
```

To adjust the duration necessary to qualify as a long press, simply pass through a minimum duration value (in seconds) to the *LongPressGesture()* call. It is also possible to specify a maximum distance from the view from which the point of contact with the screen can move outside of the view during the long press. If the touch moves beyond the specified distance, the gesture will cancel and the onEnded action will not be called:

```
let tap = LongPressGesture(minimumDuration: 10,
                                        maximumDistance: 25)

    .onEnded { _ in
        print("Long Press")
    }
```

A gesture recognizer can be removed from a view by passing a nil value to the *gesture()* modifier:

```
.gesture(nil)
```

31.3 The onChange Action Callback

In the previous examples, the OnEnded action closure was used to detect when a gesture completes. Many of the gesture recognizers (except for TapGesture) also allow the addition of an onChange action callback. The onChange callback will be called when the gesture is first recognized, and each time the underlying values of the gesture change, up until the point that the gesture ends.

The onChange action callback is particularly useful when used with gestures involving motion across the device display (as opposed to taps and long presses). The magnification gesture, for example, can be used to detect the movement of touches on the screen.

```
struct ContentView: View {

    var body: some View {

        let magnificationGesture =
                MagnificationGesture(minimumScaleDelta: 0)
            .onEnded { _ in
                print("Gesture Ended")
            }

        return Image(systemName: "hand.point.right.fill")
            .resizable()
            .font(.largeTitle)
            .gesture(magnificationGesture)
            .frame(width: 100, height: 90)
    }
}
```

The above implementation will detect a pinching motion performed over the Image view but will only report the detection after the gesture ends. Within the preview canvas, pinch gestures can be simulated by holding down the keyboard Option key while clicking in the Image view and dragging.

To receive notifications for the duration of the gesture, the onChanged callback action can be added:

```
let magnificationGesture =
                MagnificationGesture(minimumScaleDelta: 0)
    .onChanged( { _ in
        print("Magnifying")
    })
    .onEnded { _ in
        print("Gesture Ended")
    }
```

Now when the gesture is detected, the onChanged action will be called each time the values associated with the pinch operation change. Each time the onChanged action is called, it will be passed a MagnificationGesture.Value instance which contains a CGFloat value representing the current scale of the magnification.

With access to this information about the magnification gesture scale, interesting effects can be implemented such as configuring the Image view to resize in response to the gesture:

```
struct ContentView: View {

    @State private var magnification: CGFloat = 1.0

    var body: some View {

        let magnificationGesture =
                MagnificationGesture(minimumScaleDelta: 0)
            .onChanged({ value in
                self.magnification = value
            })
            .onEnded({ _ in
                print("Gesture Ended")
            })

        return Image(systemName: "hand.point.right.fill")
            .resizable()
            .font(.largeTitle)
            .scaleEffect(magnification)
            .gesture(magnificationGesture)
            .frame(width: 100, height: 90)
    }
}
```

31.4 The updating Callback Action

The *updating* callback action is like *onChanged* with the exception that it works with a special property wrapper named @GestureState. GestureState is like the standard @State property wrapper but is designed exclusively for use with gestures. The key difference, however, is that

@GestureState properties automatically reset to the original state when the gesture ends. As such, the updating callback is ideal for storing transient state that is only needed while a gesture is being performed.

Each time an updating action is called, it is passed the following three arguments:

- DragGesture.Value instance containing information about the gesture.
- A reference to the @GestureState property to which the gesture has been bound.
- A Transaction object containing the current state of the animation corresponding to the gesture.

The DragGesture.Value instance is particularly useful and contains the following properties:

- **location (CGPoint)** - The current location of the drag gesture.
- **predictedEndLocation (CGPoint)** – Predicted final location, based on the velocity of the drag if dragging stops.
- **predictedEndTranslation (CGSize)** - A prediction of what the final translation would be if dragging stopped now based on the current drag velocity.
- **startLocation (CGPoint)** - The location at which the drag gesture started.
- **time (Date)** – The time stamp of the current drag event.
- **translation (CGSize)** - The total translation from the start of the drag gesture to the current event (essentially the offset from the start position to the current drag location).

Typically, a drag gesture updating callback will extract the translation value from the DragGesture.Value object and assign it to a @GestureState property and will typically resemble the following:

```
let drag = DragGesture()
    .updating($offset) { dragValue, state, transaction in
        state = dragValue.translation
    }
```

The following example adds a drag gesture to an Image view and then uses the updating callback to keep a @GestureState property updated with the current translation value. An *offset()* modifier is applied to the Image view using the @GestureState offset property. This has the effect of making the Image view follow the drag gesture as it moves across the screen.

```
struct ContentView: View {

    @GestureState private var offset: CGSize = .zero

    var body: some View {

        let drag = DragGesture()
            .updating($offset) { dragValue, state, transaction in
                state = dragValue.translation
            }
```

```
    return Image(systemName: "hand.point.right.fill")
        .font(.largeTitle)
        .offset(offset)
        .gesture(drag)
    }
}
```

If it is not possible to drag the image this may be because of a problem with the live view in the current Xcode 11 release. The example should work if tested on a simulator or physical device. Note that once the drag gesture ends, the Image view returns to the original location. This is because the offset gesture property was automatically reverted to its original state when the drag ended.

31.5 Composing Gestures

So far in this chapter we have looked at adding a single gesture recognizer to a view in SwiftUI. Though a less common requirement, it is also possible to combine multiple gestures and apply them to a view. Gestures can be combined so that they are detected simultaneously, in sequence or exclusively. When gestures are composed simultaneously, both gestures must be detected at the same time for the corresponding action to be performed. In the case if sequential gestures, the first gestures must be completed before the second gesture will be detected. For exclusive gestures, the detection of one gesture will be treated as all gestures being detected.

Gestures are composed using the *simultaneously()*, *sequenced()* and *exclusively()* modifiers. The following view declaration, for example, composes a simultaneous gesture consisting of a long press and a drag:

```
struct ContentView: View {

    @GestureState private var offset: CGSize = .zero
    @GestureState private var longPress: Bool = false

    var body: some View {

        let longPressAndDrag = LongPressGesture(minimumDuration: 1.0)
            .updating($longPress) { value, state, transition in
                state = value
            }
            .simultaneously(with: DragGesture())
            .updating($offset) { value, state, transaction in
                state = value.second?.translation ?? .zero
            }

        return Image(systemName: "hand.point.right.fill")
            .foregroundColor(longPress ? Color.red : Color.blue)
            .font(.largeTitle)
```

```
        .offset(offset)
        .gesture(longPressAndDrag)
    }
}
```

In the case of the following view declaration, a sequential gesture is configured which requires the long press gesture to be completed before the drag operation can begin. When executed, the user will perform a long press on the image until it turns green, at which point the drag gesture can be used to move the image around the screen.

```
struct ContentView: View {

    @GestureState private var offset: CGSize = .zero
    @State private var dragEnabled: Bool = false

    var body: some View {

        let longPressBeforeDrag = LongPressGesture(minimumDuration: 2.0)
            .onEnded( { _ in
                self.dragEnabled = true
            })
            .sequenced(before: DragGesture())
            .updating($offset) { value, state, transaction in

                switch value {

                    case .first(true):
                        print("Long press in progress")

                    case .second(true, let drag):
                        state = drag?.translation ?? .zero

                    default: break
                }
            }
            .onEnded { value in
                self.dragEnabled = false
            }

        return Image(systemName: "hand.point.right.fill")
            .foregroundColor(dragEnabled ? Color.green : Color.blue)
            .font(.largeTitle)
            .offset(offset)
            .gesture(longPressBeforeDrag)
```

```
    }
}
```

31.6 **Summary**

Gesture detection can be added to SwiftUI views using gesture recognizers. SwiftUI includes recognizers for drag, pinch, rotate, long press and tap gestures. Gesture detection notification can be received from the recognizers by implementing onEnded, updated and onChange callback methods. The updating callback works with a special property wrapper named @GestureState. A GestureState property is like the standard state property wrapper but is designed exclusively for use with gestures and automatically resets to its original state when the gesture ends. Gesture recognizers may be combined so that they are recognized simultaneously, sequentially or exclusively.

32. Integrating UIViews with SwiftUI

Prior to the introduction of SwiftUI, all iOS apps were developed using UIKit together with a collection of UIKit-based supporting frameworks. Although SwiftUI is provided with a wide selection of components with which to build an app, there are many instances where there is no SwiftUI equivalent to options provided by the other frameworks. There is, for example, no SwiftUI equivalent to the MKMapView or WebView classes provided by the MapKit and WebView frameworks, or the powerful animation features of UIKit Dynamics.

Given the quantity of apps that were developed before the introduction of SwiftUI it is also important to be able to integrate existing non-SwiftUI functionality with SwiftUI development projects and vice versa. Fortunately, SwiftUI includes a number of options to perform this type of integration.

32.1 SwiftUI and UIKit Integration

Before looking in detail at integrating SwiftUI and UIKit it is worth taking some time to explore whether a new app project should be started as a UIKit or SwiftUI project, and whether an existing app should be migrated entirely to SwiftUI. When making this decision, it is important to remember that apps containing SwiftUI code can only be used on devices running iOS 13 or later,

If you are starting a new project, then the best approach may be to build it as a SwiftUI project (support for older iOS versions not withstanding) and then integrate with UIKit when required functionality is not provided directly by SwiftUI. Although Apple continues to enhance and support the UIKit way of developing apps, it is clear that Apple sees SwiftUI as the future of app development. SwiftUI also makes it easier to develop and deploy apps for iOS, macOS, tvOS, iPadOS and watchOS without making major code changes.

If, on the other hand, you have existing projects that pre-date the introduction of SwiftUI then it probably makes sense to leave the existing code unchanged, build any future additions to the project using SwiftUI and to integrate those additions into your existing code base.

SwiftUI provides three options for performing integrations of these types. The first, and the topic of this chapter, is to integrate individual UIKit-based components (UIViews) into SwiftUI View declarations.

For those unfamiliar with UIKit, a screen displayed within an app is typically implemented using a view controller (implemented as an instance of UIViewController or a subclass thereof). The subject of integrating view controllers into SwiftUI will be covered in the chapter entitled *Integrating UIViewControllers with SwiftUI*.

Finally, SwiftUI views may also be integrated into existing UIKit-based code, a topic which will be covered in the chapter entitled *Integrating SwiftUI with UIKit*.

32.2 Integrating UIViews into SwiftUI

The individual components that make up the user interface of a UIKit-based application are derived from the UIView class. Buttons, labels, text views, maps, sliders and drawings (to name a few) are all ultimately subclasses of the UIKit UIView class.

To facilitate the integration of a UIView based component into a SwiftUI view declaration, SwiftUI provides the UIViewRepresentable protocol. To integrate a UIView component into SwiftUI, that component needs to be wrapped in a structure that implements this protocol.

At a minimum the wrapper structure must implement the following methods to comply with the UIViewRepresentable protocol:

- **makeUIView()** – This method is responsible for creating an instance of the UIView-based component, performing any necessary initialization and returning it.
- **updateView()** – Called each time a change occurs within the containing SwiftUI view that requires the UIView to update itself.

The following optional method may also be implemented:

- **dismantleUIView()** – Provides an opportunity to perform cleanup operations before the view is removed.

As an example, assume that there is a feature of the UILabel class that is not available with the SwiftUI Text view. To wrap a UILabel view using UIViewRepresentable so that it can be used within SwiftUI, the structure might be implemented as follows:

```
import SwiftUI

struct MyUILabel: UIViewRepresentable {

    var text: String

    func makeUIView(context: UIViewRepresentableContext<MyUILabel>)
                                            -> UILabel {
        let myLabel = UILabel()
        myLabel.text = text
        return myLabel
    }

    func updateUIView(_ uiView: UILabel,
                 context: UIViewRepresentableContext<MyUILabel>) {
        // Perform any update tasks if necessary
    }
}
```

```
struct MyUILabel_Previews: PreviewProvider {
    static var previews: some View {
        MyUILabel(text: "Hello")
    }
}
```

With the UILabel view wrapped, it can now be referenced within SwiftUI as though it is a built-in SwiftUI component:

```
struct ContentView: View {
    var body: some View {

        VStack {
            MyUILabel(text: "Hello UIKit")
        }
    }
}

struct ContentView_Previews: PreviewProvider {
    static var previews: some View {
        ContentView()
    }
}
```

Obviously, UILabel is a static component that does not need to handle any events as a result of user interaction. For views that need to respond to events, however, the UIViewRepresentable wrapper needs to be extended to implement a *coordinator*.

32.3 Adding a Coordinator

A coordinator takes the form of a class that implements the protocols and handler methods required by the wrapped UIView component to handle events. An instance of this class is then applied to the wrapper via the *makeCoordinator()* method of the UIViewRepresentable protocol.

As an example, consider the UIScrollView class. This class has a feature whereby a refresh control (UIRefreshControl) may be added such that when the user attempts to scroll beyond the top of the view, a spinning progress indicator appears and a method called allowing the view to be updated with the latest content. This is a common feature used by news apps to allow the user to download the latest news headlines. Once the refresh is complete, this method needs to call the *endRefreshing()* method of the UIRefreshControl instance to remove the progress spinner.

Clearly, if the UIScrollView is to be used with SwiftUI, there needs to be a way for the view to be notified that the UIRefreshControl has been triggered and to perform the necessary steps.

The Coordinator class for a wrapped UIScrollView with an associated UIRefreshControl object would be implemented as follows:

```
class Coordinator: NSObject {
    var control: MyScrollView

    init(_ control: MyScrollView) {
        self.control = control
    }

    @objc func handleRefresh(sender: UIRefreshControl) {
        sender.endRefreshing()
    }
}
```

In this case the initializer for the coordinator is passed the current UIScrollView instance, which it stores locally. The class also implements a function named *handleRefresh()* which calls the *endRefreshing()* method of the scrolled view instance.

An instance of the Coordinator class now needs to be created and assigned to the view via a call to the *makeCoordinator()* method as follows:

```
func makeCoordinator() -> Coordinator {
    Coordinator(self)
}
```

Finally, the *makeUIView()* method needs to be implemented to create the UIScrollView instance, configure it with a UIRefreshControl and to add a target to call the *handleRefresh()* method when a value changed event occurs on the UIRefreshControl instance:

```
func makeUIView(context: Context) -> UIScrollView {
    let scrollView = UIScrollView()
    scrollView.refreshControl = UIRefreshControl()

    scrollView.refreshControl?.addTarget(context.coordinator,
              action: #selector(Coordinator.handleRefresh),
                                for: .valueChanged)

    return scrollView
}
```

32.4 Handling UIKit Delegation and Data Sources

Delegation is a feature of UIKit that allows an object to pass the responsibility for performing one or more tasks on to another object and is another area in which extra steps may be necessary if events are to be handled by a wrapped UIView.

The UIScrolledView, for example, can be assigned a delegate which will be notified when certain events take place such as the user performing a scrolling motion or when the user scrolls to the top of the content. The delegate object will need to conform to the UIScrolledViewDelegate protocol and implement the specific methods that will be called automatically when corresponding events take place in the scrolled view.

Similarly, a data source is an object which provides a UIView based component with data to be displayed. The UITableView class, for example, can be assigned a data source object to provide the cells to be displayed in the table. This data object must conform with the UITableViewDataSource protocol.

To handle delegate events when integrating UIViews into SwiftUI, the coordinator class needs to be declared as implementing the appropriate delegate protocol and must include the callback methods for any events of interest to the scrolled view instance. The coordinator must then be assigned as the delegate for the UIScrolledView instance. The previous coordinator implementation can be extended to receive notification that the user is currently scrolling as follows:

```
class Coordinator: NSObject, UIScrollViewDelegate {
    var control: MyScrollView

    init(_ control: MyScrollView) {
        self.control = control
    }

    func scrollViewDidScroll(_ scrollView: UIScrollView) {
        // User is currently scrolling
    }

    @objc func handleRefresh(sender: UIRefreshControl) {
        sender.endRefreshing()
    }
}
```

The *makeUIView()* method must also be modified to access the coordinator instance (which is accessible via the *representable context* object passed to the method) and add it as the delegate for the UIScrolledView instance:

```
func makeUIView(context: Context) -> UIScrollView {
    let scrollView = UIScrollView()
    scrollView.delegate = context.coordinator
.
.
```

In addition to providing access to the coordinator, the context also includes an *environment* property which can be used to access both the SwiftUI environment and any @EnvironmentObject properties declared in the SwiftUI view.

Now, while the user is scrolling, the scrollViewDidScroll delegate method will be called repeatedly.

32.5 **An Example Project**

The remainder of this chapter will work through the creation of a simple project that demonstrates the use of the UIViewRepresentable protocol to integrate a UIScrolledView into a SwiftUI project.

Begin by launching Xcode and creating a new SwiftUI Single View App project named UIViewDemo.

32.6 **Wrapping the UIScrolledView**

The first step in the project is to use the UIViewRepresentable protocol to wrap the UIScrollView so that it can be used with SwiftUI. Right-click on the UIViewDemo entry in the project navigator panel, select the *New File...* menu option and create a new file named *MyScrollView* using the SwiftUI View template.

With the new file loaded into the editor, delete the current content and modify it so it reads as follows:

```
import SwiftUI

struct MyScrollView: UIViewRepresentable {

    var text: String

    func makeUIView(context: UIViewRepresentableContext<MyScrollView>)
               -> UIScrollView {
        let scrollView = UIScrollView()
        scrollView.refreshControl = UIRefreshControl()
        let myLabel = UILabel(frame:
                    CGRect(x: 0, y: 0, width: 300, height: 50))
        myLabel.text = text
        scrollView.addSubview(myLabel)
        return scrollView
    }

    func updateUIView(_ uiView: UIScrollView,
    context: UIViewRepresentableContext<MyScrollView>) {

    }

}

struct MyScrollView_Previews: PreviewProvider {
    static var previews: some View {
        MyScrollView(text: "Hello World")
    }
}
```

Use the live preview to build and test the view so far. Once the live preview is active and running, click and drag downwards so that the refresh control appears as shown in Figure 32-1:

Figure 32-1

Release the mouse button to stop the scrolling and note that the refresh indicator remains visible because the event is not being handled. Clearly, it is now time to add a coordinator.

32.7 Implementing the Coordinator

Remaining within the *UIViewDemo.swift* file, add the coordinator class declaration so that it reads as follows:

```
struct MyScrollView: UIViewRepresentable {
.
.
    func updateUIView(_ uiView: UIScrollView, context:
UIViewRepresentableContext<MyScrollView>) {

    }

    class Coordinator: NSObject, UIScrollViewDelegate {
        var control: MyScrollView

        init(_ control: MyScrollView) {
            self.control = control
        }

        func scrollViewDidScroll(_ scrollView: UIScrollView) {
            print("View is Scrolling")
        }

        @objc func handleRefresh(sender: UIRefreshControl) {
            sender.endRefreshing()
```

```
        }
    }
}
```

Next, modify the *makeUIView()* method to add the coordinator as the delegate and add the *handleRefresh()* method as the target for the refresh control:

```
func makeUIView(context: Context) -> UIScrollView {
    let scrollView = UIScrollView()
    scrollView.delegate = context.coordinator

    scrollView.refreshControl = UIRefreshControl()
    scrollView.refreshControl?.addTarget(context.coordinator, action:
        #selector(Coordinator.handleRefresh),
                                for: .valueChanged)

    return scrollView
}
```

Finally, add the *makeCoordinator()* method so that it reads as follows:

```
func makeCoordinator() -> Coordinator {
    Coordinator(self)
}
```

Before proceeding, test that the changes work by right-clicking on the live preview button in the preview canvas panel and selecting the *Debug Preview* option from the resulting menu (it may be necessary to stop the live preview first). Once the preview is running in debug mode, make sure that the refresh indicator now goes away when downward scrolling stops and that the "View is scrolling" diagnostic message appears in the console while scrolling is in effect.

32.8 Using MyScrollView

The final step in this example is to check that MyScrollView can be used from within SwiftUI. To achieve this, load the *ContentView.swift* file into the editor and modify it so that it reads as follows:

```
.

.
struct ContentView: View {
    var body: some View {
        MyScrollView(text: "UIView in SwiftUI")
    }
}.
.
```

Use live preview to test that the view works as expected.

32.9 **Summary**

SwiftUI includes several options for integrating with UIKit-based views and code. This chapter has focused on integrating UIKit views into SwiftUI. This integration is achieved by wrapping the UIView instance in a structure that conforms to the UIViewRepresentable protocol and implementing the *makeUIView()* and *updateView()* methods to initialize and manage the view while it is embedded in a SwiftUI layout. For UIKit objects that require a delegate or data source, a Coordinator class needs to be added to the wrapper and assigned to the view via a call to the *makeCoordinator()* method.

33. Integrating UIViewControllers with SwiftUI

The previous chapter outlined how to integrate UIView based components into SwiftUI using the UIViewRepresentable protocol. This chapter will focus on the second option for combining SwiftUI and UIKit within an iOS project in the form of UIViewController integration.

33.1 UIViewControllers and SwiftUI

The UIView integration outlined in the previous chapter is useful for integrating either individual or small groups of UIKit-based components with SwiftUI. Existing iOS apps are likely to consist of multiple ViewControllers, each representing an entire screen layout and functionality (also referred to as *scenes*). SwiftUI allows entire view controller instances to be integrated via the UIViewControllerRepresentable protocol. This protocol is similar to the UIViewRepresentable protocol and works in much the same way with the exception that the method names are different.

The remainder of this chapter will work through an example that demonstrates the use of the UIViewControllerRepresentable protocol to integrate a UIViewController into SwiftUI.

33.2 Creating the ViewControllerDemo project

For the purposes of an example, this project will demonstrate the integration of the UIImagePickerController into a SwiftUI project. This is a class that is used to allow the user to browse and select images from the device photo library and for which there is currently no equivalent within SwiftUI.

Just like custom built view controllers in an iOS app UIImagePickerController is a subclass of UIViewController so can be used with UIViewControllerRepresentable to integrate into SwiftUI.

Begin by launching Xcode and creating a new Single View App SwiftUI project named ViewControllerDemo.

33.3 Wrapping the UIImagePickerController

With the project created, it is time to create a new SwiftUI View file to contain the wrapper that will make the UIPickerController available to SwiftUI. Create this file by right-clicking on the ViewControllerDemo item at the top of the project navigator panel, selecting the *New File...* menu option and creating a new file named MyImagePicker using the SwiftUI View file template.

Once the file has been created, delete the current content and modify the file so that it reads as follows:

```
import SwiftUI

struct MyImagePicker: UIViewControllerRepresentable {

    func makeUIViewController(context:
            UIViewControllerRepresentableContext<MyImagePicker>) ->
                        UIImagePickerController {
        let picker = UIImagePickerController()
        return picker
    }

    func updateUIViewController(_ uiViewController:
          UIImagePickerController, context:
            UIViewControllerRepresentableContext<MyImagePicker>) {

    }
}

struct MyImagePicker_Previews: PreviewProvider {
    static var previews: some View {
        MyImagePicker()
    }
}
```

Click on the live preview button in the canvas to test that the image picker appears as shown in Figure 33-1 below:

Figure 33-1

33.4 **Designing the Content View**

When the project is complete, the content view will display an Image view and a button contained in a VStack. This VStack will be embedded in a ZStack along with an instance of the MyImagePicker view. When the button is clicked, the MyImagePicker view will be made visible over the top of the VStack from which an image may be selected. Once the image has been selected, the image picker will be hidden from view and the selected image displayed on the Image view.

To make this work, two state property variables will be used, one for the image to be displayed and the other a Boolean value to control whether or not the image picker view is currently visible. Bindings for these two variables will be declared in the MyPickerView structure so that changes within the view controller are reflected within the main content view. With these requirements in mind, load the *ContentView.swift* file into the editor and modify it as follows:

```
struct ContentView: View {

    @State var imagePickerVisible: Bool = false
    @State var selectedImage: Image? = Image(systemName: "photo")

    var body: some View {
        ZStack {
            VStack {

                selectedImage?
                    .resizable()
                    .aspectRatio(contentMode: .fit)

                Button(action: {
                    withAnimation {
                        self.imagePickerVisible.toggle()
                    }
                }) {
                    Text("Select an Image")
                }

            }.padding()

            if (imagePickerVisible) {
                MyImagePicker()
            }
        }
    }
}
```

Once the changes have been made, the preview for the view should resemble Figure 33-2:

Figure 33-2

Test the view using live preview and make sure that clicking on the "Select an Image" button causes the MyPickerView to appear. Note that selecting an image or clicking on the Cancel button does not dismiss the picker. To implement this behavior, some changes are needed within the MyImagePicker declaration.

33.5 Completing MyImagePicker

A few remaining tasks now need to be completed within the *MyImagePicker.swift* file. First, bindings to the two ContentView state properties need to be declared:

```
struct MyImagePicker: UIViewControllerRepresentable {

    @Binding var imagePickerVisible: Bool
    @Binding var selectedImage: Image?
    .

    .
```

Next, a coordinator needs to be implemented to act as the delegate for the UIImagePickerView instance. This will require that the coordinator class conform to both the UINavigationControllerDelegate and UIImagePickerControllerDelegate protocols. The coordinator will need to receive notification when an image is picked, or the user taps the cancel button so the imagePickerControllerDidCancel and didFinishPickingMediaWithInfo delegate methods will both need to be implemented.

In the case of the imagePickerControllerDidCancel method, the imagePickerVisible state property will need to be set to false. This will result in a state change within the content view causing the image picker to be removed from view.

The didFinishPickingMediaWithInfo method, on the other hand, will be passed the selected image which it will need to assign to the currentImage property before also setting the imagePickerVisible property to false.

The coordinator will also need local copies of the state property bindings. Bringing these requirements together results in a coordinator which reads as follows:

```
class Coordinator: NSObject, UINavigationControllerDelegate,
                    UIImagePickerControllerDelegate {

    @Binding var imagePickerVisible: Bool
    @Binding var selectedImage: Image?

    init(imagePickerVisible: Binding<Bool>,
                selectedImage: Binding<Image?>) {
        _imagePickerVisible = imagePickerVisible
        _selectedImage = selectedImage
    }

    func imagePickerController(_ picker: UIImagePickerController,
                            didFinishPickingMediaWithInfo
            info: [UIImagePickerController.InfoKey : Any]) {
        let uiImage =
            info[UIImagePickerController.InfoKey.originalImage] as!
                                                            UIImage
        selectedImage = Image(uiImage: uiImage)
        imagePickerVisible = false
    }

    func imagePickerControllerDidCancel(_
                    picker: UIImagePickerController) {
        imagePickerVisible = false
    }
}
```

Remaining in the *MyPickerView.swift* file, add the *makeCoordinator()* method, remembering to pass through the two state property bindings:

```
func makeCoordinator() -> Coordinator {
```

```
    return Coordinator(imagePickerVisible: $imagePickerVisible,
                        selectedImage: $selectedImage)
}
```

Finally, modify the *makeUIVewController()* method to assign the coordinator as the delegate and comment out the preview structure to remove the remaining syntax errors:

```
func makeUIViewController(context:
        UIViewControllerRepresentableContext<MyImagePicker>) ->
                UIImagePickerController {
    let picker = UIImagePickerController()
    picker.delegate = context.coordinator
    return picker
}
.
.
/*
struct MyImagePicker_Previews: PreviewProvider {
    static var previews: some View {
        MyImagePicker()
    }
}
*/
```

33.6 Completing the Content View

The final task before testing the app is to modify the Content View so that the two state properties are passed through to the MyImagePicker instance. Edit the *ContentView.swift* file and make the following modifications:

```
struct ContentView: View {

    @State var imagePickerVisible: Bool = false
    @State var selectedImage: Image? = Image(systemName: "photo")

    var body: some View {
        .
        .
        if (imagePickerVisible) {
                MyImagePicker(imagePickerVisible:
                        $imagePickerVisible,
                        selectedImage: $selectedImage)
        }
```

33.7 **Testing the App**

With the *ContentView.swift* file still loaded into the editor, enable live preview mode and click on the "Select an Image" button. When the picker view appears, navigate to and select an image. When the image has been selected, the picker view should disappear to reveal the selected image displayed on the Image view:

Figure 33-3

Click the image selection button once again, this time making sure that the Cancel button dismisses the image picker without changing the selected image.

33.8 **Summary**

In addition to allowing for the integration of individual UIView based objects into SwiftUI projects, it is also possible to integrate entire UIKit view controllers representing entire screen layouts and functionality. View controller integration is similar to working with UIViews, involving wrapping the view controller in a structure conforming to the UIViewControllerRepresentable protocol and implementing the associated methods. As with UIView integration, delegates and data sources for the view controller are handled using a Coordinator instance.

Chapter 34

34. Integrating SwiftUI with UIKit

Apps developed before the introduction of SwiftUI will have been developed using UIKit and other UIKit-based frameworks included with the iOS SDK. Given the benefits of using SwiftUI for future development, it will be a common requirement to integrate the new SwiftUI app functionality with the existing project code base. Fortunately, this integration can be achieved with relative ease using the UIHostingController.

34.1 An Overview of the Hosting Controller

The hosting controller (in the form of the UIHostingController class) is a subclass of UIViewController, the sole purpose of which is to enclose a SwiftUI view so that it can be integrated into an existing UIKit-based project.

Using a hosting view controller, a SwiftUI view can be treated as an entire scene (occupying the full screen) or treated as an individual component within an existing UIKit scene layout by embedding a hosting controller in a *container view*. A container view essentially allows a view controller to be configured as the child of another view controller.

SwiftUI views can be integrated into a UIKit project either from within the code or using an Interface Builder storyboard. The following code excerpt embeds a SwiftUI content view in a hosting view controller and then presents it to the user:

```
let swiftUIController =
                UIHostingController(rootView: SwiftUIView())
present(swiftUIController, animated: true, completion: nil)
```

The following example, on the other hand, embeds a hosted SwiftUI view directly into the layout of an existing UIViewController:

```
let swiftUIController =
            UIHostingController(rootView: SwiftUIView())

addChild(swiftUIController)
view.addSubview(swiftUIController.view)

swiftUIController.didMove(toParent: self)
```

In the rest of this chapter, an example project will be created that demonstrates the use of UIHostingController instances to integrate SwiftUI views into an existing UIKit-based project both programmatically and using storyboards.

34.2 **A UIHostingController Example Project**

Launch Xcode and create a new iOS Single View App project named HostingControllerDemo using Swift as the programming language and with the User Interface option set to *Storyboard*.

34.3 **Adding the SwiftUI Content View**

In the course of building this project, a SwiftUI content view will be integrated into a UIKit storyboard scene using the UIHostingController in three different ways. In preparation for this integration process, a SwiftUI View file needs to be added to the project. Add this file now by selecting the *File -> New File...* menu option and selecting the SwiftUI View template option from the resulting dialog. Proceed through the file creation process, keeping the default SwiftUIView file name.

With the *SwiftUIView.swift* file loaded into the editor, modify the declaration so that it reads as follows:

```swift
import SwiftUI

struct SwiftUIView: View {

    var text: String

    var body: some View {
        VStack {
            Text(text)
            HStack {
                Image(systemName: "smiley")
                Text("This is a SwiftUI View")
            }
        }
        .font(.largeTitle)
    }
}

struct SwiftUIView_Previews: PreviewProvider {
    static var previews: some View {
        SwiftUIView(text: "Sample Text")
    }
}
```

With the SwiftUI view added, the next step is to integrate it so that it can be launched as a separate view controller from within the storyboard.

34.4 **Preparing the Storyboard**

Within Xcode, select the *Main.storyboard* file so that it loads into the Interface Builder tool. As currently configured, the storyboard consists of a single view controller scene as shown in Figure 34-1:

Figure 34-1

So that the user can navigate back to the current scene, the view controller needs to be embedded into a Navigation Controller. Select the current scene by clicking on the View Controller button circled in the figure above so that the scene highlights with a blue outline and select the *Editor -> Embed In -> Navigation Controller* menu option. At this point the storyboard canvas should resemble Figure 34-2:

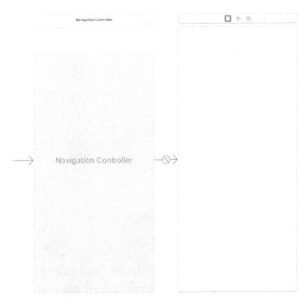

Figure 34-2

The first SwiftUI integration will require a button which, when clicked, will show a new view controller containing the SwiftUI View. Display the Library panel by clicking on the button highlighted in Figure 34-3 and locate and drag a Button view onto the view controller scene canvas:

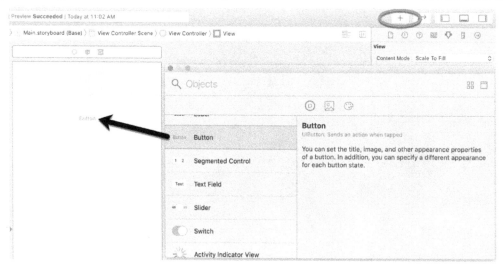

Figure 34-3

Double click on the button to enter editing mode and change the text so that it reads "Show Second Screen". To maintain the position of the button it will be necessary to add some layout constraints. Use the *Resolve Auto Layout Issues* button indicated in Figure 34-4 to display the menu and select the *Reset to Suggested Constraints* option to add any missing constraints to the button widget:

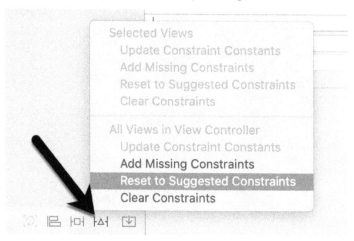

Figure 34-4

34.5 Adding a Hosting Controller

The storyboard is now ready to add a UIHostingController and to implement a segue on the button to display the SwiftUIView layout. Display the Library panel once again, locate the Hosting View Controller and drag and drop it onto the storyboard canvas so that it resembles Figure 34-5 below:

Figure 34-5

Next, add the segue by selecting the "Show Second Screen" button and Ctrl-clicking and dragging to the Hosting Controller:

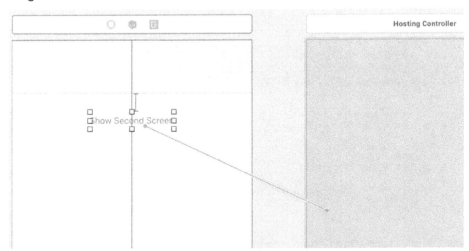

Figure 34-6

Release the line once it is within the bounds of the hosting controller and select *Show* from the resulting menu.

Compile and run the project on a simulator or connected device and verify that clicking the button navigates to the hosting controller screen and that the Navigation Controller has provided a back button to return to the initial screen. At this point the hosting view controller appears with a black background indicating that it currently has no content.

34.6 Configuring the Segue Action

The next step is to add an IBSegueAction to the segue that will load the SwiftUI view into the hosting controller when the button is clicked. Within Xcode, select the *Editor -> Assistant* menu option to display the Assistant Editor panel. When the Assistant Editor panel appears, make sure that it is displaying the content of the *ViewController.swift* file. By default, the Assistant Editor will be in *Automatic* mode, whereby it automatically attempts to display the correct source file based on the currently selected item in Interface Builder. If the correct file is not displayed, the toolbar along the top of the editor panel can be used to select the correct file.

If the *ViewController.swift* file is not loaded, begin by clicking on the Automatic entry in the editor toolbar as highlighted in Figure 34-7:

Figure 34-7

From the resulting menu (Figure 34-8), select the *ViewController.swift* file to load it into the editor:

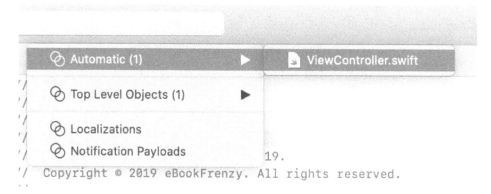

Figure 34-8

Next, Ctrl-click on the segue line between the initial view controller and the hosting controller and drag the resulting line to a position beneath the *viewDidLoad()* method in the Assistant panel as shown in Figure 34-9:

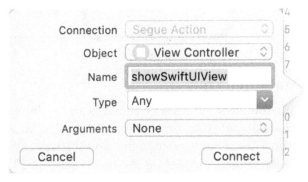

Figure 34-9

Release the line and enter *showSwiftUIView* into the Name field of the connection dialog before clicking the *Connect* button:

Figure 34-10

Within the *ViewController.swift* file Xcode will have added the IBSegueAction method which needs to be modified as follows to embed the SwiftUIView layout into the hosting controller (note that the SwiftUI framework also needs to be imported):

```
import UIKit
import SwiftUI

.

.

@IBSegueAction func showSwiftUIView(_ coder: NSCoder) ->
UIViewController? {
    return UIHostingController(coder: coder,
            rootView: SwiftUIView(text: "Integration One"))
}
```

Compile and run the app once again, this time confirming that the second screen appears as shown in Figure 34-11:

Figure 34-11

34.7 Embedding a Container View

For the second integration, a Container View will be added to an existing view controller scene and used to embed a SwiftUI view alongside UIKit components. Within the *Main.storyboard* file, display the Library and drag and drop a Container View onto the scene canvas of the initial view controller, then position and size the view so that it appears as shown in Figure 34-12:

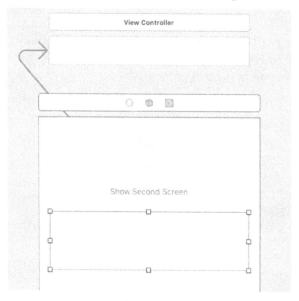

Figure 34-12

Before proceeding, click on the background of the view controller scene before using the *Resolve Auto Layout Issues* button indicated in Figure 34-4 once again and select the *Reset to Suggested Constraints* option to add any missing constraints to the layout.

Note that Xcode has also added an extra View Controller for the Container View (located above the initial view controller in the above figure). This will need to be replaced by a Hosting Controller so select this controller and tap the keyboard delete key to remove it from the storyboard.

Display the Library, locate the Hosting View Controller and drag and drop it so that it is positioned above the initial view controller in the storyboard canvas. Ctrl-click on the Container View in the view controller scene and drag the resulting line to the new hosting controller before releasing. From the segue menu, select the Embed option:

Figure 34-13

Once the Container View has been embedded in the hosting controller, the storyboard should resemble Figure 34-14:

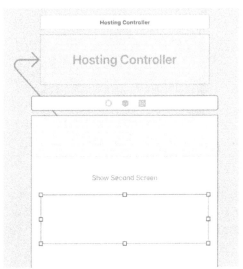

Figure 34-14

All that remains is to add an IBSegueAction to the connection between the Container View and the hosting controller. Display the Assistant Editor once again, Ctrl-click on the arrow pointing in towards the left side of the hosting controller and drag the line to a position beneath the showSwiftUIView action method. Name the action embedSwiftUIView and click on the Connect button. Once the new method has been added, modify it as follows:

```
@IBSegueAction func embedSwiftUIView(_ coder: NSCoder) ->
                                       UIViewController? {
    return UIHostingController(coder: coder, rootView: SwiftUIView(text:
"Integration Two"))
}
```

When the app is now run, the SwiftUI view will appear in the initial view controller within the Container View:

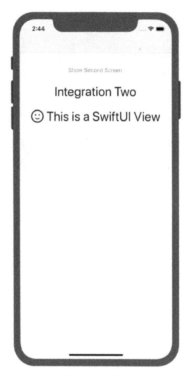

Figure 34-15

34.8 Embedding SwiftUI in Code

In this, the final integration example, the SwiftUI view will be embedded into the layout for the initial view controller programmatically. Within Xcode, edit the *ViewController.swift* file, locate the *viewDidLoad()* method and modify it as follows:

```
override func viewDidLoad() {
    super.viewDidLoad()

    let swiftUIController = UIHostingController(rootView:
SwiftUIView(text: "Integration Three"))
```

```
addChild(swiftUIController)
swiftUIController.view.translatesAutoresizingMaskIntoConstraints
                                              = false

view.addSubview(swiftUIController.view)

swiftUIController.view.centerXAnchor.constraint(
        equalTo: view.centerXAnchor).isActive = true
swiftUIController.view.centerYAnchor.constraint(
        equalTo: view.centerYAnchor).isActive = true

swiftUIController.didMove(toParent: self)
}
```

The code begins by creating a UIHostingController instance containing the SwiftUIView layout before adding it as a child to the current view controller. The *translates autoresizing* property is set to false so that any constraints we add will not conflict with the automatic constraints usually applied when a view is added to a layout. Next, the UIView child of the UIHostingController is added as a subview of the containing view controller's UIView. Constraints are then set on the hosting view controller to position it in the center of the screen. Finally, an event is triggered to let UIKit know that the hosting controller has been moved to the container view controller.

Run the app one last time and confirm that it appears as shown in Figure 34-16:

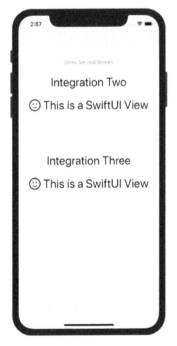

Figure 34-16

34.9 **Summary**

Any apps developed before the introduction of SwiftUI will have been created using UIKit. While it is certainly possible to continue using UIKit when enhancing and extending an existing app, it probably makes more sense to use SwiftUI when adding new app features (unless your app needs to run on devices that do not support iOS 13 or newer). Recognizing the need to integrate new SwiftUI-based views and functionality with existing UIKit code, Apple created the UIHostingViewController. This controller is designed to wrap SwiftUI views in a UIKit view controller that can be integrated into existing UIKit code. As demonstrated in this chapter, the hosting controller can be used to integrate SwiftUI and UIKit both within storyboards and programmatically within code. Options are available to integrate entire SwiftUI user interfaces in independent view controllers or, through the use of container views, to embed SwiftUI views alongside UIKit views within an existing layout.

35. Preparing and Submitting an iOS 13 Application to the App Store

Having developed an iOS application, the final step is to submit it to Apple's App Store. Preparing and submitting an application is a multistep process details of which will be covered in this chapter.

35.1 Verifying the iOS Distribution Certificate

The chapter entitled *Joining the Apple Developer Program* covered the steps involved in generating signing certificates. In that chapter, both a development and distribution certificate were generated. Up until this point in the book, applications have been signed using the development certificate so that testing could be performed on physical iOS devices. Before an application can be submitted to the App Store, however, it must be signed using the distribution certificate. The presence of the distribution certificate may be verified from within the Xcode 11 *Preferences* settings.

With Xcode running, select the *Xcode -> Preferences…* menu option and select the *Accounts* category from the toolbar of the resulting window. Assuming that Apple IDs have been configured as outlined in *Joining the Apple Developer Program*, a list of one or more Apple IDs will be shown in the accounts panel as illustrated in Figure 35-1:

Figure 35-1

Preparing and Submitting an iOS 13 Application to the App Store

Select the Apple ID to be used to sign the application and click on the *Manage Certificates...* button to display the list of signing identities and provisioning profiles associated with that ID:

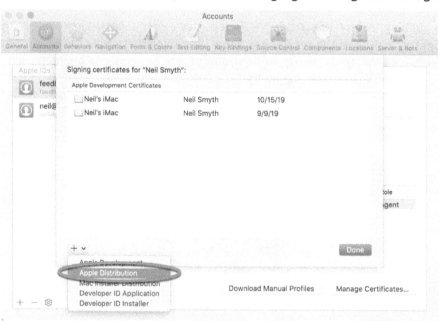

Figure 35-2

If no Apple Distribution certificate is listed, use the menu highlighted in Figure 35-3 to generate one:

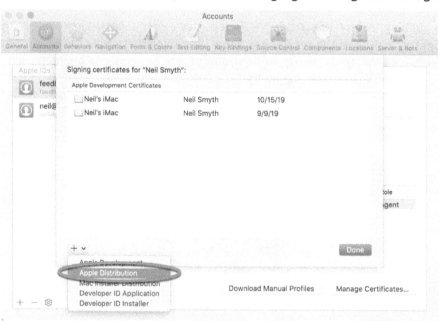

Figure 35-3

Xcode will then contact the developer portal and generate and download a new signing certificate suitable for use when signing applications for submission to the App Store. Once the signing identity has been generated, the certificate will appear in the list as shown in Figure 35-4:

Signing certificates for "Neil Smyth":

Apple Development Certificates		
Neil's iMac	Neil Smyth	10/15/19
Neil's iMac	Neil Smyth	9/9/19
Apple Distribution Certificates		
Apple Distribution	Neil Smyth	10/23/19

+ ⌄   Done

Figure 35-4

35.2 **Adding App Icons**

Before rebuilding the application for distribution it is important to ensure that app icons have been added to the application. The app icons are used to represent your application on the home screen, settings panel and search results on the device. Each of these categories requires a suitable icon in PNG format and formatted for a number of different dimensions. In addition, different variants of the icons will need to be added for retina and non-retina displays and depending on whether the application is for the iPhone or iPad (or both).

App icons are added using the project settings screen of the application project within Xcode. To view these settings, load the project into Xcode and select the application target at the top of the project navigator panel. In the main panel, select the *General* tab and scroll down to the App Icons and Launch Images sections. By default, Xcode will look for the App icon images within an asset catalog named *AppIcon* located in the *Assets.xcassets* asset catalog. Next to the *App Icons Source* menu is a small arrow (as indicated in Figure 35-5) which, when clicked, will provide access to the asset catalog of the App icons.

▼ **App Icons and Launch Images**

App Icons Source   AppIcon

Launch Screen File   LaunchScreen

Figure 35-5

When selected, the AppIcon asset catalog screen will display showing placeholders for each icon size:

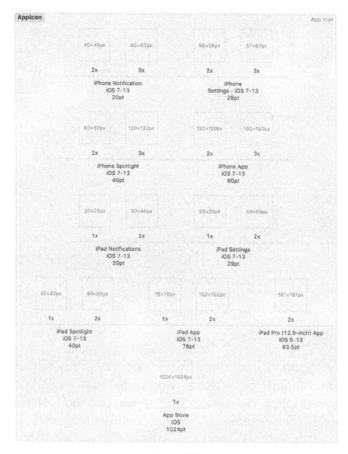

Figure 35-6

To add images, simply drag and drop the missing PNG format image files from a Finder window onto the corresponding placeholders in the asset catalog, or Ctrl-click on the catalog and select *Import* from the menu to import multiple files.

35.3 Designing the Launch Screen

The launch screen contains the content that appears when the application is starting up. The design for this screen is contained in the *LaunchScreen.storyboard* file which will have been generated automatically during the project creation process.

Load the file into Interface Builder and modify it to meet your requirements, including adding any images that may be required and keeping in mind that the layout must use Auto Layout and Size Classes to ensure that the layout appears correctly on all screen sizes. Note also that the layout is limited to UIKit classes and cannot include a WKWebView object.

35.4 Assign the Project to a Team

As part of the submission process, the project must be associated with a development team to ensure that the correct signing credentials are used. In the project navigator panel, select the project name to display the project settings panel. Click the *Signing & Capabilities* tab and within the Identity section, select a team from the menu as shown in Figure 35-7:

Figure 35-7

35.5 Archiving the Application for Distribution

The application must now be rebuilt using the previously installed distribution profile. To generate the archive, select the Xcode *Product -> Archive* menu option. Note that if the Archive menu is disabled this is most likely because a simulator option is currently selected as the run target in the Xcode toolbar. Changing this menu either to a connected device, or the generic *iOS Device* target option should enable the Archive option in the Product menu.

Xcode will proceed to archive the application ready for submission. Once the process is complete the archive will be displayed in the Archive screen of the Organizer dialog ready for upload and distribution:

Figure 35-8

35.6 **Configuring the Application in iTunes Connect**

Before an application can be submitted to the App Store for review it must first be configured in iTunes Connect. Enrollment in the Apple Developer program automatically results in the creation of an iTunes Connect account using the same login credentials. iTunes Connect is a portal where developers enter tax and payment information, input details about applications and track the status of those applications in terms of sales and revenues.

Access iTunes Connect by navigating to *https://itunesconnect.apple.com* in a web browser and entering your Apple Developer program login and password details.

First time users should click on the *Agreements, Tax, and Banking* option and work through the various tasks to accept Apple's terms and conditions and to input appropriate tax and banking information for the receipt of sales revenue.

Once the administrative tasks are complete, select the *My Apps* option and click on the + button followed by *New App* to enter information about the application. Begin by selecting the *iOS* checkbox and entering a name for the application together with an SKU of your own creation. Also select or enter the bundle ID that matches the application that has been prepared for upload in Xcode:

Figure 35-9

Once the application has been added it will appear within the My Apps screen listed as *Prepare for submission*:

InAppDemo2018

iOS 1.0 Prepare for Submission

Figure 35-10

35.7 **Validating and Submitting the Application**

To validate the application, return to the Xcode archives window, make sure the application archive is selected and click on the *Validate App* button. Enter your iOS Developer program login credentials when prompted to do so. If more than one signing identity is configured within Xcode, select the desired identity from the menu.

Xcode will connect to the iTunes Connect service, locate the matching app entry added in the previous step and display the summary screen shown in Figure 35-11:

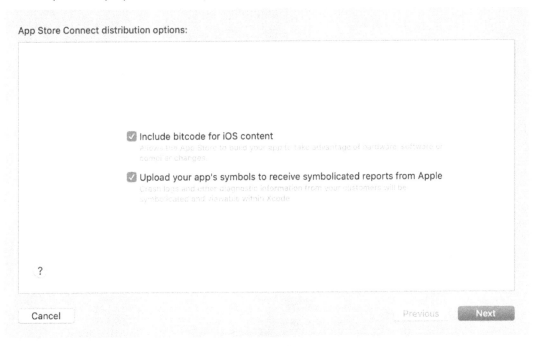

Figure 35-11

This screen includes the following options for selection:

- **Include bitcode for iOS content** – Bitcode is an intermediate binary format introduced with iOS 9. By including the app in bitcode format, it can be compiled by Apple so that it is optimized for the full range of target iOS devices and to take advantage of future hardware and software advances. Selection of this option is recommended.

- **Upload your app's symbols** – If selected, Apple will include symbol information for the app. This information, which includes function and method names, source code line numbers and file paths, will be included in the crash logs provided to you by Apple in the event that your app crashes when in use by a customer. Selection of this option is recommended.

The next screen will provide the option to allow Xcode to automatically manage signing for the app, or to allow you to make manual certificate selections. Unless you are part of a team that uses multiple distribution certificates, automatic signing is usually a good choice:

Figure 35-12

The final screen summarizes the certificate, profile and entitlements associated with the app:

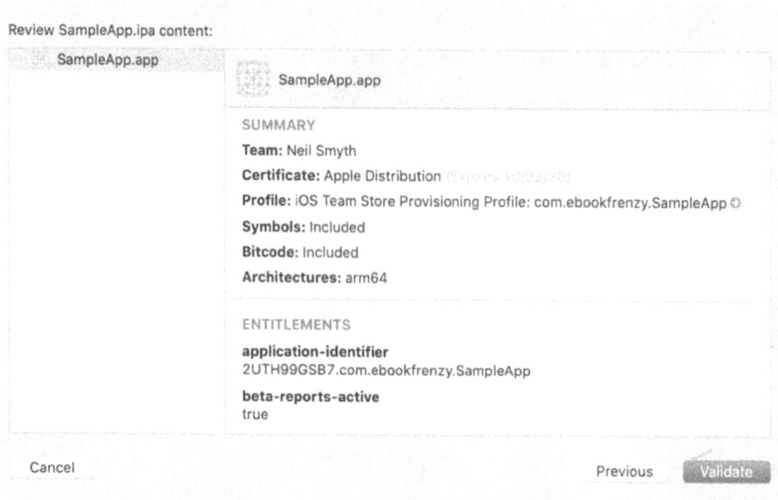

Figure 35-13

Click the *Validate* button to perform the validation and correct any problems that are reported. Once validation has passed, click on the *Done* button to dismiss the panel:

Archive validation complete:

App "SampleApp" successfully validated.

Figure 35-14

The application is now ready to be uploaded for App Store review.

Make sure the application archive is still selected and click on the *Distribute App* button. Work through the screens, selecting the *App Store Connect* and *Upload* options, enter your developer program login credentials when prompted and review the summary information before clicking on the *Upload* button. Wait for the upload process to complete at which point a message should appear indicating that the submission was successful:

Archive upload complete:

App "SampleApp" successfully uploaded.

Figure 35-15

35.8 **Configuring and Submitting the App for Review**

On the My Apps screen of the iTunes Connect portal, select the new app entry to display the configuration screen where options are available to set up pre-release test users, designate pricing, enter product descriptions and upload screenshots and preview videos. Once this information has been entered and saved and the app is ready for submission to the App Store, select the *Prepare for Submission* option (marked A in Figure 35-16) followed by the *Submit for Review* button (marked B):

Figure 35-16

Once Apple has completed the review process an email will arrive stating whether the application has been accepted or not. In the event that the application has been rejected, reasons for the rejection will be stated and the application may be resubmitted once these issues have been addressed.

Index

Index

Index

Index

Index

CPSIA information can be obtained
at www.ICGtesting.com
Printed in the USA
BVHW061448220421
605636BV00001B/191

9 781951 442057